Accountancy and the British Economy 1840-1980

The Evolution of Ernst & Whinney

❀

Accountancy and the British Economy 1840-1980

The Evolution of Ernst & Whinney

❀

EDGAR JONES

Introduction by Professor Peter Mathias

B. T. Batsford Ltd London

ISBN 0 7134 3776 6

Typeset and printed in Great Britain by
Butler & Tanner Ltd
Frome and London
for the publishers
B. T. Batsford Ltd
4 Fitzhardinge Street
London W1H 0AH

❀❀ CONTENTS ❀❀

❀❀ LIST OF ILLUSTRATIONS ❀❀

For permission to use illustrations from their collections, the author would like to thank Price Waterhouse & Co for 11; Midland Bank Archives for 17; and the Institute of Chartered Accountants in England and Wales for 1, 2, 3 and 18; 10, 13 and 14 belong to the author.

❧ LIST OF TEXT FIGURES, TABLES AND MAPS ❧

❀❀ PREFACE ❀❀

This book was commissioned to mark recent events significant for the firm and for the accounting profession. First, the merger in 1979 of the two international accountancy firms of Whinney Murray & Co and Turquands Barton Mayhew & Co, and then of the joint firm with Baker, Sutton & Co. Next, following the formation on 1 January 1979 of Ernst & Whinney International, the adoption on 1 July 1979 of the world-wide practising name of Ernst & Whinney. Finally, and of significance for us all, the Centenary in 1980 of the Institute of Chartered Accountants in England and Wales.

With all the changes that have taken place, the continuing development of the firm may soon obliterate the last traces of the more comfortable, intimate and traditional partnership in which many of us have developed our skills. Before the next leap forward, we believed a backward glance was appropriate. We decided not just to record the histories of the predecessor firms, which would have been of limited interest, but to put the development of the profession as a whole in its historical and economic context. We hope that this will have a wider appeal.

Although publication is a year after the Institute's Centenary, I hope the book, the aim of which is to trace the growth of the accountancy profession and its contribution to the economy of the country, will be acceptable as a fitting tribute to the Institute's first hundred years. As a firm we have a long historical affinity with the Institute: the first two presidents were senior partners of predecessor firms of Ernst & Whinney, and Frederick Whinney was the fourth holder of that office.

Our thanks are due to Professor Mathias for his overall supervision of the project and to Edgar Jones for the scholarly work which he has written.

PETER GODFREY,
Senior partner, Ernst & Whinney
January 1981

❄❄ ACKNOWLEDGEMENTS ❄❄

The author's thanks are due first and foremost to Professor Peter Mathias, who has supervised this study, its research and writing, and made many valuable comments. In addition, a debt of gratitude is owed to Mr Michael Bywater, Librarian of the Institute of Chartered Accountants in England and Wales, for suggesting and making available so many sources and for correcting many errors in the text. Dr R. Ferrier and Mr Richard Roberts (now at Sussex University) have supplied much information from British Petroleum's archives and given valuable assistance, while Mr T. A. B. Corley of Reading University, as Burmah Oil's historian, has similarly provided a wealth of source material as well as commenting on the early drafts. Thanks are also due to Dr W. J. Reader, who kindly allowed the author to read the manuscript of his history of Bowaters and arranged access to that company's records. Valuable advice and assistance have been offered by Dr Leslie Hannah (of the Business History Unit), who patiently read and commented upon the complete text, Dr John Stevenson, who provided a number of leads and encouragingly discussed its content and to Mr Alan Cave, who provided an insight on the workings of the professions. Mr Edwin Green, Archivist to the Midland Bank, has supplied much source material relating to Whinney, Smith & Whinney and his assistance is much appreciated. Both Professor R. H. Parker of Exeter University and Professor B. S. Yamey of the London School of Economics have assisted with the book's research by suggesting new lines of inquiry and the existence of further sources. Thanks are also due to Dunlop Holdings, Price's Patent Candles and Price Waterhouse & Co, who have each surrendered much of their time to supplying information and answering questions. Mr Andrew Harding, senior partner of Macfarlanes, solicitors, devoted much time to elucidating the history of Sir R. P. Harding; his efforts are much appreciated.

I am deeply indebted to all the past and present members of Ernst & Whinney, particularly to the History Committee (Peter Godfrey, David Barton, Dennis Garrett, Hugh Patterson, John Whinney and Julian Potter), who have devoted their energies to correcting misconceptions and provided much assistance in the study's execution. A list of the many retired members of the firm, who have given priceless help, is contained in Appendix 3. Finally, a special note of thanks is owed to Julian Potter, the Partnership Secretary, who has guided the history from its inception and has offered constant encouragement and advice. However, the errors, which surely remain, are alas entirely of the author's making and are his responsibility alone.

EDGAR JONES

Kensington,
December 1980

❦ INTRODUCTION ❦

Early in 1979 I was approached by the partners of Whinney Murray & Co and Turquands Barton Mayhew & Co (as the practices were then styled) with a view to writing their history. Other commitments prevented me from accepting the invitation, but I agreed to advise them on the choice of an author and to help where I could. In the event, Mr Edgar Jones was commissioned to write the book, which now appears under his authorship. While I have advised Mr Jones over the research, participated in some of the interviews and subsequently commented upon various drafts of the text, this is his book, a product of much hard work concentrated within two years. This severe constraint of time has been mitigated by the incomplete survival of records (particularly for Turquands Barton Mayhew and the non-London partnerships), but it has imposed a cost because, within this brief period, the archives in London and several provincial centres had to be mobilized, all the research done, many interviews conducted and the text written and revised.

I am glad to pay tribute to the partners of Whinney Murray and Turquands Barton Mayhew, and now of Ernst & Whinney, for taking a broad view about the kind of history they felt was appropriate to celebrate their adoption with Ernst & Ernst of a world-wide practising name and thus making this book of greater interest to economic historians and a wider public concerned to understand how the present business world has evolved. They sought an academic historian to be its author precisely because they wished to avoid a narrow 'house' history, confined to documenting the careers of individual partners and the genealogies of the various partnerships. They asked that the evolution of the various accountancy practices which had come together as Whinney Murray in 1965, as Turquands Barton Mayhew in 1972 and as Ernst & Whinney in 1979 should be placed in the wider contexts of the accountancy profession, the business world and the British

economy more generally. The resulting study is, to my knowledge, the first 'economic history' of an accountancy firm which
has enjoyed such wide terms of reference.

Mr Jones was given full access to all surviving documents,
which must be a condition for professional academic standards,
and although errors of fact and judgement were corrected in early
drafts, thanks to the partners' advice, the text stands as the author,
receiving my assessments as adviser, would have it. Academics
must accept professional responsibility for any text they put their
names to, and thus it is with this book.

★   ★   ★

The 'business professions', banking apart, have not yet been seriously studied by economic historians. That is to say that their
contribution to the national economy, their role in the evolution
of business, their place in the nation's economic fortunes have not
been assessed. Indeed, the basis for such an assessment has been
lacking. Despite much evidence about the evolution of accountancy as a set of financial procedures from external sources in the
public domain – particularly published books about accountancy,
and more recent technical periodical literature, publications of the
various Institutes of accountants and the like – very little information has been forthcoming about the evolution of accountancy as
a profession or about the evolution and mode of operation of
accountancy firms, through which the evolution of the role of
accountancy in the operations of business and hence its contribution to the economy more widely is embodied. This dimension of
the historical evolution of accountancy in the economy can only
be provided through access to the archives of accountancy practices; the essential 'internal' documentation without which the full
critical history of any profession, or firm, or trades union, or any
other institution can never be written.

To provide a framework for the text which follows, the more
general significance of the expansion and development of services
in the British economy, of which the accountancy developments
described by the present book form a part, deserves some comment. It is an integral feature of a much neglected aspect of
Britain's recent economic development (as, indeed, of structural
changes in all the richest, most industrialized and most moder-
nized economies). Economic historians have concentrated their
attentions much more upon production – the evolution of agri-

culture, mining and industry – than upon distribution and services. In particular, when considering the sources of growing productivity, the progressive improvement in the efficiency of the economy from which a rising national income and improving standards of living ultimately derive, they have been mesmerized by dramatic technology – the machine – which is the icon of industrial man. Even at the present time, reflected in certain aspects of government policy (such as the selective employment tax; or the large claims made for engineering in the Finniston Report) no less than in more popular presuppositions, productivity is assumed to be just what happens within the factory and inside the farm gate.

With this has gone a popular suspicion that the supplier of services does not create wealth as does the producer. Indeed, that at worst, the bankers and insurance companies, the accountants, the brokers, agents, dealers, salesmen, shopkeepers, in particular the advertisers and public relations men (who doubtless have double doses of original sin to expiate), and all the other intermediaries are the parasites of the system, the drones in the hive. The economy has productive workers and then the rest; there are wealth-creators and wealth-consumers. *Homo fabricator*, he who makes, justifies his existence; those who serve the market and support the business system have to be justified. A market just happens; economic efficiency is just a function of high levels of investment.

These atavistic, instinctive assumptions, which have a propensity to break surface when all is not well with the economic performance of the country, have long historical roots. Medieval hostility to financial and commercial intermediaries of all kinds, expressed in standing laws against 'forestalling, regrating and engrossing', and in the championship of the 'just price' against the unfettered operation of the market, established the tradition.

In fact, since these same early centuries, the objective process of economic evolution has seen the providers of services become steadily more important as necessary collaborators with the producers, whether of farm or workshop. The larger the scale of output from the single plant or locality, the greater the productivity of the machine, the wider the marketing range, the more extensive the capitals, the more complex the organization of production, then the potential for expansion, together with the possibilities of realizing the full technical limits of productivity, are alike dependent upon more effective provision of services which cocoon the productive function on all sides. Such providers of business services are part and parcel of the evolving system which has produced greater wealth: a necessary, if not sufficient, condition of that evolution.

In fact, the growth of services relative to physical production (whether measured by value of net output or by differential growth in the labour force) has proved to be a consequence of modernization and the growth of wealth. With increases in income beyond certain thresholds the utility or satisfaction derived from more services increases faster than that from more goods. In all advanced societies the role of government, and the services dispensed by government, has increased relative to the national income. The parameters of sophistication and costs in health, education, entertainment, travel, leisure activities and the like expand exponentially with income. But the progressive expansion of services in the richest, most sophisticated economies and societies is also a consequence and integral aspect of evolution of business and industry itself. The mass production of goods utilizing the full potential of improving technology implies an incremental development of design, planning, distribution and marketing services. An increasing scale or complexity of business organization requires greater financial and managerial controls. Widening markets demand increased investment in transport and communications. Such relative trends towards services are, in fact, greater than the occupational censuses usually reveal because of the growth of 'white-collar' functions within the occupational groups designated as employed in industry.

These broad structural trends can be quickly documented. In the richest economies in the world the proportion of the national income contributed by 'services' (excluding wholesale and retail trade, communications and transport) is now above 30% – and this has been rising rapidly since 1945: in the U.S.A. from 26% to 37%; in Sweden from 26% to 38%; in West Germany from 21% to 32%; in France from 20% to 31%; in the United Kingdom from 25% to 33%. The inclusion of trade, transport and communications would bring the present percentage up to 50% of the national income. In countries of middling wealth – such as Argentina or Brazil – the equivalent percentage contributed to their national income by services is 23–25% and for the poorest range of countries, such as India, it is usually 14-15%.* Thus the great rise in wealth, led by the advanced nations, since the Second World War, as long before, has been associated with this progressive trend towards a 'services economy' and relatively away from agriculture and industry; while in the spectrum between the richest and the poorest nations at a single point of time there is also a very close correlation between the level of national wealth per capita and the relative importance of the contribution of services to the total national income. It needs to be said that this process of 'de-industrialization', if such be its name, follows a long-term evolutionary trend, not being just the product of short-term depression or crisis; nor, as a gradual phenomenon, is it the immediate cause of high unemployment or stagnation (although it may well be associated with slower rates of growth amongst the richest economies).

More specific measurement is possible to document the growth of financial services in the British economy during recent decades; a trend which has been little short of dramatic but much overlooked.† Since 1954 the most rapidly expanding large occupational group of the total working population has been that of those providing 'financial, business, professional and scientific services'. They more than doubled in strength from 2.26 million in 1954 to 4.77 million in 1977, their share of the working population almost doubling from 9.3% to 18.1%; whereas the share of the workforce in manufacturing industry shrank steadily from 37.9% (9.12 million) of the whole to 27.9% (7.35 million), and that of the labour force in construction from 6.2% (1.49 million) to 4.8% (1.27 million). Numbers of those employed in 'accountancy services' alone rose from 78,000 in 1959 to 90,000 in 1977. Since 1951 'insurance, banking, finance and business services' has been consistently the fastest growing sector of the economy in terms of output, save only for 'gas, electricity and water'.

The latter chapters of the book show how Whinney Murray, Turquands Barton Mayhew and other major accountancy firms developed an international dimension to their practices – symbol-

---

* All data from United Nations Statistical Yearbooks. 'Other services' include 'financing, insurance, real estate and business services, community social and personal services, public administration and defence'. The individual categories are not separately shown.
† Central Statistical Office, *Annual Abstract of Statistics* (H.M.S.O.).

ized by the formation of the international partnership, Ernst & Whinney International, in 1979 with Ernst & Ernst of the United States. The accountants in the twentieth century, like the banks, insurance companies and shipping firms from the nineteenth century, developed their international commitments originally on the basis of providing services for their British clients, who were themselves operating overseas, or for British-based multi-national companies. This was a natural extension of Britain's own business commitments in the international economy. From this base, however, overseas business independent of British firms is rapidly developing, as has happened, for example, with shipbroking and auctioneering, and the partnership of the international practice itself is becoming multi-national.

The direct overseas earnings of the accountancy practices have not been significant as contributions to the balance of payments on the same scale as insurance companies or banks, but their operations have been integral with the expansion of British business overseas which has contributed very greatly, both to export earnings and more particularly to 'invisible' earnings through the supply of services (commercial, financial, technical and professional) in the world economy. This expansion of services, in fact, has wrought a quiet revolution in Britain's balance of payments during the past generation no less than in the structure of the national economy. Net surpluses earned by services have been offsetting deficits in the balance of commodity trade since the eighteenth century, but their relative importance and the contribution of different constituent services have changed markedly in recent times.

Net earnings from shipping, for example, which were previously by far the largest of all the surpluses from services, making up about two-thirds of the whole before 1914, have gone into deficit, while the earnings of financial services* have risen most rapidly. The net surplus produced from all invisibles (interest and profits as well as earned income from services) rose from £273 million in 1967 to virtually £2,000 million in 1977, while the visible trade deficit grew from under £600 million to over £1,700 million. The role of services in total exports increased from less than a fifth to over a quarter, Credits from financial services alone increased from just over £100 million in 1964 to

* Insurance, banking, commodity trading, merchanting of other goods, brokerage, legal earnings – and accountancy earnings.

over £1,360 million in 1977. Moreover some earnings from financial services lie outside these totals, being hidden within other categories, such as contributions to the earnings of British firms overseas or repatriated business profits. Swift expansion overseas by British accountancy firms, in company with banks and insurance companies, may be one reason why finance and insurance services contribute a significantly higher percentage to gross domestic product in the United Kingdom (11.7% in 1970) than in either France (8.5%) or Germany (6.4%).

Such are the new dimensions being wrought in the British economy, and in its dealings with the world, by the contributions of services – business, financial and professional services in particular, with the accountancy firms prominent among the leaders.. Laments over the export performance and poor productivity record of British industry too-often divert attention from the excellent record which British business has enjoyed in supplying commercial, financial and professional services to the world. Overseas success in such diverse fields as international banking, insurance, aviation (if no longer shipping), shipbroking, the construction metal exchanges and commodity markets, retailing, merchanting, auctioneering, accountancy, and – dare one add? – British medical, professional and academic expertise, stands as proof of internationally competitive standards in sectors of the economy of progressive importance.

This has been a silent revolution, still largely undocumented by historians. Success does not breed evidence like failure. Quite apart from the predilections which historians, like governments, have had for production, services have not spawned the documentary data which have provided the staple fare for historians of industry. There have been no armies of oppressed workers in coal mines, satanic mills or the sweated trades to induce elaborate parliamentary investigations, and then the detailed reports of official inspectors; no great legislative battles in Parliament to stir the nation and produce bibliographies of oppression or crisis; no great strikes to dominate the consciousness of a generation; no threats of nationalization, or reports from the Monopolies Commission; no extensive record of failure, with lame ducks to be supported or the National Enterprise Board to be wooed. This is not to say that the path of expansion has always been smooth, but compared with the history of textiles or shipbuilding or mining the contrast stands. Historians of the business professions do not have their evidence presented in such obvious ways: it has to be sought out in nooks and crannies, unearthed and put together. This book seeks to open a window on one such story which has been too long neglected in the evolution of British business and the British economy.

PETER MATHIAS

All Souls College, Oxford
15 November 1980

CHAPTER 1

Introduction and Early Days

The evolution of the accountancy profession in Britain is inextricably linked with the history of its Industrial Revolution. The latter began towards the end of the eighteenth century, some sixty years before the foundation of either Turquand, Youngs or Whinney, Smith & Whinney – two of the oldest English accountancy practices. We shall, therefore, open by looking at the character of these early but fundamental links before taking up the story of these two firms in the 1840s. In a letter to Mrs Piozzi, Dr Johnson advised the mother of a wealthy heir, 'Let your boy learn arithmetic, dear Madam, he will not then be a prey to every rascal which this town [London] swarms with: teach him the value of money and how to reckon it.'[1] The arithmetic that Johnson referred to included basic book-keeping and it was the continued refinement of these methods, initially by entrepreneurs, which encouraged the creation of a specialist profession of accountants. They, in turn, were responsible for further innovation and the development of advanced procedures designed to measure and control the financial performance of companies. It is the nature of the changing connection between accountancy and business that this study seeks to elucidate.

The story has a long pre-history, virtually as old as western civilization. In fact, crude accounts have been kept in various forms since antiquity and the art of book-keeping was practised in chanceries and merchant houses throughout medieval Europe. However, Greek and Roman accounting had been designed not to measure notions of profit and loss, but to keep an accurate record of acquisitions and outgoings and to expose any losses due to dishonesty or negligence.[2] The same was largely true of the charge-and-discharge system developed during the twelfth century in the royal Exchequer and subsequently re-applied to the larger ecclesiastical and lay estates in England. Its principal aim was to prevent fraud or loss by recording the respective liability

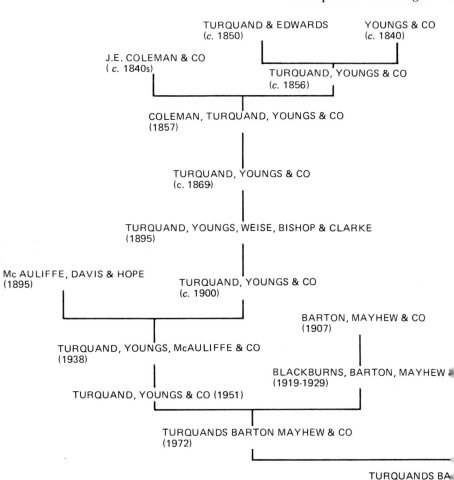

TURQUAND & EDWARDS
(c. 1850)

YOUNGS & CO
(c. 1840)

J.E. COLEMAN & CO
(c. 1840s)

TURQUAND, YOUNGS & CO
(c. 1856)

COLEMAN, TURQUAND, YOUNGS & CO
(1857)

TURQUAND, YOUNGS & CO
(c. 1869)

TURQUAND, YOUNGS, WEISE, BISHOP & CLARKE
(1895)

McAULIFFE, DAVIS & HOPE
(1895)

TURQUAND, YOUNGS & CO
(c. 1900)

BARTON, MAYHEW & CO
(1907)

TURQUAND, YOUNGS, McAULIFFE & CO
(1938)

BLACKBURNS, BARTON, MAYHEW
(1919-1929)

TURQUAND, YOUNGS & CO (1951)

TURQUANDS BARTON MAYHEW & CO
(1972)

TURQUANDS BA
WHINNEY MURR

Ernst & Wh

Whinney's Predecessor Firms

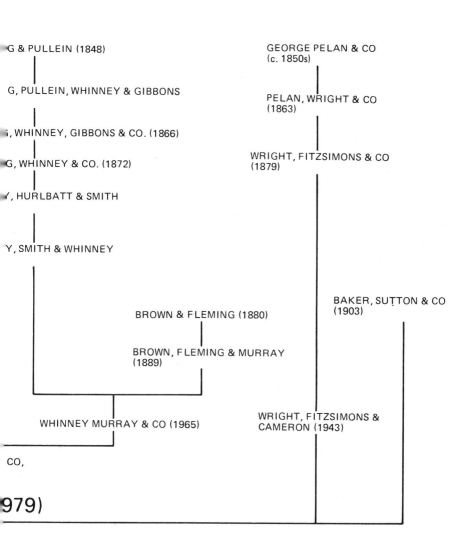

G & PULLEIN (1848)

G, PULLEIN, WHINNEY & GIBBONS

G, WHINNEY, GIBBONS & CO. (1866)

G, WHINNEY & CO. (1872)

Y, HURLBATT & SMITH

Y, SMITH & WHINNEY

GEORGE PELAN & CO
(c. 1850s)

PELAN, WRIGHT & CO
(1863)

WRIGHT, FITZSIMONS & CO
(1879)

BROWN & FLEMING (1880)

BROWN, FLEMING & MURRAY
(1889)

BAKER, SUTTON & CO
(1903)

WHINNEY MURRAY & CO (1965)

WRIGHT, FITZSIMONS &
CAMERON (1943)

CO,

979)

of officials in their daily dealings on behalf of the lord or bishop. Under this system each, within the hierarchy of officers, had to account for the outgoings and incomings under his control; yet not all merchants or manors conformed to this charge-and-discharge model, many preferring to improvise their own methods.[3] The reigns of Edward I and II witnessed the authorship of a number of treatises on estate management, most drawing on Exchequer models for their accounting precedent. During the latter part of the thirteenth century the law was amended to facilitate action against defrauding officials and this encouraged more intensive farming of the lord's estate. The economic and political impetus towards more profitable estate management, in turn, created a need for more reliable accounting and the incidence of manors keeping orderly accounts increased, while others which had already devised rudimentary systems improved their accuracy by adopting the approved form of reeve's account.[4] From the outset, therefore, accountancy behaved as a service, responding to events rather than initiating change. It is also thought that the thirteenth century generated a new class of accounting clerks conversant with the charge-and-discharge system, who were either resident on large estates or itinerant, travelling from manor to manor assisting the local reeve.[5] We can thus regard these men in several senses as the precursors of the professional accountant in practice.

The next major step forward in accounting knowledge occurred in the early fourteenth century when Florentines and Venetians developed the double-entry system, though the method was not written about until 1494 – Luca Pacioli's *Summa di Arithmetica*, printed in Venice, being the first published exposition of double-entry book-keeping. The new practice gradually spread through Europe to England following the well-worn channels of commerce. Its pedigree is well illustrated by an early accounting text printed in England. Jan Ympyn Christoffel's version of Pacioli, as the title page declared, had been 'Translated with great diligence out of Italian toung into dutche, and out of dutche into french, and out of french into English'; it was published in London in 1547.[6] The first original work in English on accountancy, by James Peele, was published by Richard Grafton a few years later in 1553 under the title, *The maner and fourme how to keepe a perfecte reconyng, after the order of the moste and worthie and notable accompte, of debitour and creditour*. As in Italy, however, publication followed practice, the earliest example of double-entry book-keeping in England being Sir Thomas Gresham's journal kept for the years 1546–1551,[7] although Thomas Howell, a member of the Draper's Company, trading chiefly in Spain, where he was resident between 1522 and 1527, produced in that country the first double-entry book-keeping in the English language.[8]

Despite such early individual instances, in general the Italian system of double-entry book-keeping made slow headway in England during the next three centuries.[9] Professor Yamey's examination of surviving material suggests that double-entry was not commonly used by substantial merchants even as late as the eighteenth century. Indeed, its widespread diffusion was a feature of the following century and then, too, its adoption was often greatly delayed. For example, the Sun Fire Office, founded in 1710, did not introduce this system until 1890, while the Capital and Counties Bank, which was to merge with Lloyds in 1918, was still using various single-entry methods at the time of the amalgamation, a factor slowing their practical union.[10] Such instances of the failure to adopt double-entry for so long were probably as unrepresentative of the general position by the end of the nineteenth century as was the precocious adoption of the system by Gresham and Howell in the sixteenth. The main impetus behind these developments undoubtedly came from the progressive spread of industrialization and, in particular, its attendant commercial expansion. In the eighteenth century, the Industrial Revolution remained limited in its impact with small-scale workshops, artisan technology and restricted family and partnership enterprise still characterizing the organization of business and the nascent accountancy profession. Although a canal and turnpike road network had been laid down, mills, mines, foundries and potteries set up, it was not until the early decades of the nineteenth century that the momentum of industrialization and urban growth became widely apparent and took an obvious hold on the nation's fortunes.

Economists traditionally divide an industrial nation into three sectors: the primary (concerned with agriculture, forestry and fishing), the secondary (industry, mining and construction) and the tertiary sector (transport, commerce, government and services generally).[11] Nineteenth-century services may broadly be further divided into three main groups: retail and wholesale trade including auctioneers and land agents; secondly, finance (banking, insurance and brokerage); and thirdly, professional services, of which accountancy, along with surveying and the law, is one.[12] One way, therefore, of identifying the Industrial Revolution is to say that it involved fundamental structural change in the economy with both absolute and relative growth in the size of the secondary and tertiary sectors.[13] In 1801 Britain's service sector contained 1.4 million people (34% of the total occupied population), which by 1901 had risen to 7.2 million (45%).[14] This expansion was accompanied by increased specialization within the service sector as jobs which were formerly performed by the entrepreneur himself 'were developed [in the nineteenth century] as independent professionalisms operating as separate business units'.[15] Thus, the Industrial Revolution (or rapid and sustained economic growth) should not be seen simply in terms of the growth of physical output and increased productivity in coal, iron, manufacturing and commerce, but in addition, should be viewed in the light of heightened efficiency in the service sector, resulting from evolved skills, better expertise and increased specialization.[16] The greater the advances in output and productivity in the factory and on the farm produced by the miracles of technical advance, the greater the economy's dependence upon improving efficiency in the network of services that surrounds production technology, if such progress is to be sustained.[17] Thus the growth of the economy (and the prosperity of the nation) has been much dependent upon links between the growth of business and the professional services which support it. One of the aims of this history is to try to throw fresh light upon this fundamental connection, though it is limited generally to accountancy and concentrates more specifically on a number of firms within that profession.

In the early stages of the Industrial Revolution, as in the Middle Ages, the entrepreneur or merchant often performed such accountancy as was necessary with the assistance of his own clerks qualified in elementary book-keeping. The businessman invented his own methods to suit his trade or particular transactions, rather than call in a specialist to deal with his accounts. For example, Josiah Wedgwood, who employed a relatively large number of workers performing a variety of different functions, devised a complex system of cost accounting to cope with the peculiarities of the pottery trade.[18] His method, dating from the late 1770s, took note of depreciation, interest on capital, losses incurred through breakages, accidents and imperfect pieces.[19] It was sufficiently detailed to take account of the cost of book-keeping itself and was both accurate and flexible enough to influence wages, techniques of manufacture, quantities produced and prices charged.[20] Wedgwood, however, was scarcely representative of eighteenth-century businessmen. Most conformed to a much simpler concept of the role of accounting with more basic procedures and a limited range of account books. At this stage, therefore, many entrepreneurs did not feel the need for an independent accountant. Undertaking simple (if detailed) book-keeping in the counting house, they were capable of performing virtually all the calculations required for the practical operation of their businesses. Later, as companies became more complex, with much of their capital subscribed by outsiders, specialist skills were demanded, so that accountants increasingly found themselves employed on a consultancy basis.

As an illustration of the difficult accounting problems faced by entrepreneurs in the early stages of the Industrial Revolution, the case of the Soho Manufactory of Boulton and Watt in Birmingham may be cited. In the 1790s when equipping the foundry, James Watt Junior could not think of a way to account for machinery made on the premises. He asked advice from George Lee, a Salford mill owner, whose reply demonstrates that, although accounts were not then being used as an aid to management, there was at least a growing feeling that their accounting methods were in need of improvement.[21]

I wished [Lee wrote on 11 March 1797] I could communicate to you any information respecting the mode of keeping manufacturing books – in the introduction of machinery we never yet could reduce it to regular piece work or divide the labour of making and repairing it in such a manner as to determine the distinct cost of each. In the manufactory I have attain'd rather more accuracy but yet far short of my hopes and wishes.

Previously, in 1786, Matthew Boulton had said to Watt, with an insight which was not to be taken seriously for a further century that, 'the best engine and mill in the world is not sufficient without *exact* and shrewd management....'[22] But as will be seen, cost accounting developed by engineers and accountants in industry was not widely adopted until the 1880s in America and much later in Britain (see p. 112).

Even Wedgwood's sophisticated accounting system did have its limitations, failing to interlock the various components to achieve a coherent financial analysis.[23] This was, in fact, a general criticism of late eighteenth-century accountancy, while the particular conceptual and operational problems of handling capital costs (as distinct from current costs), depreciation and the ability to assess the effect of technical innovation were not properly understood.[24] For example, the study of Thomas Grigg's retail clothing business at Ballingdon, Essex, has shown that in the 1740s 'neither the valuation of assets, nor the estimate of profits gives a comprehensive survey of capital or income.... Even when in partnership with others, when malting for retail or when stock grazing, although keeping accounts, Griggs struck no formal balance.'[25] At this time money spent on capital improvements was not generally distinguished from cash spent on maintenance.[26] Men engaged on production jobs were often switched to construction work when fresh plant was needed, while owners ploughed back their salaries and savings, often taking household expenses from the business, without taking account of this in their levels of profit, or even identifying such items separately.

Accordingly, until well into the nineteenth century, accountancy remained an area of some indeterminacy, where entrepreneurs devised their own methods of control with greater or lesser degrees of success. In the 1830s Hague & Cook, a West Riding firm, mixed their banking, merchanting and manufacturing accounts without attempting to distinguish the precise areas of profitability or loss. Similarly, for some years the Eastern Counties Railway failed to untangle its accounts as a result of the 'perplexity and confusion' in which they had been left by the late secretary in 1839.[27] As late as 1856 Robert Hyde Greg, head of a distinguished family partnership of cotton mill owners, criticized his son's management of Calver Mill, Derbyshire, on the grounds that, 'You call me nervous and boast of your being a perfect manager. I keep strict accounts which you do not, and I know the incomings and accumulations, where any and so forth, and the responsibilities of my situation as a man of business.'[28]

Having noted that businesses as a whole did not see the need to employ specialist accountants, the latter part of the eighteenth century did witness a gradual growth in the numbers of men describing themselves as such. Normally performing a broad range of tasks, they were not as well qualified as their Victorian counterparts. Most were little more than book-keepers who often also advertised themselves as 'writing masters'.[29] One gentleman mentioned in the *Liverpool Directory* of 1790 as a 'mercantile accomptant' rather devalued his professional specialization by describing himself in addition as a 'dealer in tin plates'.[30] Just as the entrepreneur performed a broad range of tasks in the eighteenth century, so the accountant also offered a wide range of services. Other more closely related functions included work as notaries and general agents, while Frederick Whinney quoted an 1837 London directory which mentioned the jobs of auctioneer and appraiser among an accountant's tasks.[31]

A further indication of the rising demand for accountancy services in the latter part of the eighteenth century was the proliferation of accounting manuals and text books published at the time. Most of the authors including Charles Snell, Richard Hayes, John Clark and James Dodson (who wrote *The Accountant, or, the method of book-keeping deduced from clear principles*, London, 1750) were private tutors whose works had been written in part for their fee-paying students.[32] They were practical guides rather than academic studies, designed to assist merchants and book-keepers in ordering their affairs. Charles Snell, 'Master of the Free-Writing School in Foster Lane, near Cheapside', was also author of *The Tradesman's Director; or, a short and easy method of keeping his books of accompts*, London (1697), while *The Merchant's Counting-House*, London (1720), was designed to teach 'merchants accompts in the true Italian way ... a method of book-keeping which making reason its guide admits no entrance but what is truth, or according to reason....'[33] John Cooke's *The Compting House Assistant or Book-keeping made easy*, London (1764), declares unashamedly in the preface that '... it is principally intended for the perusal of youth at school and in the compting-house, I have, therefore, endeavoured ... to avoid burthening it with tedious rules ... and accompanied the examples with such explanatory notes as cannot fail of making them plain to the most common capacities'.[34] Although most of these eighteenth-century works focused on mercantile accounting, a few were directed at estate management: George Clerke's *The Landed-Man's assistant; or, the steward's vade mecum. Containing the newest most plain and perspicuous method of keeping the accompts of gentlemen's estates yet extant*, London (1715).[35]

Towards the end of the eighteenth century the titles of contemporary accounting literature began to reflect the impact of the Industrial Revolution. Edward Jones's *An Address to Bankers, merchants, tradesmen* was published in 1795 at Bristol, then Britain's fourth largest port. Works were also now being printed in the new industrial towns. James Luckcock's *Practical English Book-keeping* (1802), published in Birmingham, was intended for 'young apprentices and for tradesmen on a contracted scale' and contained 'a copious illustration of the nature of profits and discounts'.[36] The broadening role of the accountant is reflected in Thomas Mortimer's definition: 'Accountant or Accomptant, is a book-keeper or person conversant with accounts; it is also applicable to persons in public offices etc, as the accountant of the bank....'[37]

Trade directories reveal that the numbers of persons identifying themselves as accountants were steadily increasing throughout the latter part of the eighteenth and early nineteenth centuries. For example, in 1776 one accountant was listed in London directories, 11 in 1799,[38] 24 in 1809-11, 47 in 1817, 99 in 1826-27 and 107 in 1840, rising to 264 in 1850.[39] The picture for Manchester is much the same, with two accountants listed in 1790, 14 in 1815, 24 in 1829 and 52 in 1840.[40] Bristol, an old-established mercantile city, had 20 accountants recorded in 1824, 28 in 1830 and 74 in 1861. Irish accountancy history, more closely analogous to English rather than Scottish, followed this pattern, the number of accountants in Dublin Trade Directories rising from 4 in 1795 to 7 in 1800 and 16 by 1820.[41] Using a wider definition of the term, the 1841 Census for England and Wales enumerated a total of 4,974 accountants in the country.[42] While this dramatic rate of growth doubtless reflects changes in nomenclature to some extent, as book-keepers increasingly came to regard themselves as accountants, such a change in consciousness, with the identification of an independent and valued role, is itself important in the evolution of the profession.

If it is possible to argue that a particular decade was critical for the development of the English accountancy profession, then this was the 1840s. Both government legislation and the growth in the size and complexity of businesses at this time meant that the expanding numbers of accountants were drawn into strategic positions within the economy and, once there, consolidated their hold.

Incorporation for manufacturing industry and any possibility of limited liability for shareholders had been virtually prohibited by the Bubble Act of 1720 (limiting in the case of banks any partnership to six members),[43] actually passed before the bursting of the South Sea Bubble to prevent growing competition and speculation. The repeal of this Act in 1825,[44] but more particularly the joint stock company legislation of 1844-45, relaxed the legal constraints upon incorporation and encouraged the expansion of business, while the 1856 and 1862 Acts made limitation of liability for such public companies universally available in law. In the eighteenth and early nineteenth centuries industrial units had remained relatively small, which meant that they could be managed on a family or close partnership basis, obviating any need for incorporation or limited liability. Such a structure of business organization did not provide powerful incentives for the employment of specialist independent accountants. In time, the pressure for further economies of scale and continued growth of output in larger-scale plant resulted in larger organizations demanding, amongst other things, improved financial services and better transport links. The 1840s were important in both these respects. The decade saw the projection and part completion of England's basic railway network. Parliament granted railway companies, like the canals before them, the right to raise the vast sums of money needed for their construction by the sale of shares to the public. In finance and organization they were the antithesis of small family businesses as joint stock companies were controlled by managers and financed by investors, remote from the board of directors, anxious to see a return on their capital. As matters stood few safeguards existed in law against the fraudulent use of money subscribed by shareholders. The government recognized that these vast enterprises, with capitals running into millions of pounds for the larger companies, had overstepped the traditional limits of the family partnership and hence required greater public controls.

Initially early Railway Acts did not normally make provision for shareholders to examine the relevant accountancy records, nor were periodic financial statements to be published.[45] Later Acts amended this omission and in 1835 the Great Western Railway's Act required that half-yearly financial statements be laid before the shareholders at a general meeting. These new regulations naturally brought extra work for the growing body of public accountants. 'Perhaps that which added most to our duties', recalled Frederick Whinney, 'was the great creation of companies in the years 1844 and 1845, principally connected with the railways', though he also suggested that the speculative nature of 'the rail mania of 1845 brought us a very great acquisition of business not only in audits, but also in the winding-up of companies'.[46]

Sir Robert Peel as Prime Minister, with Gladstone at the Board of Trade, was concerned that great and growing financial enterprises should not get out of hand as had happened in the South Sea Bubble, yet, at the same time, he did not wish to stifle entrepreneurial energies. In an attempt to regulate and safeguard the dealings of these new companies, Peel passed an Act for the Registration, Incorporation and Regulation of Joint Stock Companies in 1844.[47] It provided them with an administrative and financial framework requiring that the names and addresses of directors together with their annual balance sheets be filed with the Registrar of Companies. In addition, the auditors, 'one of whom at least shall be appointed by the shareholders', were to be given open access to the company's books while compiling their report on the balance sheet which was to be a 'full and fair' statement of its financial condition.[48] Even so the Act did not prescribe the preparation of a profit and loss account, nor did it specify the form of the balance sheet and its contents.[49]

In the following year Peel's government passed the Companies Clauses Consolidation Act which took matters further.[50] It determined that 'every auditor shall have at least one share in the undertaking' and – most important for the future – that 'it shall be lawful for the auditors to employ such accountants and other persons they may think proper, at the expense of the company'.[51] This represents an intermediate stage in auditing, between the appointment of independent shareholders as auditors and later the election of individual practising accountants; later still the firm of auditors itself was appointed. The 1845 Act went further in defining the balance sheet, requiring that,[52]

... an exact balance sheet shall be made up, which shall exhibit a true statement of the capital stock, credits and property of every description belonging to the company, and the debts due by the company ... and a distinct view of the profit and loss which shall have arisen. ...

Neither of these Acts provided in itself for incorporation with limited liability. Their main aim was to provide shareholders and creditors with a clear statement of a company's solvency and to reassure them that dividends had not been paid out of capital. To distinguish capital transactions from current income and expenditure in a systematic way, while determining in detail accounting conventions governing the valuation of capital assets, was to transform the significance of accounting procedures.

Although these new financial controls developed, unscrupulous directors still had ample opportunity for fraud. George Hudson, christened the 'Railway King' for putting together a virtual empire of railway companies through mergers, sometimes deliberately delayed or suppressed the publication of accounts to conceal his manipulation of the figures. *The Railway Magazine* in 1844 criticized auditors for not scrutinizing totals more carefully and making 'occasional suggestions to the companies in which they are engaged'.[53] By transferring expenditure from revenue to capital account, George Hudson, as chairman of the Eastern Counties Railway, paid out £115,000 more in dividends than the books said the company had earned between 1845 and 1848. It was in response to popular protests that shareholder auditors called in public accountants.[54]

Railway companies, by the nature of their size and financial complexity, presented a host of specialized problems which further encouraged the employment of public accountants as auditors and advisers. Because of the very large capitals involved and the high proportion of fixed costs (often of a technical type), including annual payments of interest on a scale which no earlier business had faced, depreciation created particular problems in railway accounts. Early on, some companies had naïvely imagined that when the cost of replacement locomotives rose, then the value of their assets went up by an equivalent amount.[55] This ignored the fact that as their engines aged so they became less efficient, more prone to breakdown and so less valuable. In that non-inflationary age, unlike our own, the principal reason why replacements were more expensive was not because locomotives had become more valuable in monetary terms, but because new engines were technically improved and demanded more skilled man-hours to build.

The double-account system had been specifically designed to cope with railway accounting problems. William Deloitte, as the auditor of the Great Western Railway, laid claim to having devised the method, though Quilter, Ball & Co also demanded credit. It was argued that special reserve funds to take account of capital depreciation need not be set up by railway companies as they had of necessity to ensure that their networks were properly maintained. Current expenditure on repairs and renewals was considered sufficient to compensate for any possible depreciation of capital assets. While the system worked reasonably well in practice, it had some teething troubles. Deciding upon the effective life of an asset has always required a subjective judgement to be made by businessmen and accountants in advance of known results. For example, engineers initially thought that wrought-iron rails would last a hundred years, but experience taught them that a life of twenty years was good (steel tracks available from the 1850s were to last longer). Having found favour with the railways, in 1868 Parliament made the system compulsory for all railway companies and then in 1871 for gasworks as well.[56] Accordingly it became a requirement that the engineer-in-chief sign and publish with the annual accounts a certificate declaring that the physical condition of the assets had remained unchanged; in the case of railway companies, that the track, buildings, locomotives and rolling stock had been adequately maintained, which additionally proved a safeguard against fraud. Although considered rigorous and sound by nineteenth-century standards, the double-account system fell behind the advances made in other areas of accounting and was finally phased out under the 1948 Companies Act.

Another significant piece of legislation enacted in 1844 was the Joint Stock Banking Act, which required these banks provide their shareholders with an annual balance sheet and a profit and loss account (an obligation absent from other joint stock companies) in an attempt to make them more secure.[57] Provision was also made for the election of auditors by the shareholders, while the banks were bound to publish a monthly statement of assets and liabilities. This legislation not only encouraged the appointment of public accountants to assist the auditors, but also resulted in the banks themselves appointing salaried accountants to regulate their daily financial dealings.[58]

The preceding examples have shown that innovation in railway accounting came from the shareholder auditors appointing public accountants to assist them. As men who had taken the trouble to acquire the skills, the latter were particularly concerned to see their widespread application. The 1840s also proved to be a significant decade in witnessing the establishment of a number of leading accountancy practices, which in time were not only to grow in size but were also to exercise a powerful influence on the character of the profession: Deloittes (in 1845), Price Waterhouse

(1849), Harding & Pullein (1848) Turquand & Edwards (*c.* 1850) and Youngs & Co (*c.* 1840). This is further evidence that the changes in legislation and business practices in this decade made it critical for the evolution of accountancy as a profession.

Harding & Pullein (the firm which Frederick Whinney [1829–1916] joined in December 1849) have Day Books which go back to August 1848, but both principals were practising accountants before they came together in partnership.[59] A Victorian hand-written manuscript records that 'Mr Robert Palmer Harding [1821–1893] commenced business as an accountant ... in July 1847', a belief which is confirmed by his obituary.[60] It is thought that Harding had originally been a fashionable West End hatter whose business had got into difficulties. When his books were produced in court, the official said that he had never seen better kept business records and that Harding would be far better en-gaged in accountancy.[61] R. P. Harding is not mentioned in the *Post Office Directory* for 1845 to 1847 but does appear in 1850 as 'Harding & Pullein, accountants and arbitrators, 16 Gresham Street'.[62] Nothing further is known of Edmund Pullein as he, too, goes unrecorded until 1850.

More information exists on the Whinney family. In 1850 William Whinney [b. 1820], Frederick's half-brother (both sons of Thomas Whinney [1793–1853] a licensed victualler who later joined William at his livery stable), is recorded as being the owner of a livery stable at 28 Shepherd's Street, Mayfair.[63] The same directory contains an entry that there was a Frederick Thomas Whinney who was an accountant in the firm of Free & Whinney at 79 Basinghall Street.[64] A further complication is that the 1856 *Directory* mentioned a Frederick Whinney who was a 'ship and insurance broker' in partnership with a Mr Young at 114 Fenchurch Street.[65] Meantime, William Whinney had moved to a livery stable at 30 Clarges Street, Piccadilly,[66] and in 1870 appears at 33 Grosvenor Mews, Grosvenor Square.[67] It is possible that the Frederick Thomas was Frederick himself (there is no record of anybody with those two christian names in the family tree) and that this was an early but abortive attempt to set up an accountancy practice. Frederick Whinney's private ledger details dealings for a Young & Whinney between 1854 and 1855; his grandfather in South Shields had been a ship broker and his uncle continued the business, suggesting that his family might have been a source of work.[68] However, Harding & Pullein's Cash

Books reveal that Frederick Whinney began work as a clerk on 8 December 1849 when he was paid £1 5s per week.[69] Almost from the outset Whinney received more than the half-dozen other clerks and he appears to have been employed in a senior capacity. This suggests, therefore, if Frederick was the Whinney in Free & Whinney or the ship and insurance broker, then these must have been part-time enterprises.

Still less is known of Turquand, Youngs' early history. William Turquand's [1819-1894] father was one of the first official assignees appointed under the Bankruptcy Act of 1831[70] and the son is recorded as being an official assignee at 13 Old Jewry in 1846-47.[71] The connection with government continued after he had entered private practice when Turquand was appointed an inspector by the Board of Trade to investigate and report on companies wishing to obtain a certificate of registration under the 1855 Companies Act.[72] By 1852 he had entered into partnership with a Mr Edwards* at which point they were described as 'accountants, arbitrators and referees', still based in Old Jewry.[73] In 1857 William Turquand and the brothers Young joined J. E. Coleman, the first *Directory* describing the partnership as Coleman, Turquand, Youngs & Co, at 16 Tokenhouse Yard, Lothbury, being in 1859. Turquand achieved a degree of recognition in 1855 when he had been involved in a major legal case – Royal British Bank v. Turquand (6 E. & B., 327) – which had established the principle that a third party in dealing with a company need not have to examine its internal organizational rules to ensure that its officers had obtained the necessary authority. It was, therefore, an important case in laying the foundations for sound business practice.

John [d. 1888] and Alexander Young [d. 1907] were the sons of a farmer of Windmill, near Gordonstown, Moray. John Young first served an apprenticeship in law with Alexander Cooper in Elgin, but then decided to move to London where he entered the office of Robert Fletcher & Co as a junior clerk; Fletcher, another Scotsman, had been a founder member of the Aberdeen Society, drawn to the capital to assist with the financial reorganization of the London, Chatham & Dover Railway.[74] Apparently in 1840

---

* It is possible that this was William Edwards, F.C.A., who, starting on his own in 1843, had been responsible for training 'a considerable percentage of the chartered accountants now in practice in London', including S. L. Price (*The Accountant*, No. 527, 10 January 1885, p. 15).

John then set up on his own and was later joined by his brother. Having refused various offers of partnership the two merged in c.1856 with William Turquand, being joined a year later by J. E. Coleman.[75] They were by no means alone in being the sons of Scots farmers. Other such accountants, Richard Brown, T. P. Laird and Sir William Peat, enjoyed similar Scottish origins, reflecting the general point that mid nineteenth-century accountants tended to be of middle-class parents of modest means, which is to be expected of an emergent profession.[76] James Edward Coleman had established a considerable reputation as a City accountant by the late 1840s and was often called by the Bank of England to investigate the solvency of suspect firms, including Trueman & Cook, colonial brokers. His success was recalled by Ernest Cooper [1848-1926] who added, 'I am not sure that I ever saw him, but he was reported to be living in a park as a Buckinghamshire squire.'[77]

An important feature of accountancy practices in the mid-nineteenth century, like merchanting, banking and manufacturing more generally, proved to be the connection with Non-conformist sects. Cooper Brothers, founded in 1854 by William Cooper, were staunch Quakers.[78] Ware, Ward & Co, a practice established at Bristol in 1867, was set up by Charles Ware, a Plymouth Brother, and then handed on to his children who were also Brethren.[79] Samuel Lowell Price's [1821-1887] (founder of Price Waterhouse) brother Charles, a pottery manufacturer based in Bristol, married the daughter of a Baptist minister, suggesting that if the Price family were not Dissenters, then they had certainly formed close commercial and social connections with Nonconformist groups. Edwin Waterhouse [1840-1917] (the other founder of Price Waterhouse), son of Arthur a Liverpool merchant, was born into a Quaker family, but in later life he joined the Church of England. Later in the century, Basil Pike [1871-1957], founder of Pike, Russell & Co, London chartered accountants, was the son of a third-generation Baptist minister, though his son later joined the Presbyterian Church of England.[80] Whilst William Deloitte [1818-1898] was not a Dissenter he was an outsider to established English society in a different sense, as his grandfather had been an émigré fleeing France in 1793.[81] Being a Roman Catholic, he was debarred by the Test and Corporation Acts from holding official posts, while popular anti-French prejudice must initially have made life difficult.

It is an interesting question why so many accountants, entrepreneurs and merchants were Dissenters. Part of the answer doubtless lies with restrictive legislation, particularly the Test and Corporation Acts, passed in 1672. Non-conformists loyal to their faith were not allowed to hold civil or military office, sit in Parliament or local government assemblies, be appointed as Justices of the Peace or go to Oxford or Cambridge. Although the repeal of the Test and Corporation Acts in 1829 allowed them to hold governmental posts, most other restrictions remained, which encouraged the pursuit of business and commercial careers.

In addition, Non-conformist groups had set up a number of exceptionally proficient academies which were organized to provide a practical education consolidating and perpetuating this commitment to business. Unlike so many Anglican or Catholic schools, they did not concentrate on the classics, but taught bookkeeping, mathematics, foreign languages and elementary sciences.[82] They also instilled the virtues of hard work, prudence, honesty and advancement (to the point where some historians have argued that it was occasionally a cynical attempt to improve output),[83] all of which were qualities calculated to make a successful accountant. By 1700, Lancashire, already a developing commercial region, probably had some 20,000 Dissenters. Norwich, in another important manufacturing and business region, had a sizeable Non-conformist element which included the Gurneys, established Quaker cloth traders and bankers-to-be.[84] The strongest concentrations were the Quakers of the Midlands and the West Country, particularly in Bristol and spreading into South Wales. These were soon to become the heartlands of the Industrial Revolution and places where accountants were to derive a fair proportion of their work. Nevertheless, London still remained the principal port, financial and business centre in the land, also with a powerful Non-conformist community.

Unfortunately, little is known of Frederick Whinney's religious background and it remains most likely that he was Anglican, as is the present family. However, John Smith, of Whinney, Smith & Whinney, was described by Harold Whinney as a 'bearded old Quaker'. The name Turquand is not English, and like Deloitte, William Turquand could well have been descended from an *émigré* family. *The General London Guide* for 1794 recorded the existence of a silk manufacturing firm, Turquand, Grugeon & Turquand at 10 Old Jewry, this being an industry much characterized by immigrants.[85] Devin of Buckley, Hall, Devin & Co in Hull was the grandson of D'Vin, a French aristocrat who had fled the revolution and settled in Richmond. Thomas Shuttleworth (of Shuttleworth & Haworth, an old established Manchester practice, which much later merged with Turquand Barton Mayhew), a signatory of the 1880 Charter of Incorporation of the English Institute, was a leading Methodist in Bury at the turn of the century.

Another important feature of these early accountancy firms was the emphasis placed on family continuity. The founders of Cooper Brothers, Ware, Ward and Thomson McLintock all placed their children in the business. Relations of both the Harding and Whinney families entered the partnership. Frederick Whinney's two sons Arthur and Frank became partners, while in turn, Arthur's two youngest sons Ernest and Douglas also joined the firm, Ernest becoming senior partner in 1960. Today his son Jack Whinney and Douglas's son John Whinney are both partners. Turquand, Youngs rigorously upheld the tradition of Victorian family succession into the twentieth century and it was not until 1932 that the first outsider was admitted to the partnership, when F. C. Hanna replaced Stanley Young who had died, joining the three other partners, Adam Turquand-Young, Leonard Osmond (the eldest grandson of Alexander Young) and John Bishop. This exclusive recruitment was, however, exceptional and most leading City firms, though retaining the custom of family involvement, also admitted talented members to the partnership from outside. The strong family tradition and the steady rise in status revealed by the nineteenth-century history of Whinney, Smith & Whinney offers a close parallel with the Forsyte Saga, which faithfully reflects the characteristic path of successful professional families in these same generations[86] Galsworthy, a barrister by training, detected and described this pattern evident from the genealogies of the prosperous middle-class households of his day.

References

1 *Johnsoniana*, London (1845), p. 70.
2 W. T. Baxter and Sidney Davidson (Editors), *Studies in Accounting*, London (1977), B. S. Yamey, 'Some Topics in the History of Financial Accounting in England 1500-1900', pp. 11-12. And Dorothea

Oschinsky, *Walter of Henley and other treatises on estate management and accounting*, Oxford (1971), pp. 214–15.

3 Yamey, 'History of Financial Accounting', *op. cit.*, pp. 13–14.

4 Oschinsky, *op. cit.*, p. 227.

5 *Ibid*, p. 234.

6 *Historic Accounting Literature*, London (1975), p. 69.

7 Yamey, 'History of Financial Accounting', *op. cit.*, p. 17.

8 A. C. Littleton and B. S. Yamey (Editors), *Studies in Accounting*, London (1956), Peter Ramsey, 'Some Tudor Merchants Accounts', p. 187.

9 Yamey, 'History of Financial Accounting', *op. cit.*, p. 17.

10 R. S. Sayers, *Lloyds Bank in the History of English Banking*, Oxford (1957), p. 273.

11 J. D. Gould, *Economic Growth in History*, London (1972), pp. 59–61.

12 C. M. Cipolla, *The Fontana Economic History of Europe*, Vol. III, Brighton (1976), R. M. Hartwell, 'The Service Revolution: the growth of services in the modern economy 1700–1914', p. 363.

13 R. M. Hartwell, *The Industrial Revolution and Economic Growth*, London (1971), p. 210.

14 Hartwell, 'The Service Revolution', *op, cit.*, p. 370.

15 Hartwell, *The Industrial Revolution*, *op. cit.*, p. 210.

16 *Ibid*, p. 211.

17 *Ibid*, p. 209.

18 N. McKendrick, *The Economic History Review*, XXIII (1970), 'Josiah Wedgwood and Cost Accounting in the Industrial Revolution', p. 47.

19 *Ibid*, pp. 51–2.

20 *Ibid*, pp. 59–60.

21 Quoted from Jennifer Tann, *The Development of the Factory*, London (1970), p. 39.

22 *Ibid*.

23 McKendrick, *op. cit.*, p. 63.

24 S. Pollard, *The Genesis of Modern Management*, London (1965), pp. 212, 223.

25 B. S. Yamey (Editor), *The Historical Development of Accounting, A Selection of Papers*, New York (1978), K. H. Burley, 'Some Accounting Records of an Eighteenth-Century Clothier', p. 53.

26 F. Crouzet (Editor), *Capital Formation in the Industrial Revolution*, London (1972), S. Pollard, 'Capital Accounting in the Industrial Revolution', pp. 124–5, 129.

27 Pollard, *Genesis of Management*, *op. cit.*, p. 227.

28 Mary Rose, *The Gregs of Styal*, Quarry Bank (1978), p. 17.

29 Richard Brown, *A History of Accountancy and Accountants*, Edinburgh (1905), pp. 233–4.

30 *Ibid*.

31 *The Accountant*, No. 656, 2 July 1887, p. 387.

32 Pollard, *Genesis of Management, op. cit.*, p. 116.

33 Charles Snell, *The Merchant's Counting-House: or, Wast-Book Instances*, London (1720), p. 3.

34 John Cooke, *The Compting House Assistant or Book-keeping made easy: Being a complete treatise on Merchants Accompts*, London (1764), pp. i–ii.

35 *Historic Accounting Literature, op. cit.*, p. 76.

36 *Ibid*, p. 86.

37 Thomas Mortimer, *A General Dictionary of Commerce, Trade and Manufactures*, London (1810).

38 A. C. Littleton, *Accounting Evolution to 1900*, New York (1933), p. 269.

39 Brown, *op. cit.*, p. 234.

40 *Ibid.*

41 Howard W. Robinson, *A History of Accountants in Ireland*, Dublin (1964), pp. 11–13.

42 *Census for 1841, Occupation Abstract*, Vol. XXVII (1844), p. 57.

43 6 Geo I c. 18 (1719), which came into force in June 1720.

44 6 Geo IV c. 91 (1825).

45 Sheila Marriner, *Business and Businessmen, Studies in Business, Economic and Accounting History*, Liverpool (1978), T. A. Lee, 'Company Financial Statements: An essay in business history 1830–1950', p. 237.

46 *The Accountant*, No. 656, *op. cit.*, p. 387.

47 7 & 8 Victoriae c. 110 (1844), p. 425.

48 *Ibid*, pp. 434–5.

49 Littleton and Yamey (Editors), *op. cit.*, H. C. Edey and P. Panitpakdi, 'British Company Accounting and the Law 1844–1900', p. 362.

50 8 & 9 Victoriae c. 16 (1845), p. 550.

51 *Ibid*, p. 551.

52 *Ibid*, p. 552.

53 Quoted from E. P. Jeal, *The Accountant* (1937), 'Some Reflections on the Evolution of the Professional Practice of Accountants in Great Britain', p. 525.

54 Littleton and Yamey, *op. cit.*, p. 340.

55 *Ibid*, p. 343.

56 31 & 32 Victoriae c. 119 (1868), and J. Kitchen and R. H. Parker, *Accounting Thought and Education: Six English Pioneers*, London (1980), p. 5. See also Gasworks Clauses Act (1871); Electric Lighting Act (1882).

57 7 & 8 Victoriae c. 113 (1844), p. 473; and Edey and Panitpakdi, *op. cit.*, p. 359.

58 S. C. Checkland, *Scottish Banking, A History 1695–1973*, London (1975), p. 381.

59 Harding & Pullein Day Book 1848–1854, p. 1.

60 *The Accountant*, No. 995, 30 December 1893, p. 1093.

61 Philip Magnus, The History of the Institute of Chartered Accountants of England and Wales 1880–1958, (unpublished), pp. 52–3.

62 *The Post Office London Directory* (1850), p. 791.

63 *Ibid*, p. 1080.

64 *Ibid*, pp. 754, 1080.

65 *The Post Office London Directory* (1856), pp. 1467, 1498.

66 *Ibid*, p. 1467.

67 *The Post Office London Directory* (1870), p. 1338.

68 Frederick Whinney's Private Ledger 1851–1855, p. 125.

69 Harding & Pullein Cash Book 1848–1853, 15 December 1849, p. 27.

70 Magnus, *op. cit.*, p. 25; Robson's London Directory for 1833, p. 405.

71 *The Post Office London Directory* (1846), p. 1022.

72 Magnus, *op. cit.*, p. 25.

73 *The Post Office London Directory* (1852), p. 1035.

74 R. H. Parker, *British Accountants: A Biographical Source Book*, London (1981), p. 6.

75 *The Accountant*, No. 732, 15 December 1888, p. 813; *The Post Office London Directory* (1858), p. 1458.

76 Parker, *op. cit.*, p. 4.

77 *Institute of Chartered Accountants of England and Wales, Proceedings of the Autumnal Meeting*, London (1921), Ernest Cooper, 'Fifty-seven years in an Accountant's Office', p. 46.

78 *A History of Cooper Brothers 1854–1954*, London (1954), pp. 1–3.

79 'Ware, Ward & Co, A History of the Firm', Bristol (1973), pp. 2–3.

80 *Pike, Russell & Co, An Account of a London Firm of Chartered Accountants 1903–1973*, London (1973), pp. 8–10. London (1977), pp. 2–15.

81 *Deloitte and Co 1845–1956*, Oxford (1958), p. 8.

82 Charles Wilson, *England's Apprenticeship 1603–1763*, London (1965), p. 341.

83 E. P. Thompson, *The Making of the English Working Class*, London (1963), pp. 390–5.

84 Wilson, *op. cit.*, p. 341.

85 *The General London Guide; or Tradesman's Director*, London (1794), p. 90. *Pigot & Co's London and Provincial New Commercial Directory for 1823-4*, p. 67, recorded that Turquand's father was then a stockbroker at Shorter's Court, Bank.

86 John Galsworthy, *The Man of Property*, London (1906), Penguin edition pp. 11–12.

CHAPTER 2

Victorian Accountancy

Shortly after Harding and Pullein had come together in partnership in August 1848, they employed Frederick Whinney as their senior clerk. In April 1854 he recorded in his pocket diary that he was 'in future to have 15£ per calendar month',[1] his name disappearing from the clerks' weekly wages list in the firm's Cash Books. He continued to progress and on 1 November 1857 was admitted as a partner.[2] It was agreed, however, that the 'style of the firm shall ... be Harding & Pullein' until 1 January 1859, when Whinney's name would be included.[3] But in December 1858 the three admitted a fourth partner, James Boatwright Gibbons, and on the stipulated date the firm's style became Harding, Pullein, Whinney & Gibbons.[4] The practice was divided between the main office at No. 4 Lothbury and a smaller one at No. 5 Serle Street, Lincoln's Inn. Frederick Whinney initially worked at the latter,[5] which had probably been opened for its proximity to the courts, allowing members of the firm readily to attend cases of bankruptcy.

Edmund Pullein retired in 1866 and died later that year. When Gibbons died in 1872, the style of the firm changed to Harding, Whinney & Co. Two years earlier William Hurlbatt and John Smith had been introduced as salaried partners, but it was agreed that the firm's title would remain unaltered so that their two names were not included until 1886.[6] When R. P. Harding was appointed Chief Official Receiver in 1883, he had to resign from the partnership. Arthur Whinney, Frederick's son by his second marriage to Emma Morley, then became a partner in 1891, and on Hurlbatt's death in May 1894, the firm's style changed again. This time it was to remain the same for seventy-one years. As the partners wrote to the Cashier at the Bank of England, 'we beg to advise you that on account of Mr. Hurlbatt's decease, we have changed the name and title of our firm ... to Whinney, Smith & Whinney'.[7] Frederick Whinney was the senior partner, John

Smith and Arthur Whinney [1865-1927] the other two. By this name the practice became well known in the twentieth century.

Frederick Whinney had four sons by his first marriage and a further ten children by his second. Only two of this large number joined the firm: Arthur Francis born in 1865 (his third child by his second marriage) and Frank Toller, his twelfth child born in 1874, the latter to become a partner in 1903 and retiring in 1925. John Smith having resigned in 1902, Arthur Whinney succeeded as senior partner on his father's retirement in 1905, though Frederick lived until 1916. Thus dynastic succession, typical of Victorian professional firms, was achieved.

By comparison little is known of the Victorian chronology of Coleman, Turquand, Youngs. By 1869 Coleman had retired and his name had been dropped. Three further partners had been admitted by 1885, when the style changed to Turquand, Youngs, Weise, Bishop & Clarke. Alexander Young, who in 1894 had succeeded William Turquand as senior partner, was described in his obituary in *The Times* as 'one of the most important men in the City of London'. Like Turquand, he had built up a considerable reputation in insolvency and this, combined with Young's knowledge of Romantic painting, enabled him to assemble one of the finest galleries of Corots – a collection which sold on his death in 1906 for the record sum of £525,000.

But to look at the changing composition of the partnership is to consider only a small part of these firm's histories. They were in existence to make profits. Hence, the ways in which they did so, and with what degrees of success, remain the most important lines of inquiry. Fortunately Whinney, Smith & Whinney's fee roll survives virtually unbroken from the foundation of Harding & Pullein in 1848 until the merger with Brown, Fleming & Murray in 1965, apart from a short break from 1872 to 1873. Although Turquand, Youngs were established earlier, fewer of their records survive, most having been destroyed by a recent fire. However, a number of Private Ledgers did escape the flames and, though providing no information about clients, they do contain details of the fee roll for the periods 1859-1873, 1876-1886 and 1894-1905.

The natural measure for the scale and changing fortunes of Victorian accountancy practices is the annual total of their fee income. In order to gain a picture of how these firms fared through the century the monetary totals of their fees year by year have been adjusted by a price index to offset the effect of annual price movements and these figures have then been represented on a graph (Fig.1).[8] It can readily be seen that Harding & Pullein grew steadily from their foundation in 1848.[9] The first sharp upturn in their fortunes corresponds with the general economic and financial collapse of 1857. This was a depression year with a financial crisis (no doubt given a psychological fillip by the Indian Mutiny), which had been heightened by an American banking panic requiring a special note issue by the Bank of England to restore liquidity.[10] The peak indicated on the graph for 1858 is a strong indication that Harding & Pullein derived a considerable proportion of their fee income from bankruptcy work. Indeed, Table I, p. 47, reveals that in 1858 £13,478 or 93.2% of their fees came from insolvencies. Sustained growth in total fee income was the trend (Fig. 1) for both Harding, Pullein, Whinney & Gibbons and Turquand, Youngs between 1857 and 1866, when there was again a startling rise in their income, and most particularly in the latter's case. This resulted from the Overend & Gurney banking crash, which produced the worst panic in the City since 1825, as the bank had failed with liabilities totalling £18 million causing widespread and deeply felt repercussions: Friday 11 May 1866 went down to history as 'Black Friday'.[11]

William Turquand was duly appointed receiver of Overend & Gurney with R. P. Harding as his deputy – in retrospect a remarkable coincidence, which was later to be reflected in the establishment of the English Institute. Turquand was offered the position as a result of his experience in insolvency work, while Harding had already been appointed auditor of Overend & Gurney by the directors earlier in 1866 when their mounting difficulties were acknowledged as serious. It proved to be a particularly lucrative commission. The receivers earned £71,000 in fees and £14,000 in expenses over a period of thirty years.[12] Whinney, Smith & Whinney were employed on the matter for twenty-eight years, from 1867 to 1893, and received £43,205, while insolvency fees from another liquidation, the European Bank (1866-83), amounted to £37,351. Turquand, Youngs' fee income more than doubled in 1867, rising to a peak of £90,287 in 1868, but fell back to £37,532 the following year.[13] Major bankruptcies such as these often provided a substantial income for a decade or more as the receivers sought to collect the debts outstanding for the stricken company and pay its creditors.

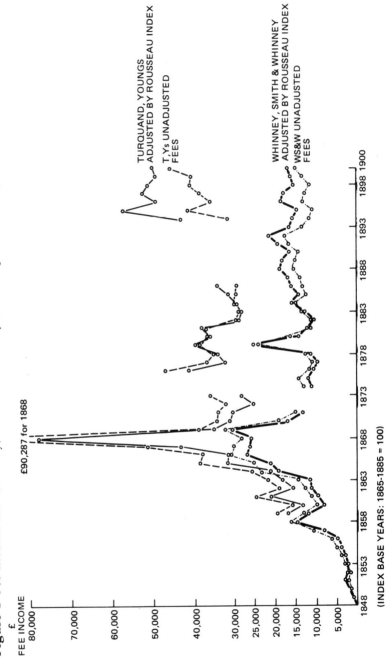

Figure I Fee Income for Whinney, Smith & Whinney and Turquand, Youngs (1848–1900)

Once the 1866 crisis had passed, Whinney, Smith & Whinney grew with fluctuations of a less marked character to 1900. The only jumps in income occurred in 1879 and in 1891-92. The first was a depression year, heightened in agriculture by the influx of cheap American wheat, while the rise in 1891-92 followed the financial crisis of 1890, which had exhibited all the early signs of being the greatest collapse of the century.[14] Barings, the important merchant bank, had virtually failed. Had they been allowed to go bankrupt, then the repercussions would have outweighed the catastrophe following the Overend & Gurney crash. In the event, having learned the lesson of 1866, the Bank of England intervened and stood half Barings' losses, minimizing the crisis. Nevertheless, there were bankruptcies and Whinney, Smith & Whinney's fee roll rose accordingly, but not to the extent that it had profited in 1866-69 or in 1879-80.

Two general points emerge from the graph. First, both practices grew in real terms during the latter half of the nineteenth century; in the case of Whinney, Smith & Whinney their average annual fee income rose from £13,460 for 1855-65 to £19,200 for 1880-1900, a percentage gain of 42.6%. If, however, these monetary figures are adjusted to take account of falling prices, the firm's expansion may be seen in a more dramatic light; Whinney, Smith & Whinney's real income rose on average from £11,390 per annum in 1855-65 to £22,490 in 1880-1900, a gain of 97.5%. The same is largely true of Turquand, Youngs' fees over the equivalent period, as the graph shows. Secondly, it appears that accountants did particularly well in times of financial disaster and depression, when bankruptcies brought extra and highly lucrative work. They were the rich undertakers of the economic world and gained disapprobation in consequence of profiting from the misfortunes of others.

Contemporaries have left a number of general descriptions of accountants' work during the Victorian period that may serve as a starting point for an inquiry into the character of their business. Frederick Whinney himself noted in 1883 that the 'winding-up of joint stock companies is a subject which calls for a large share of the attention of accountants', adding that 'this business runs back to the year 1848 when official managers came into existence'.[15] He was here referring to the 1848 Winding-Up Act, which regulated the control of liquidations, making the appointment of a public accountant, as the official manager, a virtual necessity.[16]

Ernest Cooper, recalling his youth in the 1860s, wrote that 'If an accountant were required, he would be found at the bar of the nearest tavern to the Bankruptcy Court in Basinghall Street. . . .'[17] In the 1870s the ornate letterhead of Joe Sharp, a member of the Society of Accountants in England, who practised in Huddersfield 'adjoining the County Court', described him as 'Public Accountant & Auditor, Receiver, Trustee, Official Liquidator in Bankruptcy and Chancery, Estate Agent etc'. A vivid picture of the variety of tasks performed by an accountant in the 1860s is provided by Edwin Waterhouse's recollections of his three years as a clerk in the offices of Coleman, Turquand, Youngs. He had started work there in 1861, but he wrote in his diary for 1864,

. . . I was given little matters of audit or investigation to carry through myself. . . . I remember the examination into the accounts of the Manager of the Union Workhouse on which I made a long report, while yet a novice at my work. For many weeks I was engaged in assisting the principal clerk in putting in order the accounts of some Army Agents in Westminster. . . . I was occasionally sent to the offices of the L. & N.W.R. to assist in Mr. Coleman's work as accountant in the service of the auditors. Mr. Coleman was connected also with the L.C. & D.R., then carrying out its metropolitan extensions, and I gained not a little experience in examining into the trade claims for loss of business on exchange of premises, and in sometimes giving evidence in the court of arbitration.

These contemporary impressions can be verified by an examination of Harding & Pullein's Day Books which record the nature of individual jobs and the fees charged. A survey of selected years (Table I) reveals that from the outset, insolvency work contributed the lion's share of Harding & Pullein's fees: 73.2% in 1848, 74.1% in 1853, 93.2% in 1858, and 93.9% in 1865. The influence of the Overend & Gurney crash is evident in the high monetary total (£25,447) for insolvencies in 1867, though the reduced percentage (85.3%) results from the high level of general accountancy work (10.8%), presumably due to the cumulative effect of the 1862 Companies Act (see p. 52). The 1867 Report from the Select Committee on Limited Liability Acts recorded that Harding, Whinney & Gibbons and Coleman, Turquand, Youngs had cornered the market in liquidations.[18] William Henderson, a City accountant, had compiled the following table:[19]

Liquidators in 1866	No. of Companies	Amount, £s.
Harding, Whinney & Gibbons	61	20,259,600
Coleman, Turquand, Youngs & Co	29	18,416,000
Kemp, Cannan, Ford & Co	12	13,660,000
Price, Holyland & Waterhouse	8	5,200,000
Chatteris & Nichols	5	4,915,000
Quilter, Ball & Co	5	1,100,000
Sundries consisting of 91 persons	139	28,558,600
Total	259	92,109,200

Henderson's conclusion was that 'the firm of Harding & Co represent one fourth of all capital in liquidation. The firm consists of three partners, who, on the average, would have 20 companies each to liquidate and they could not possibly give more than about 20 minutes a-day to each. One of the partners (Mr Whinney) has his own name to 30 companies; he could not give more

Table 1 The Percentage Composition of Whinney, Smith and Whinney's Fee Income*

YEAR	Insolvency		Accounting		Auditing		Trustee & Executorship		Special Work		TOTAL
	%	£	%	£	%	£	%	£	%	£	£
1848 (6 months)	73.2	153	1.9	4	–		17.2	36	7.7	16	209
1849	74.6	600	8.2	66	–		11.9	96	5.2	42	804
1853	76.9	1,861	17.2	410	–		4.2	101	1.8	44	2,416
1854	69.4	2,488	27.0	970	–		1.3	45	2.1	76	3,579
1855	80.6	3,937	13.3	648	–		6.1	298	–		4,883
1858	93.2	13,478	6.2	1,091	–		0.6	106	–		14,675
1860	85.8	7,610	7.6	672	2.4	220	3.6	319	0.6	52	8,873
1865	93.9	22,814	3.3	808	1.1	255	1.6	387	0.04	10	24,274
1867	85.3	25,447	10.8	3,221	2.1	637	1.7	501	0.1	39	29,845
1870	93.6	17,751	2.4	451	2.2	413	1.7	329	0.07	14	18,958
1875					4.3	617	ONLY CATEGORY POSITIVELY IDENTIFIED				
1880	72.3	9,965	11.2	1,544	10.9	1,506	3.5	478	2.2	297	13,790
1884	66.2	9,773	8.6	1,281	19.8	2,920	3.7	548	1.7	244	14,766
1885	60.0	7,420	8.7	1,073	26.0	3,217	4.6	573	0.7	84	12,367
1890	45.6	6,490	10.0	1,436	36.8	5,237	4.3	606	3.3	468	14,237
1895	15.1	1,464	22.7	2,193	54.3	5,244	2.1	204	5.7	549	9,654
1900	19.9	2,844	16.9	2,421	52.9	7,544	5.6	794	4.7	671	14,274

* For a fuller explanation of the 'Total' figures see p. 78.

than about ten minutes per day to each. Coleman & Co represent upwards of one-fifth of the capital, and have four partners engaged in liquidations. These have an average of nine and a half companies each. . . . These two firms have very nearly one half of the total capital in liquidation under their control.' In fact their share is well under half and the time calculations slightly spurious as these insolvent companies did not all demand attention at the same time, being staggered throughout the year, while all routine transactions would doubtless have been handled by subordinates. Nevertheless, the two firms have an impressive record, founded on a solid reputation for insolvency work.

The 1831 Bankruptcy Act had established the bankruptcy court and provided for the appointment of 'official assignees' – 'merchants, brokers, accountants or persons who were engaged in trade' – to liquidate the estate on behalf of the creditors.[20] Under this system official assignees increasingly employed public accountants to perform investigation work and prepare a balance sheet. For example, in 1848 52.6% and in 1849 38.3% of Harding & Pullein's fees were derived from bankruptcies, while a further 20.6% and 29.7% came from liquidations. However, the 1869 Bankruptcy Act abolished the position of official assignee and created that of trustee in its place. This meant that public accountants could be appointed directly by the courts. The removal of the middleman (restored again by the 1883 Act) resulted in a greater volume of bankruptcy work going to accountancy practices.

Paradoxically the accountant's involvement in insolvency work was further heightened by the grant of limited liability to joint stock companies in 1856 and 1862. Initially the privilege (designed to encourage the expansion of business through injections of public capital) was a mixed blessing as large numbers of short-lived, speculative or unsound companies were formed. 25.6% of all public companies set up between 1856 and 1865 ended in insolvency, 30.3% of those from 1866–74 and 33.4% of those founded between 1875 and 1883.[21] Half of the doomed companies formed between 1856 and 1865 failed within the first six years of their life, half of those of 1866–74 within the first five years, and half of those of 1875–83 within the first four years. There was, therefore, a growing tendency for Victorian companies to go bankrupt and fall after a shorter space of time – all of which meant rising levels of insolvency business for public accountants in the 1870s and 1880s. When Turquand was interviewed by the 1877

Select Committee on the Companies Acts and asked, 'Have you in your business had much to do with joint stock companies?' he did not mention auditing, but replied, 'With the liquidation of them I have had a great deal to do ... mostly ... compulsory liquidations.'[22] Harding too was questioned and recorded that he 'personally administered 62 companies and my firm have had the administration of 140 altogether'.[23] Whinney, Smith & Whinney's best years for insolvency fees were indeed the 1860s and 1870s when the proportion of total income was above 85% and often over 90%.

The major bone of contention in the period before the abolition of the official assignee and the creation of the trustee in bankruptcy concerned the payment of liquidator's fees. Remuneration was in the form of fixed rates, the official liquidator, created by the 1862 Companies Act receiving £1 for 'a day of eight hours, and the clerk at one shilling an hour', which, as Ernest Cooper suggested, 'shows the estimation of the value of an accountant's services at that time'.[24] Turquand certainly objected to this system, arguing that it was often likely to lead to delay, while he felt that the commission system as operated from 1869 to 1883 was more efficient – 'if the liquidator is paid by the result, that is a strong inducement to him to make the most of the assets'.[25]

The 1883 Bankruptcy Act,[26] which in a sense resurrected the official assignee now called an Official Receiver, broke the direct link between the courts and the public accountant by abolishing the trustee in bankruptcy, a post usually filled by an accountant with no intermediary. However, a number of leading accountants were appointed as Official Receivers under R. P. Harding, who had resigned from Harding & Whinney to take the post of Chief Official Receiver.[27] When he retired in 1890, he was knighted and so became the first accountant to receive such an honour. The re-introduction of the middleman performing some insolvency accounting resulted in the loss of valuable business by public accountants who were again employed indirectly by these officials and subject to their discretion. The tremendous outcry which greeted these changes was not directed simply at trying to re-capture lost business, but it was also suggested that political considerations had influenced this legislation. Critics argued that Joseph Chamberlain, as President of the Board of Trade, had given 51 of the 65 appointments to Liberal supporters.[28] Whinney, Smith & Whinney's insolvency fees for 1884 and 1885 (66.2% and

60.0% respectively) certainly show a marked drop in monetary totals and percentages in comparison with 1870 or 1880. However, this is in part a reflection of the more general decline in the importance of insolvencies, contributing a mere 15.1% in 1895 and 19.9% in 1900.

To return to their first ten years Harding & Pullein performed virtually no audit work. Accounting on the other hand was a small but growing area of business, though insolvency contributed the major share of their fee income. In 1849 accounting earned a mere £66, 8.2% of total fees, but by 1854 it had risen to £970 and in 1858 it produced £1,091 or 6.2% of fee income. Typical entries in the Day Books included,[29]

Richard Beard, King William Street, Attending you to a new set of books, which you were desirous of opening – discussing the peculiarity of your business etc, when we at length arranged that the 'Columna'' system was well adapted....

or an entry from the 1855 Day Book,[30]

... making up the books and partnership accounts of Mackay & Champion for a period between five and six years, the books being by your directions balanced at the end of each year and six distinct balance sheets prepared.

This period preceded the general grant of limited liability and a small, recently established accountancy practice, such as Harding & Pullein, could not expect to secure the audit of railway companies or important banks after such a short period of time, prestigious clients demanding prestigious auditors. However, the passing of the 1856 and 1862 Companies Acts, resulting in the formation of hundreds of joint stock companies each requiring an annual audit, opened the doors to this kind of work. Auditing first appears to be of consequence in 1860 when it contributed £220 or 2.4% of fees. In fact the firm's first audit had been performed as early as 1853, when an entry recorded:[31]

Brown Jansen & Co, Bankers, City. For time occupied in examining and investigating the accounts and balance sheet herein and in preparing a report.

This was no major task as the fee was extremely small – £6 18s. Although audit's percentage contribution did not rise to over 20% until the 1880s, the level of fees rose steadily, reaching £2,902 in 1884. In 1890 audit work and insolvency were both contributing about 40% to total income but by 1895 auditing had become the major source of income, generating just over 50% of the firm's fees. The monetary total continued to rise in 1900, though the audit percentage fell slightly with the small increase in insolvency work. Accounting similarly exhibited continuous expansion in monetary terms, while its percentage composition varied.

Contemporary assessments of the changing character of an accountant's duties suggest that Whinney, Smith & Whinney's experience was fairly typical. As Frederick Whinney himself noted in 1883, '. . . during the last few years . . . the business of the accountant has very widely spread, and at the moment the administration of assets makes up a large part of an accountant's duty . . . the auditing of accounts is a very important item in an accountant's work'.[32] Pixley's study of a chartered accountant, published in 1897, concluded that 'the auditing of the accounts of individuals, firms and public companies, also of executors and trustees and corporations, forms the foundation of the practice of professional accountants'.[33] Lisle, writing two years later, judged auditing as one of the two main branches of the accountant's business, the other he classified rather vaguely as general accounting.[34] The *Encyclopaedia of Accounting* (1905) placed auditing at the head of the list, accounting second, while winding-up came low down. Joseph Patrick argued in 1905 that 'fifty years before there was virtually no reference to auditing', a task completely omitted from the list of accountant's duties contained within the Edinburgh charter petition of 1853 and the 1855 Glasgow counterpart, but clearly mentioned in the English charter granted in 1880.[35]

What, then, were the reasons for the growing importance of audit work? Undoubtedly the major factor was the company legislation of the 1850s and 1860s. The 1856 and 1862 Companies Acts were of paramount importance for business; they allowed a company to sell shares to the public in order to raise capital for improvements and expansion with the protection of limited liability.[36] Until then, despite earlier statutes, only canals and railways, projects demanding huge inputs of capital, had been readily granted this facility. Legislators increasingly realized that if the economy were to continue to grow, then factories, foundries and business enterprises generally must be provided with the financial means to extend their operations. Family partnerships had served this purpose hitherto, but signs demonstated that, in sectors of the economy where technology and the scale of operations were already large and growing, many were reaching their financial limits.[37] In the first nine years of limited liability, 1856-65, 4,859 companies registered,[38] while the first year of the

1862 Act witnessed the registration of 165 businesses, 790 in 1863, 997 in 1864 and a further 1,034 in 1865.[39] In total, between 1866 and 1883, 15,662 limited companies were formed.[40]

There was still no statutory obligation for these companies to take their accounts to a public accountant for audit. Although the 1856 Companies Act[41] provided a model set of articles, they remained voluntary and such compulsory accounting provisions as had been contained in the 1844 Act were repealed.[42] Nevertheless, various advances in accounting practice can be detected in the 1856 legislation. New recommendations included that 'such accounts shall be kept upon the principle of double-entry, in Cash Book, Journal and Ledger'.[43] The model balance sheet provided for an analysis of assets and liabilities in substantial detail, and though not providing a standard form for a profit and loss account, it did make reference to its desirable inclusion.[44] Assets and liabilities were classified by type, trade and expense creditors separated from bills payable, interest due and law expenses, while limited allowance was made for depreciation, the balance sheet providing for a 'deterioration in value'. The 1862 Act[45] consolidated previous joint stock legislation and required that a profit statement and balance sheet be presented at the annual general meeting. Details of the contents of both the profit and loss statement and balance sheet were given but not made binding, and no guidance was offered concerning the accounting methodology to be followed. A more general point may be made here about the timing of company legislation. These Acts corresponded with upswings in the trade cycle.[46] The Bubble Act was repealed in 1825 during a boom, the Letters Patent Act of 1834 and the Chartered Companies Act of 1837, both of which eased the formation of corporations, were passed during a period of recovery, while the 1844-45 Companies Acts coincided with an upswing. 1856 and 1862 were also good years. In a sense, therefore, accountants could not go wrong; in times of depression they gained valuable insolvency work and in times of prosperity company legislation brought additional accounting and audit responsibilities.

As has been seen, the 1845 Companies Clauses Consolidation Act provided for the election of auditors from among the shareholders and permitted them to employ public accountants as their assistants. The latter's presence was resented by the directors from the outset. When, for example, William Deloitte was called in to inspect the books of the Great Western Railway in 1849 there was a furore on the board.[47] Their minutes recorded that 'the auditors have been assisted for the first time throughout a laborious examination of all books, accounts and documents of the company by a public accountant, which they appointed without previous communication with any individual connected with the company'.[48] No railway company had been tackled in this way before. This soon became the accepted practice, and when in 1867 J. E. Coleman resigned as the London & North Western Railway's public accountant, Price, Holyland & Waterhouse were appointed 'to assist the auditors'.[49] Coleman had been selected in 1849 following the widespread financial misdemeanours which hit the railway world and was appointed not simply to lend technical expertise to the auditor's report but to restore the shareholders' confidence.[50] The election of public accountants as auditors was only possible after the passing of the 1867 Railway Companies Act, which also deemed that auditors need no longer be shareholders.[51] There had been some objection to this requirement amongst the accountancy profession. William Quilter, himself employed by the auditors of the Eastern Counties Railway, had argued before the Lords' Committee on Railway Accounts that the auditor 'ought to be an independent individual, not interested in putting a favourable appearance upon the face of the accounts'.[52] Directors were often at pains to keep their shareholders in the dark. At best they regarded them as a nuisance and a hindrance to their freedom of action. In *The Man of Property*, Jolyon Forsyte, Chairman of the New Colliery Company, remarked to the Company Secretary who thought that their company was particularly enlightened, ' "You mean what they [the shareholders] *do* know isn't worth knowing!" '[53]

The tradition that the auditor himself should hold shares in the company continued into the twentieth century. When Arthur Whinney wrote unsuccessfully to the Metropolitan Carriage & Wagon Company in February 1896 asking to be considered as their auditor, he mentioned that 'the old company had a provison that the auditors must be shareholders, and that if the new company has a similar regulation, it is one with which we can easily comply'.[54] This also appears to be an example of touting. There had been quite an outcry against soliciting for business in this way in the late 1880s when *The Accountant* had carried a series of articles criticizing the practice.[55] An editorial reported that a large number of West Yorkshire accountants had 'commenced as rent and debt collectors and to further their business started some sort of a trade association; which was, or ... became an association in name only. The taint contracted from such an origin, and from semi-touting practices which it brought in its train...'.[56]

In the second half of the nineteenth century auditing was not generally as it is now, a matter of reporting on prepared accounts; Victorian auditors were, as Frederick Whinney commented in 1891, 'frequently asked to finish the balance sheet and take out the balance and write up the books'[57] – a judgement which Lisle echoed in his 1899 text book. Recalling the same period, de Paula remarked, adding testimony to the slow spread of double-entry book-keeping,[58]

In practice in those days, the majority of our new audits represented virgin soil, that is the books of account of that business had never before been examined by a professional accountant. In this way strange systems of book-keeping came to light. It was by no means uncommon [in the 1890s] to find primitive records upon a single entry basis or alternately most complicated double-entry systems.... A great part of the work of practising accountants in those days was introducing double-entry systems.... It [also] commonly fell to the auditor to balance the books and prepare the annual accounts.

Edwin Waterhouse recorded how in 1872, when called by Joseph Pease & Partners to put 'their large colliery and ironstone departments on a firm footing and audit them in future half yearly', the task was made doubly difficult because 'the methods of book-keeping were antiquated and the staff, to a large extent Quakers of mature years, averse to change'.[59]

In a sense, this parlous state of business accounting is not suprising. Regular calculations of profit and statements of the value of assets were of little interest to the entrepreneur closely and continuously involved in his own business operations.[60] Provided he was not accountable for part of his profit to others, little thought needed to be given to its precise and periodic calculation. For example, although the Dowlais Iron Company, a family business, undertook a wide range of accounting calculations in the 1860s to try to assess the foundry's financial performance, there was never any attempt to draw up a profit and loss account.[61] As the owners of the business, they were intimately involved in its and hence required the accounts to tell them how efficiently the works operated, not ways in which any profits might be divided. It was only with the advent of shareholders, remote from the actual production line, or (in lesser degree) the advent of partners outside the family circle and the need to calculate their dividends or share of the profits while providing an outward measure of the viability of operations, that public accountants tended to be called in to examine and report on a company's or firm's accounts.

A further pressing reason for the need to employ professional accountants as auditors was the prevalence of fraud. The popular image of Victorians as righteous and reliable, if rather dull and phlegmatic, is upset by a study of the welter of nineteenth-century frauds and failures.[62] Edwin Waterhouse recounted the discovery of numerous frauds in the execution of his duties as an auditor. In 1880 he unearthed a particularly ingenious case of 'fraud at the offices of the Metropolitan Railway. . . . The man had manipulated the depositors' pass books in every conceivable way, duplicating some and stitching duplicated leaves into others with singular cleverness. There was great difficulty in ascertaining the amount of his frauds.'[63] When in 1856 the Great Northern Railway discovered a fraud in their Registration Department involving some £150,000, Deloitte was called upon to investigate and present a report, the directors of the G.W. and L. & Y. Railways also instructing him to examine their stock registers to allay shareholders' anxiety. The great collapse of the City of Glasgow Bank in 1878 resulted in the imprisonment of several directors who had lent recklessly and perpetrated deliberate frauds in the attempt to make quick profits.[64] Lisle's *Encyclopaedia of Accounting* contained a lengthy section on fraud because the subject was 'one which is always more or less claiming the attention of professional and commercial men. . . .'[65] Dicksee declared in 1892 that 'the detection of fraud is a most important portion of the auditor's duties' and put it above the other two objects of an audit – the discovery of technical errors, and errors of principle, which today is exactly the reverse.[66]

It was common not only for clerks to manipulate the books but also for managers to falsify the stock returns. 'We auditors', wrote Frederick Whinney, 'are very largely dependent upon the honesty and fidelity of those who prepare the stock list. And here will come in something which is not to be taught – that is, the facility to judge whether the man or men who have prepared the list have done so honestly or not.'[67] It was not enough, therefore, for an auditor to be expert in accounting; he needed to have a reasonable knowledge of the company's technical operations and always to be a good judge of people to check that all was as it should be. For example, when Edwin Waterhouse was called upon to report on the financial state of the British Ice Making Company in 1864, he recorded that he had 'inspected the machinery and works of the company at Barking. The machinery is apparently in perfect working order....'[68] The ingenuity and daring of some Victorian frauds would have amazed a real-life Sherlock Holmes. One workhouse superintendent, who had several buildings under his authority, invented an additional block, devised a complete set of account books and drew up records for its putative inmates, transferring the funds so obtained into his own pocket. Every year he conducted the auditors around one of the other buildings a second time to persuade them of his imaginary block's existence. It was many years before his ghost workhouse was discovered. Fraud was a disease endemic in the Victorian economy, and public accountants were the physicians employed to drive it out.

In addition to audit and insolvency work, late nineteenth-century accountants performed a number of other tasks of a varied but related nature. Speaking at the English Institute's Jubilee Celebrations, Frederick Whinney distinguished seven major areas of work: preparation of books of accounts, making up partnership accounts, giving evidence as experts, acting as trustees in bankruptcy, liquidations, investigations into businesses about to go public and the detection of fraud.[69] Other functions included secretarial work for companies. Harding & Pullein did such work for the Caledonian Railway, preparing lists and 'directing envelopes to shareholders ... enclosing circulars'.[70]

Harding, Whinney & Co's Day Book recorded in 1880: 'for services rendered in preparing their accounts [William Clowes & Sons] and arranging the details of forming their business into a company'.[71] Although the same accountant might not always secure the annual audit, much business resulted from the preparation of prospectuses in the latter part of the nineteenth century. The importance of the 1856 and 1862 Acts as a source of this work is illustrated by the following letter from C. R. Trevor (founder of the Manchester practice of Shuttleworth & Haworth) concerning his investigation of a growing business in 1874.[72]

This is the engineering business [agricultural machines and engines] at Hull about which I wrote you.... This is one of the soundest and most reliable undertakings which has ever come under negotiation for joint stock enterprise. . . . The business was established about 27 years ago by the present proprietors on a small scale and has gradually grown to its present dimensions which the enclosed paper will show are pretty considerable; at present the demand home and continental . . . is so far in excess of the capabilities of supply as call for extensions beyond the capacity of the firm in its private partnership. . . .

Accountants were valued advisers not simply when balancing the books, but in general management and judging the appropriate moment to go public. Through the range of his experience, the public accountant built up an acumen and insight beyond the reach of a single entrepreneur.

Public accountants also found employment as investigators commissioned to examine the financial condition of businesses. In 1887 Frederick Whinney, then President of the English Institute, was asked to investigate the accounts of Woolwich Arsenal. He chose Edwin Waterhouse to be his assistant, but as the latter recorded, he felt an opportunity had been missed, since the report did not,[73]

. . . point out how the very great cost of the account keeping of the departments might be made productive of greater and more useful information . . . there is no general exchange statement showing in money values to what services of the State the amount spent in materials and wages has ultimately to be allocated on the issue of these stores, or to what extent the reserves of finished materials have been strengthened or drawn upon. . . .

On another occasion Harding, Whinney & Co, as prestigious City accountants, were asked to inquire into the affairs of the Channel Islands Bank, which was considering going public. William Hurlbatt, who conducted the investigation, found that the bank was in a sound financial condition with assets sufficient to satisfy all liabilities and form an additional reserve fund, while the books had been well kept.[74] After presenting their report Harding, Whinney & Co became the bank's auditors. Hence, when the Birmingham & Midland Bank took over the Channel Islands Bank in 1897 there was no change of auditors.[75]

Accountants are not today normally associated with wage and rate arbitration work, but in the nineteenth century they appear to have been much involved in such judgements. Edwin Waterhouse recalled how early in 1870 he was employed by Fox Heads Company to 'determine a proportion of their profits, which under a profit sharing scheme was apportionable as a bonus on the wages paid to their men. . . .'[76] In the following year his experience in arbitration decisions led the Consett Iron Company to settle similar wage disputes. Waterhouse decided that in future 'an independent accountant might ascertain the average selling values and that the wages of the men should rise or fall in accordance therewith under a sliding scale to be agreed upon. . . .'[77] In January 1876 he was called in by colliery owners in Cardiff, Newport and Aberdare to arbitrate in other disputes. West Ham Parish employed Waterhouse in February 1865 to determine the rates payable by the Great Eastern Railway. Writing to the company for their traffic returns, he explained that he needed to calculate their average income on 'such portion of your line as lies in the parish'.[78]

Until the English Institute of Chartered Accountants forbade other forms of employment by their members,★ accountants often performed a variety of associated occupations. Mason & Sons, a firm of chartered accountants, continued to act as licensed valuers long into the twentieth century, while Harding & Pullein were described in the *Post Office Directory* for 1850 as 'accountants and arbitrators'.[79] Earlier London trade directories described a number of accountants as also being appraisers, auctioneers or agents.[80] Indeed, it appears that R. P. Harding's father, Robert [1772–1862], was an auctioneer, appraiser and house agent in 25 New Broad Street.[81] The firm's Letter Books reveal that R. P. Harding continued to act as an house agent in the Norwood, Beulah Hill and Peckham area throughout the 1860s and early 1870s.[82] However, by 1880 (after the inauguration of the English Institute's Fundamental Rules), this aspect of Harding, Whinney & Co's work seems to have disappeared.[83] In fact rule three expressly stated that 'a member shall not directly or indirectly accept or agree to accept [commissions] from an auctioneer, broker or other agent employed for the sale or letting of . . . any real or personal property'.[84] Doubtless the growing scale of business, as well as the imposition of professional rules of conduct, had led to this increased specialization of function.[85]

In Manchester, Richardson & Trevor was described in the *Post Office Directory* for 1873 as 'public accountants [and] agents for the Scottish Provident Institution'.[86] Their letter book for 1874–75 shows regular dealings in insurance policies, one of their best clients being the Soho Works in Birmingham,[87] while Thomas

---

★ In July 1881 the Council concluded that 'it is not inconsistent with the business of an accountant to take out a license as a valuer . . . provided that he does not hold himself out to the public by advertisement or otherwise as a valuer'. Council Minute Book 'A' 1880–1885, 6 July 1881, p. 104.

Smethurst, another Manchester accountant, was 'an agent for the County Fire Insurance Company'.[88] The Council decided in October 1881 that the holding of an insurance agency was not 'inconsistent with the business of a public accountant'.[89] Among the Institute's aims was the desire that there should be no conflict of interest in the various tasks performed by an accountant and that he should concentrate his attention on the jobs which he was best qualified to undertake.

Another activity commonly performed by public accountants in the early and mid-nineteenth century and which has since been discouraged was the collection of debts. Several entries in the Day Books record that Harding & Pullein had secured a 5% commission on all debts recovered.[90] The firm derived only a small income between 1849 (£53 or 6.6%) and 1854 (£2) from debt collecting, rising to a maximum of £68 in 1853, but this merely represented 2.8% of total fees. Thomas Smethurst, a leading Manchester accountant (whose practice merged with Whinney, Smith & Whinney in 1928), regularly wrote in the following vein:[91] 'in reply to your advertisement in *The Guardian*, I should be glad to undertake the collection of rents and entire management of the property referred to – I have good experience in the business and my terms are 5% for weekly and $2\frac{1}{2}$% for quarterly property'.[92] The function of debt collecting also formed part of the duties of a receiver or liquidator, whose task it was to recover assets to repay creditors.

Public accountants keen to offer their services to management also sought directorships – again an activity discouraged among practitioners today and prohibited should the accountant be auditor of the same company. Frederick Whinney was himself a director of the London, Tilbury & Southend Railway,[93] while another partner in Whinney, Smith & Whinney audited the company from 1892 to 1912 (when it was taken over by the Midland Railway) thereby creating a possible conflict of interest. He owned a number of shares in the L.T. & S.R. qualifying him to serve either as its auditor or as a director,[94] and there remained no statutory reason why an accountant should not hold the post of director so long as he had no professional obligation to the shareholders. In this case Frederick's son, Arthur, always performed the audit to reduce any possible division of loyalty.[95]

In any history of the development of accountancy, the clients themselves provide a different and profitable line of inquiry.

Indeed, in certain respects the history of accountancy is as much the history of the evolution of the clients as that of the accountants. It has been argued by Brown, Stacey and others that the latter half of the nineteenth century witnessed a move towards specialization in accountancy. 'There is no doubt', claimed Joseph Patrick in 1905, 'a growing tendency on the part of firms ... to devote themselves more particularly to one branch of work. ... Now we hear of men being specially marked out as railway accountants, company promoters, court accountants, bankruptcy trustees and the like.'[96] Not only did accountants specialize in particular forms of activity (winding-up, secretarial work and so forth), but those who were heavily involved in audits often also exhibited special-isms within that field. Although both Cooper Brothers and De-loittes accommodated a range of audit clients by occupation and size, they specialized within this broader grouping. Deloittes established a reputation as railway company auditors,[97] and fo-cused more generally on engineering, mining and manufacturing businesses, opening an office in Cardiff in 1912 and another later in Swansea.[98] Cooper Brothers' nineteenth-century clients similarly exhibited a wide range of business with concentrations in bank-ing, iron and steel production, engineering, mines and land fi-nance.[99]

Whinney, Smith & Whinney also built up a well-balanced practice. Being a City firm of a gentlemanly character, banks and financial institutions featured prominently in their client lists: the Union Bank of London (from 1883), International Financial Society and the Law Union Life Insurance Company (both 1863), Birmingham & Midland Bank (1885), Channel Islands Bank (1886) and the Equitable Life Assurance Society (1894), originally a personal appointment for Frederick Whinney. Provincial banks often appointed City auditors as a way of boosting public confid-ence in their security. Widespread failures at Leeds in 1864 en-couraged the Barnsley Bank to appoint a London firm of audi-tors.[100] Later notions of prestige also influenced the directors of the Birmingham & Midland Bank who appointed Whinney, Smith & Whinney as their auditors before opening a London branch. As an expanding bank with broad horizons, they felt the need for an established and distinguished firm of City auditors. The annual reports of the Birmingham & Midland Bank relate how V. W. Houghton, a Birmingham chartered accountant, was appointed as their first auditor in 1880 for until then 'the directors have not submitted the accounts ... to any official auditor'.[101] When his health failed in 1885, Houghton tendered his resignation and it was 'resolved that the manager be instructed to ascertain whether Mr Whinney of the firm of Harding, Whinney & Co ... would be willing to undertake the auditorship at a remuneration not exceeding two hundred guineas and travelling expenses'.[102] The suggestion was accepted and terms agreed.

A further factor in the 1880s was the desire amongst many joint stock banks 'to avail themselves of the advantages afforded by limited liability. On revising their constitution, they had to give consideration to the subject of audit and were inclined to make use of the services of public accountants.'[103] Accordingly, Edwin Waterhouse was appointed joint auditor of the National Provincial Bank of England and 'about the same time ... accepted a similar appointment with the London & Westminster Bank jointly with Mr. Turquand, my old master....'[104] Turquand, Youngs also secured the audit of Parr's Banking Company in the 1890s.[105]

City accountancy firms also benefited from London's position as the finance capital of the world, picking up the audit of a number of companies based overseas and throughout the Empire, but controlled from the City. Within this category Whinney, Smith & Whinney audited the Union Bank of Australia (from 1880), Central Argentine Land Company (1886), Pundaloya and Bogawantalawa Tea Companies (1897) and the Natal Bank (pre-1901). In 1877 Turquand, Youngs were appointed auditors of the National Mortgage and Agency Company of New Zealand on its formation, already being auditors of the Australian Mercantile Land Finance Company (founded in 1863). Both were substantially funded from Scotland and presumably desired an established City accountancy firm with strong Scottish connections.[106] From this base British accountants subsequently followed British business overseas, needing to operate wherever important clients became established in the world.

As has been seen, railway auditing had played an important part in the development of the accountancy profession, both as a source of work and as a proving ground for new accounting techniques. Whinney, Smith & Whinney, who audited the London, Tilbury & Southend Railway, also secured the audit of the Grand Trunk Railway's London agency in 1893,[107] while *Bradshaw's Railway Manual and Shareholder's Guide* for 1869 reveals that John Young was auditor of the mighty Caledonian Railway, the Cambrian Railways and the Great Western of Canada Railway – Turquand, Youngs being the auditors of the Oude & Rohilkund Railway in India.[108] R. P. Harding is listed as being the auditor of the Central Argentine Railway.[109] By 1890 Turquand, Youngs audited nine railway companies (mostly overseas enterprises financed by British capital) and Alexander Young had taken over the audit of the Caledonian Railway jointly with John Graham, C.A., of Glasgow – preserving the Scottish connection at the London end.[110]

Although neither Turquand, Youngs nor Whinney, Smith & Whinney concerned themselves much with industrial companies – Ernest Whinney recalled that until 1900 such work was 'considered not fully respectable'[111] – they did audit businesses. Morgan Brothers (later Morgan Crucible), the Battersea iron founders, became a Harding & Whinney client in 1878 largely because R. P. Harding and Octavius V. Morgan, brother of William the founder, were close friends and neighbours in Queen's Gate, Kensington. It was a fortunate connection as the Battersea works, established in 1851, grew by the turn of the century to be the largest manufactory of crucibles in the world. The prestige and experience of an established City accountancy firm was considered important. Many Irish firms were handicapped by the reluctance of companies there to appoint them as auditors. For example, when Arthur Guinness & Sons became a public company in 1886, it appointed Turquand, Youngs as its auditors,[112] while Whinney, Smith & Whinney audited the Guinness Trust from 1890, Turquand, Youngs remaining auditors of the Dublin Guinness Company when it became a separate but wholly owned subsidiary in 1952. Oxford colleges, whose investments in this period were over-whelmingly in land, featured among Whinney, Smith & Whinney's clientele and included All Souls, Balliol, Christ Church, Pembroke, St John's and Somerville (with, in addition Oriel, Lincoln and University Colleges from 1883/4 to 1888), whilst the firm also audited the Oxford University Fund, the Randolph Hotel and the Oxford Electric Lighting Company. This Oxford work had originated in 1877 when Frederick Whinney, who was sitting on the Parliamentary Commission to inquire into the University's finances, was appointed by All Souls to tidy up their muddled accounts. Today Whinney, Smith & Whinney's dominance of Oxford college audits has been lost to firms with local offices, Ernst & Whinney retaining the audit of All Souls, Christ Church and St John's.[113]

The balance which is evident in the size and scope of these clients is also reflected in the level of their fees. In 1858, 34 clients each paid over £50 per annum in fees. Of these 22 were paying more than £100 and of those eight were paying £500 and over.[114] The Royal British Bank (£5,291, conducted jointly with Turquand, Youngs), the Athenaeum Life Assurance Society (£985) and the Mexican & South American Company (£2,930) contributed the most, but they were all liquidations. The overall picture was much the same for 1870 when 15 clients of a varied character all paid over £100 per annum, 11 of these being over £500. Again the largest four – the East of England Bank (£1,295), the Hop Planters' Association (£1,310), the European Bank (£4,277) and Overend & Gurney (£2,287) – were all liquidations. As has been seen, insolvency work generated 94% of Whinney, Smith & Whinney's fees in 1870 and it was not until the 1890s that auditing assumed a sizeable proportion of the firm's income.

It has proved impossible to discover the exact geographical location of all Whinney, Smith & Whinney's nineteenth-century clients, as addresses are seldom given in the Day Books. However, in the early days, the clerks did occasionally record the location of new clients. Of those quoted in the 1855–1858 Day Book 30 of 34 were in London, the remainder being situated variously in Portsmouth, Brighton, Luton and Salisbury. Since travelling time and costs were chargeable expenses, it encouraged businesses to employ local accountants. By the latter part of the century both Turquand, Youngs and Whinney, Smith & Whinney had attracted a number of audit clients from as far afield as Ireland and the north of England at a time when their reputations as trusted City auditors overcame any desire to save money on travel and hotel expenses.

The character and location of Whinney, Smith & Whinney's accounting and audit clients may be further explained by setting the firm back in its Victorian business context. The City of London was not then, as it is now, dominated by office blocks belonging to major commercial and financial institutions, but functioned as a much more coherent organic body. Housing a much wider range of businesses, it was not simply a place where commuters travelled to work but was the home and market place for a substantial resident population. Before becoming the premises of Whinney, Smith & Whinney, Brown, Fleming & Murray, Price Waterhouse and several other accountancy firms, Frederick's Place, an elegant Georgian court, was largely occupied by solicitors, surgeons, wine and other types of merchant in the 1870s. Victorian London supported three major industries: clothing, furniture and footwear production,[115] which, in their turn, surrounded themselves with a host of specialist advisers, accountants included. In 1894 Viney, Price & Goodyear described themselves as 'Chartered Accountants and sellers of drapery and other stocks by tender'.[116] J. D. Viney's obituary in *The Draper's Record* recorded his close involvement with 'the drapery world and the City warehouses where his genial and kindly disposition and professional skill ... won for him ... universal respect'.[117]

The furniture trade concentrated in the Shoreditch, Bethnal Green and Stepney areas, spreading to Hoxton Square and Great Eastern Street at the turn of the century.[118] It was here that Baker, Sutton gained a number of clients and later as a result of this experience became secretaries of the Cabinet Traders Federation and the Furnishing & Allied Trades Protection Society.[119] In addition, printing and publishing were important and long-established occupations in central London. William Clowes & Son (from 1879), Richard Clay & Son (1888) and Wightman & Co (1897), all printers, took their accounts to Whinney, Smith & Whinney, as from 1901 did Strong, Hanbury & Co, paper merchants, while Chapman & Hall (from 1880) and Hurst & Blackett (1901) were both publisher clients.

Traditionally offices also contained substantial warehousing space for finishing and packing as well as storage, so that clerical and sales activities formed only part of a building's functions. The warehousing and movement of goods was an important and now largely defunct aspect of the City's economic role. Accountants had not simply to check a company's books but to check the stock and ensure that these processes were running smoothly. Because the resident population demanded all the services typical of a major town, the range of businesses that required accounting skills was much broader in the Victorian City than it is today. Although this town character has now disappeared, it is apparent from Whinney, Smith & Whinney's nineteenth-century client lists, which include: Frederick Braby & Co (corrugated iron manufacturers, clients from 1865), W. & C. Nightingale (bedding manufacturers, 1891), Grimble & Co (vinegar producers, 1901), Nubian Manufacturing Co (makers of boot polishes, 1901), Monkwell Street Warehouse Co (1901), London Commercial Sale Rooms (1893), London Road Car Co (1886), Maypole Dairy (1898) and the Chancery Lane Safe Deposit Co (1894).

Much of the change in the City and central districts of London may be ascribed to increased specialization as the more general traders have been forced away through rising rents and land values and the falling resident population, while the larger commercial and financial institutions have expanded in their place. Although the range of functions performed in Victorian London was broader, even then there existed a tendency to form increas-

Map 1 The Location of Ernst & Whinney's Various Predecessor Firms in the City of London

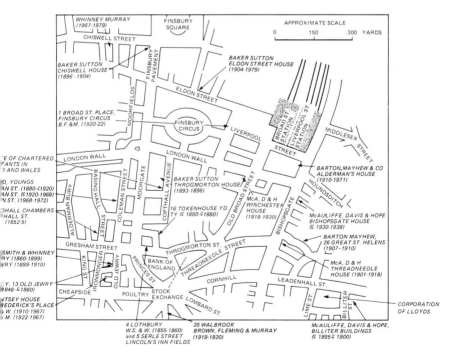

ingly specialist districts. Accountants themselves concentrated in the Gresham Street, Old Jewry, Basinghall and Coleman Street area.[120] 'The City of London', remarked *The Builder* as early as 1868, '... is becoming more and more the office of the world. Stately buildings replace the ... houses of the Georgian era, and these buildings are almost entirely parcelled out in offices. The City lives out of town.'[121] Growth in the size of accountancy firms has meant that their accommodation demands could no longer be satisfied by the elegant Georgian and Regency residences which once formed these streets and courts.[122] The increasing scale of insurance, banking, accountancy and other services came to require larger and more impressive buildings both to house their various operations and to serve as architectural expressions of their wealth, respectability and reliability.[123] Soon speculative office blocks were built wholly for sub-letting - later examples being Dauntsey House in Frederick's Place, Eldon Street House, Alderman's House, Bishopsgate, and 175 West George Street, Glasgow, where Whinney, Smith & Whinney, Baker, Sutton & Co, Barton, Mayhew & Co and Brown, Fleming & Murray respectively first occupied a few rooms but expanded to fill the greater part of the building.

The 1830s had witnessed the creation and growth of several statistical societies, the first being at Manchester in 1833, followed some months later by the London Society and by Birmingham (1835), Bristol (1836), Liverpool (1838) and Leeds (1838).[124] Accountants, with their related technical skills, might at first sight appear to have been obvious candidates for membership. They were not, however, notable amongst their first generation of members. For although these bodies called themselves statistical societies, their primary aim was not to collect and evaluate numerical data, but to use this information to initiate social reform. Doctors, clergymen, bankers and philanthropic entrepreneurs founded these groups in the largest industrial conurbations where the problems of poverty and disease existed on the greatest and most obvious scale.[125] The statistics were a means to an end rather than a fascination in themselves.

Accountants joined statistical societies towards the end of the nineteenth century when their membership had expanded and broadened in character. One further reason for the delay in accountants' involvement was that they had been preoccupied with securing recognition for their own profession, so that only when they had justified their immediate role in society could they take the opportunity to tackle its wider problems. One of the Manchester Statistical Society's Presidents, Edwin Guthrie (1888-90), was a chartered accountant who had started life as a book-keeper in Liverpool, rising to become a partner in the Manchester practice of Thomas, Wade & Guthrie.[126] Amongst the Society's publications were several papers dealing with accountancy problems, including: 'On the Audit of Public Accounts' (1865-66) by W. Rees, 'Local Taxation' (1894-95) by Guthrie, 'The Companies Act 1862 and Subsequent Acts and Suggested Amendments' (1891-92) by R. M. Pankhurst, and H. L. Price's (President of the Incorporated Society of Accountants, 1907-10) 'Some Financial and Commercial Aspects of Trade Insolvency' (1905-6).[127] In the Edwardian period the Society regularly invited distinguished visitors to their annual dinner to express their opinions and among these was Sir William Plender, President of the English Institute of Chartered Accountants in 1911-12.[128]

With the grant of a Royal Charter in 1880, English accountancy rose to the status of a profession, an initiative which directly involved Harding, Whinney Gibbons & Co and Turquand, Youngs as leading City practices concerned with its advancement. The first English association of accountants had been the Incorporated Society of Liverpool Accountants founded in January 1870,[129] but there clearly existed a wider need to regulate the growing body of men who called themselves accountants. Contemporary opinion often judged that accountants were 'mixed up in money lending, bogus company promoting, book-making and other shady occupations',[130] while William Hazlitt, son of the writer and Senior Registrar of the Bankruptcy Division, argued that 'an accountant was a person unaccountable for his actions'.[131] As Frederick Whinney recalled, London in the 1870s contained a number 'who thought they had nothing whatever to do to become accountants but to put up a plate and designate themselves as such in order to become rich men'.[132] Hence, in November 1870 following the Liverpool and Scottish examples, a group of leading City accountants formed the Institute of Accountants in London.[133] It began as an informal meeting of nine men in the offices of Quilter, Ball & Co under the presidency of William Quilter, while William Turquand, John Young and J. B. Gibbons were also present.[134]

One of their first resolutions followed the Scottish precedent, setting out to secure recognition through the grant of a Royal Charter – the Edinburgh Society and Glasgow Institute had thus been recognized in 1854 and 1855 respectively.[135] Thirty-seven accountants signed the draft rules devised in 1870, including R. P. Harding. At the first Council meeting on 13 December 1870, William Turquand was elected Vice President and when Quilter retired in 1877 succeeded him as President, with John Ball becoming Vice President.[136] It was probably these early London Institute connections which prompted Turquand in 1883 to approach Quilter, Ball & Co with proposals for an amalgamation. Harding, in a letter to Whinney, suggested that he might put in a rival bid as 'the fact of his [Harding's] retirement [from the partnership] opens the door to an arrangement',[137] although nothing came of these approaches.

In the meantime other bodies had been set up in the major commercial and manufacturing centres: the Manchester Institute of Accountants, founded in 1873, and the Institute of Accountants in Sheffield, 1877. Pressure soon followed to unite these disparate organizations into a single authority which could effectively regulate the profession throughout England and establish common standards of entry.[138] Although the London Institute had opened its doors to accountants from all parts of the United Kingdom in 1872, it had not developed into a truly national organization, this being possible only if these various bodies came together in a single institute. Indeed, the Society of Accountants in England, a rival organization established in 1872, also based in London, grew rapidly in the latter part of the decade, outpacing the London Institute; the former's membership had reached 286 by 1880 in comparison with the latter's 188.[139]

When Frederick Whinney was elected to the London Institute's Council in 1877, a more forceful policy developed to parry the challenge offered by the Society of Accountants in England. Turquand as the former's President accompanied by S. L. Price and R. P. Harding, giving evidence before Disraeli's select committee into the 1862 and 1867 Companies Acts, did much, by participating in the Parliamentary process, to pave the way for official recognition. However, success depended upon unity and this led the major English accountancy bodies to join forces initially in a campaign for the grant of a Royal Charter. Changing tactics, they submitted a Bill to Parliament entrusted to Lord Redesdale in the Lords and Sir John Lubbock in the Commons, hoping to secure recognition by an Act.[140] The Duke of Richmond, Lord President of the Council in Disraeli's government, advised them to abandon the Bill and return to their original plan to petition the Queen in Council for a Charter of Incorporation, which they duly did. The application declared that it was their intention to encourage[141]

the elevation of the profession of public accountants as a whole, and the promotion of their efficiency and usefulness by compelling the observance of strict rules of conduct ... and by setting up a high standard of professional education.

Their petition was granted on 11 May 1880. On the death of John Ball in August 1879, R. P. Harding had been elected as Vice President, so that he and William Turquand actually received the Charter.[142]

The various bodies, including the Society of Accountants, united formally as the Institute of Chartered Accountants in England and Wales. Admission was solely by examination and students were obliged to serve articles for five years (only three for university graduates), although practising accountants of ten years' experience could gain admittance under a transitional provision. Membership existed at two levels (in contrast to Scotland's unitary system), either as Fellows or Associates. William Turquand, its first President, served from 1880 to 1882 when he was succeeded by R. P. Harding, 1882–83. Arthur Cooper followed from 1883 to 1884, being succeeded by Frederick Whinney who held office for four years until 1888. Whinney's involvement in every aspect of the English Institute's business is clear from the Council's minute books.[143] Of the eight separate committees formed in 1882, Frederick Whinney extraordinarily sat on all but one (only the Finance Committee not hearing his voice), while Turquand sat on those concerned with General Purposes, Investigation, Bankruptcy and the Benevolent Association.[144] In addition, Harding, Turquand and Whinney, together with Cooper and Kemp, had been delegated to negotiate with the Board of Trade on any matters which might affect the profession.[145] As Whinney's successor was William Deloitte, the first five presidents, all men of distinction in the City, represented firms which have since grown or merged to rank among the leading five in Britain.

Accountants had been by no means alone among the professions in seeking legal recognition in the latter part of the nineteenth century. A hundred years previously only the Church, physicians and barristers (not surgeons or attorneys) had achieved professional status.[146] One of the most noticeable and influential social developments of the period proved to be the rise of the qualifying professional associations. The first, the Institution of Civil Engineers, was followed by the Institute of British Architects, established respectively in 1818 and 1834 and granted their Royal Charters in 1828 and 1837; solicitors formed a professional association in 1825, later called the Law Society, receiving a Royal Charter in 1831, surgeons, vets and pharmacists achieving professional standing in their wake.[147] By the 1870s a pattern in England had emerged. Bodies seeking recognition were required to demonstrate that they performed valuable work, that they could control entry and standards of work and that their members were men of integrity. For example, land surveyors pursued an almost parallel approach to the accountants in their attempts to secure legal recognition. The Land Surveyors Club, formed in 1834, had remained largely a dining society so that it was not until 1868 with the creation of the Institution of Surveyors that their campaign produced tangible results. The motivation, as in the accountants' case, followed renewed agitation for protection against imposters and their first act on receiving a Royal Charter in 1881 was to impose standards of entry by examination.[148]

By virtue of their ancestry and the particular tasks they performed, the professions ranked in a distinct hierarchy. Even when granted a Charter, Whinney declared that 'we cannot, however, regard ourselves as on a line with the old professions'. Progressive specialization in the economy had 'called into existence the semi-professions, of which we form one, and that not the least distinguished'.[149] Justice Quain's much quoted remark of 1875 that 'the whole affair[s] of bankruptcy had been handed over to an ignorant set of men called accountants . . .'[150] represented a common view which persisted into the twentieth century. Certainly in 1857, when Byerley Thomson published *The Choice of a Profession*, there had been no mention of accountancy, although engineers and architects gained inclusion.[151]

Accountants took the unusual step among the professions of adding a set of Fundamental Rules to their Charter.[152] Generally professional bodies did not promulgate codes of conduct as these were felt to be antithetical to their Victorian philosophy. Members, as gentlemen, it was argued, ought instinctively to know how to play the game without having the rules laid down in a formal fashion. The gentlemanly code of behaviour came to be known as 'professional ethics' or 'etiquette'. This view persisted well into the twentieth century when it was articulated by D. V. House, a past President of the English Institute. 'As a nation', he reasoned, 'we prefer a man to be judged by his peers, rather than condemned or exonerated by the written word and we can still pride ourselves upon knowing instinctively what is "done" or "not done".'[153] But in the case of accountancy where the membership was potentially large and embraced some of uncertain character, a public showing of regulation helped somewhat to overcome popular prejudice against the profession.[154] The rules did not make any attempt to regulate accounting procedures but confined themselves to defining ways in which an accountant might go about his daily business, or rather the things he might not do. Under the 1880 regulations members could not accept commissions from solicitors (an important source of work) and were debarred from following 'any business or occupation other than that of public accountant', with certain approved exceptions, while advertising was banned.[155] Accordingly in 1881 Mr C. E. Mason (Mason & Son merged with Whinney Murray in 1978) received a caution because he 'had joined a firm of brewery agents who did not appear in the Directory as accountants and were not so described in their advertisements....'[156] A detailed set of procedural regulations governed the internal organization of the Institute itself.

Typically these *laissez faire* regulations left certain areas of grey which attracted controversy in the 1890s. Although advertising was prohibited, members continued to tout for business. Accountants often wrote offering their services in response to announcements in the press, Arthur Whinney and Thomas Smethurst being by no means exceptional in following this custom. 'I notice', wrote Whinney in May 1893, 'in this morning's *Gazette* that you are presenting a petition against the Volcanic Acration Company and that if you are desirous of having a liquidator other than the Official Receiver, I shall be pleased to act....'[157]

Shortly afterwards, inspired by the English Institute's example, the Incorporated Society of Accountants and Auditors* was formed in 1885.[158] Articles were an expensive matter, as firms

* In 1908 the Society changed its name to the Society of Incorporated Accountants and Auditors, dropping the 'and Auditors' in 1954.

normally demanded payment of 500 guineas for the period of training, while in addition, parents had to provide for the clerk's daily expenses. For the less well-off, the Incorporated Society devised a ten-year apprenticeship, the pupil being paid during his articles without having to provide a costly premium. The English Institute's success, in turn, fired Irish accountants to campaign for a Charter of Incorporation. Towards the end of 1887 Robert Stokes of Dublin organized a petition (also signed by William FitzSimons and William Mayes of Belfast) and a Charter was duly granted on 14 May 1888, as in England their first concern being to ban advertising and draft a table of bye-laws.[159]

What, in general terms, therefore, were the characteristics and aims of the Victorian professions? From his examination of the architects' experience, Kaye concluded that a professional was an expert whose relationship with his client, a layman unable to judge the competence of his services except in the long run, was fundamentally based upon trust.[160] Professional men founded associations to. safeguard this relationship of trust by regulating the competence and integrity of their members. The oldest professions – priests, physicians and barristers – performed tasks which they alone were considered competent to perform by virtue of their long training or privileged position. The qualifying professions of the nineteenth century, by contrast, were really the offshoots of the entrepreneur's broad skills, the result of growing specialization and the need to have increasingly precise and detailed information. Engineers, surveyors, accountants, architects and actuaries all existed in the past but in the eighteenth century had usually combined such work with various other tasks and consequently made no exclusive claim for their execution. As these jobs became more complex and required greater expertise, so men specialized and felt the need to safeguard their hard-won skills. Indeed the professions have, with varying degrees of success, sought to secure a monopoly. In January 1896, for example, Frederick Whinney introduced proposals for a Bill to widen the membership of the English Institute while at the same time granting it sole audit rights in the country. The Council remained unimpressed and members defeated the motion by 1,064 votes to 613.[161]

In the mid-nineteenth century the number of qualifying associations multiplied, particularly in the 1880s when engineers, chemists, librarians, auctioneers and company secretaries along with accountants, all achieved formal recognition from government. This was not a direct response to improved educational facilities, though it certainly reflected them. Rather it resulted from the tireless actions of dedicated members who wished to build an improved foundation for study, protection and raising standards.[162] The rise of the professional classes, like the rise of the trade unions, was a direct social and institutional response to the Industrial Revolution. The middle classes, expanding in size and riches, prospering from the new commercial and industrial opportunities, demanded a greater degree of professional advice and expertise, while in their general outlook they provided intellectual fuel for the developing professional philosophies.

References

1 Frederick Whinney's *Pawsey's Pocket Diary and Almanack for 1854*, London (1854), 11 March, p. 45; Harding & Pullein's Cash Book 1853-1858, 1 May 1854, p. 2.

2 Article of partnership, 1 November 1857, p. 1.

3 *Ibid*, p. 2.

4 Article of partnership, 29 December 1858, p. 1.

5 *Pawsey's Pocket Diary and Almanack for 1860*, London (1860). This address is written in Frederick Whinney's hand on the endpaper.

6 Harding, Whinney & Gibbons Letter Book 1867-1902, Letter 26 May 1871, p. 229; Letter, to the Chief Cashier of the Bank of England to inform him of their change of style to Harding, Whinney, Hurlbatt & Smith, 17 February 1887.

7 *Ibid*, 20 August 1894, p. 348.

8 Throughout the study two price indices have been used: the Rousseau index has been adopted for the period 1848 to 1913 and the Sauerbeck-Statist index from 1900 to 1938. The annual fee income is multiplied by 100 and then divided by the index figure for the given year. B. R. Mitchell and P. Deane, *Abstract of British Historical Statistics*, Cambridge (1962), pp. 471-5.

9 Figures derived from the firm's Day Books, which run in unbroken series from 1848 to 1963.

10 Peter Mathias, *The First Industrial Nation*, London (1968), p. 356.

11 *Ibid*, p. 359.

12 Richard Brown, *A History of Accounting and Accountants*, Edinburgh (1905), p. 326.

13 Turquand, Youngs & Co Private Ledger 1863-1868, pp. 13-17.

14 Mathias, *op. cit.*, p. 359.

15 *The Accountant*, No. 440, 12 May 1883, p. 12.

16 11 & 12 Victoriae c. 45 (1848), An Act to Amend the Acts for facilitating the Winding-Up ... of Joint Stock Companies, pp. 154-61.

17 *A History of Cooper Brothers 1854-1954*, London (1954), p. 4.

18 *Report from the Select Committee on Limited Liability Acts*, Vol. X (1867), p. 393.

19 *Ibid*, p. 463.

20 Quoted from *The Accountant*, 10 April 1937, E. F. Jeal, 'Some Reflections on the Evolution of a Professional Practice of Accountancy in Great Britain', p. 524.

21 E. M. Carus-Wilson, *Essays in Economic History*, Vol. I, London (1954), H. A. Shannon, 'The Limited Companies of 1866-1883', p. 387.

22 *Report from the Select Committee on the Companies Acts 1862 and 1867*, Vol. VIII (1877), p. 457.

23 *Ibid*, p. 517.

24 *Institute of Chartered Accountants in England and Wales, Proceedings of the Autumnal Meeting*, London (1921), Ernest Cooper, 'Fifty-seven years in an Accountant's Office', p. 43.

25 *1877 Select Committee, op. cit.*, p. 466.

26 46 & 47 Victoriae c. 52 (1883).

27 *The Accountant*, No. 995, 30 December 1893, p. 1093.

28 *The Accountant*, No. 484, 15 March 1884, p. 4.

29 Day Book 1848-1854, 1849, p. 34.

30 Day Book 1855-1858, 1855, p. 21.

31 Day Book 1848-1854, 1853, p. 150.

32 *The Accountant*, No. 440, 12 May 1883, p. 10.

33 Francis W. Pixley, *The Profession of a Chartered Accountant*, London (1897), p. 7.

34 George Lisle, *Accounting Theory and Practice*, Edinburgh (1899), p. 1.

35 Brown, *op. cit.*, p. 314.

36 19 & 20 Victoriae c. 47 (1856) and 25 & 26 Victoriae c. 89 (1862).

37 Mathias, *op. cit.*, pp. 384-5.

38 Shannon, *op. cit.*, p. 382.

39 Stacey, *op. cit.*, p. 8.

40 Shannon, *op. cit.*, p. 382.

41 Edey and Panitpakdi, *op. cit.*, p. 362.

42 Marriner, *op. cit.*, p. 239.

43 1856 Companies Act, *op. cit.*, section 69.

44 Littleton and Yamey, *op. cit.*, pp. 364, 366.

45 Marriner, *op. cit.*, p. 239.

46 C. A. Cooke, *Corporation, Trust and Company*, Manchester (1950), p. 151.

47 Stacey, *op. cit.*, p. 15; *Deloittes 1845-1956, op. cit.*, p. 17.

48 P.R.O. Rail 250/65 Great Western Railway Directors' Report Book, 14 February 1850.

49 *Accounting Research*, Vol. VIII, Cambridge (1957), Harold Pollins, 'Railway Auditing - A Report', p. 20. Edwin Waterhouse's Diary, 1867, pp. 101-2.

50 Pollins, *op. cit.*, p. 21.

51 30 & 31 Victoriae c. 127 (1867).

52 *House of Lords Sessional Papers*, Vol. XXIX (1849), The Audit of Railway Accounts, pp. 215-16.

53 John Galsworthy, *The Man of Property*, London (1906), Penguin edition, p. 150.

54 Harding, Whinney & Gibbons Letter Book 1867-1902, 29 February 1896, p. 385.

55 Michael Chatfield (Editor), *The English View of Accountants' Duties and Responsibilities 1881-1902*, New York (1978), p. 55.

56 *The Accountant*, No. 773, 28 September 1889, pp. 497-8.

57 *The Accountant*, No. 886, 28 November 1891, p. 841; George Lisle, *Accounting in Theory and Practice, A Text Book for the Use of Accountants*, Edinburgh (1899), p. 2.

58 Quoted from, J. Kitchen and R. H. Parker, *Accounting Thought, op. cit.*, p. 3.

59 Edwin Waterhouse's Diary, p. 147.

60 Baxter and Davidson, *op. cit.*, p. 26.

61 J. R. Edwards and C. Baker, *Accounting and Business Research*, Vol. 9 (1978-79), 'Dowlais Iron Company: Accounting Policies and Procedures for Profit Measurement and Reporting Purposes', pp. 140-1.

62 Robinson, *Irish Accountants, op. cit.*, p. 40.

63 Waterhouse, *op. cit.*, p. 211.

64 Edwin Green, *The Making of a Modern Banking Group, A History of the Midland Bank since 1900*, London (1979), p. 3.

65 George Lisle, *Encyclopaedia of Accounting*, Vol. II, Edinburgh (1903), pp. 113-49.

66 Lawrence R. Dicksee, *Auditing: A practical manual for auditors*, London (1892), p. 6.

67 *The Accountant, op. cit.*, 28 November 1891, p. 840.

68 Price Waterhouse Letter Book 1864-1871, p. 22.

69 *The Accountant*, No. 656, 2 July 1887, p. 388.

70 Harding & Pullein Day Book 1848-1854, pp. 6, 15.

71 Harding & Whinney Day Book 1874-1883, p. 262.

72 C. R. Trevor's Letter Book 1874-1875, 5 October 1874, p. 215.

73 Waterhouse's Diary, *op. cit.*, p. 345.

74 *Report, 27 May 1886*.

75 W. F. Crick and J. E. Wadsworth, *A Hundred Years of Joint Stock Banking*, London (1936), pp. 444-5.

76 Waterhouse's Diary, *op. cit.*, p. 132.

77 *Ibid*, pp. 134-6.

78 *Ibid*, p. 156.

79 *Post Office Directory*, London (1850), p. 791.

80 *Pigot & Co's London and Provincial Directory*, London (1822-23), p. 21.

81 *Post Office Directory*, London (1847), p. 768.

82 Letter Book, *op. cit.*, pp. 58, 79.

83 *Ibid.*

84 *Institute of Chartered Accountants in England and Wales, Charter of Incorporation and Bye-laws*, London (1882), p. 19.

85 See pp. 70-1.

86 *The Post Office Directory of Manchester*, London (1873), p. 423.

87 Trevor's Letter Book, *op. cit.*, p. 82.

88 Thomas Smethurst's Letter Book (1885-1893), 18 January 1886, p. 15.

89 Council Minute Book 'A', *op. cit.*, 5 October 1881, p. 114.

90 Harding & Pullein Day Book 1848-1854, p. 12.

91 Thomas Smethurst's Letter Book, *op. cit.*, *passim*.

92 *Ibid*, 6 January 1886, p. 13.

93 *Bradshaw's Railway Manual, Shareholder's Guide and Directory*, London (1900), p. 193.

94 Frederick Whinney's Private Ledger 1886-1895, passim.

95 *Bradshaw's Railway Manual, op. cit.*, p. 193.

96 Brown, *op. cit.*, p. 322.

97 *Deloittes, op. cit.*, pp. 13-14.

98 *Ibid*, p. 14.

99 *Coopers, op. cit.*, p. 5.

100 Crick and Wadsworth, *op. cit.*, p. 223.

101 Midland Bank Archives (M.B.A.) Annual Report of the Birmingham & Midland Bank, 30 June 1879.

102 M.B.A. Ref. AA61 Board Minutes of the Birmingham & Midland Bank, 23 February 1885.

103 Waterhouse's Diary, *op. cit.*, p. 209.

104 *Ibid*, p. 210.

105 *Parr's Banking Company and the Alliance Bank Ltd., Report 11 January 1893*, Auditors, Turquand, Youngs, Weise, Bishop and Clarke jointly with Stead, Taylor & Stead.

106 J. D. Bailey, *A Hundred Years of Pastoral Banking, A History of the Australian Mercantile Land and Finance Company 1863-1963*, Oxford (1966), pp. 61-6; Gordon Parry, *National Mortgage and Agency Company of New Zealand, The Story of its First Century 1864-1964*, Dunedin (1964), pp. 5, 31, 246.

107 Day Book 1886-1894.

108 *Bradshaw* (1869), *op. cit.*, pp. 48, 52, 387, 403.

109 *Bradshaw* (1869), *op. cit.*, p. 407.

110 *Bradshaw* (1890), *op. cit.*, p. 39.

111 E. F. G. Whinney, *E. & E.*, Cleveland (1961-62), 'Whinney, Smith & Whinney', p. 43.

112 Robinson, *op. cit.*, p. 59.

113 *University of Oxford Accounts of the Colleges 1977-1978*, Oxford (1978), p. 12.

114 Day Book 1855-1858.

115 P. G. Hall, *The Industries of London since 1861*, London (1962), p. 92.

116 *Viney, Merretts, Chartered Accountants for 150 Years in the City of London*, London (1978), p. 2.

117 *Ibid*, 6 August 1910.

118 Hall, *op. cit.*, pp. 72, 78-9.

119 Baker, Sutton & Co Fee Book No. I (1903-1926), 1903, pp. 1-7.

120 D. J. Olsen, *The Growth of Victorian London*, London (1976), p. 88.

121 *The Builder*, Vol. XXVI (1868), p. 501.

122 See Plate 11.

123 Olsen, *op. cit.*, p. 121.

124 T. S. Ashton, *Economic and Social Investigations in Manchester 1833-1933, A Centenary History of the Manchester Statistical Society*, London (1934), pp. 3, 4.

125 *Ibid*, pp. 4, 5, 6, 11-12.

126 *Ibid*, pp. 138-9; Kitchen and Parker, *op. cit.*, pp. 8-9.

127 *Ibid*, pp. 150, 157, 160.

128 *Ibid*, p. 135.

129 Stacey, *op. cit.*, p. 23.

130 Beresford Worthington, *Professional Accountants, An Historical Sketch*, London (1895), pp. 1-2.

131 *Ibid*, p. 4.

132 *The Accountant*, No. 656, 2 July 1887, p. 387.

133 *The History of the Institute of Chartered Accountants in England and Wales*, London (1966), p. 5.

134 *Ibid*, p. 6.

135 Brown, *op. cit.*, pp. 207, 211.

136 *History of the English Institute*, *op. cit.*, pp. 7-8.

137 Letter from R. P. Harding to F. Whinney, 6 December 1883.

138 Stacey, *op. cit.*, p. 24.

139 *History of the English Institute*, *op. cit.*, pp. 12-13.

140 *Ibid*, p. 20.

141 *Ibid*, p. 21.

142 Institute of Chartered Accountants in England and Wales, Council Minute Book 'B' (1879-1880), 29 October 1879, p. 55.

143 Council Minute Book 'A' 1880-1885.

144 *Ibid*, 28 June 1882, p. 165.

145 *Ibid*, 2 June 1881, p. 102.

146 W. J. Reader, *Professional Men*, London (1966), p. 11.

147 Geoffrey Millerson, *The Qualifying Associations*, London (1964), p. 23; Barrington Kaye, *The Development of the Architectural Profession* *in Britain, A Sociological Study*, London (1960), p. 88; Reader, *op. cit.*, p. 54.

148 F. M. L. Thompson, *Chartered Surveyors, The Growth of a Profession*, London (1968), pp. 94, 129-30.

149 *The Accountant*, No. 656, 2 July 1887, p. 388.

150 Quoted from Stacey, *op. cit.*, p. 24.

151 H. Byerley Thomson, *The Choice of a Profession*, London (1857), pp. 1-2.

152 Millerson, *op. cit.*, p. 163.

153 *The Accountant*, No. 4269, 13 October 1956, pp. 367-73.

154 Millerson, *op. cit.*, pp. 51-2.

155 *Institute's Charter and Bye-Laws* (1882), *op. cit.*, pp. 6, 7, 19, 46.

156 Council Minute Book, *op. cit.*, 3 August 1881, p. 111.

157 Letter Book 1892-1894, 31 May 1893, p. 44.

158 A. A. Garrett, *History of the Society of Incorporated Accountants*, Oxford (1961), pp. 1-6.

159 Robinson, *op. cit.*, pp. 85-7, 89-90.

160 Kaye, *op. cit.*, p. 15.

161 Cooper, *Reflections, op. cit.*, p. 62.

162 Millerson, *op. cit.*, pp. 24, 28.

Note to Tables I and II

The totals recorded in each of these tables are in all cases slightly lower than the corresponding figures given in Appendix I (A). The difference is around 10% but in the majority of cases much smaller. While the latter are simply a summation of all the entries in the Day Books, and should therefore tally with the totals quoted in the two tables, it proved impossible to identify every individual entry when assembling these figures. In this case the fee charged was omitted and not recorded in Tables I and II. Hence, the difference between the two 'total' figures of fee income represents the unclassified entries. There is no evidence to suppose that these unidentified entries fell within one specific category (insolvency, auditing and so forth), but that they are spread across the whole range of the accountant's work. Either the client's name was not known or the description of the tasks performed was too vague for any positive categorization.

CHAPTER 3

Accountants in Scotland

Having traced the evolution of the accountancy profession in England, we will now return to the 1850s to examine its important antecedents in Scotland. Professional societies in Edinburgh (1854), Glasgow (1855) and later Aberdeen (1867) predated the English Institute of Chartered Accountants (1880) by over twenty years, prompting the question, what were the reasons for Scotland's advance? Were there qualitative differences in the professions, did accountants perform different functions in the two countries, or was the Scottish profession blessed with particularly favourable circumstances? It is fortunate that Brown, Fleming & Murray and Reid & Mair in Glasgow, together with Wallace & Somerville and Davidson Smith, Wighton & Crawford in Edinburgh (all predecessor firms of Ernst & Whinney),★ though not founder firms of their respective societies, were closely associated with these bodies from an early date. This has made it possible not only to discover something of their operation and character, but also to trace the growth of these professional bodies through the individual histories of these firms.

Significantly one of the earliest references to Scottish accountants occurs in an industrial context, recorded in the Minute Book of the New Mills Cloth Manufactory, Haddingtonshire. Over the period 1681–1703, there are many references to Alexander Herreot, or Heriot, who appears to have been a stockholder and by profession a book-keeper employed part-time by the company. Engaged annually at a salary of £10, he was called upon to adjust entries, examine accounts, check balances and cash and supervise stocktaking. By 1697 he had established himself in Edinburgh as a teacher of book-keeping and had compiled a treatise on mercantile tables.[1] That the teaching of accountancy was taken more

---

★ Reid & Mair merged with Turquands Barton Mayhew in 1978, Wallace & Somerville amalgamated with Whinney Murray in 1969 and Davidson Smith, Wighton & Crawford also joined Turquands Barton Mayhew in 1978.

seriously in eighteenth-century Scotland than in England is indicated by the fact that the master of the academy at Kelso, William
Perry, had written in 1774 *The Man of Business and Gentleman's
Assistant....Book-Keeping by Single and Double Entry....Adapted
to the Use of Gentlemen, Merchants, Traders and Schools.*[2] English
schools did not generally treat accountancy so seriously nor was it
so widely taught.

In the latter part of the eighteenth century accountants appear
to have been no more numerous in Scotland than they were in
England. An Edinburgh directory for 1773, for example, records
that seven accountants practised in the city;[3] ten years later the first
Glasgow directory listed six.[4] However, even at this early stage
certain distinctions had emerged. In Edinburgh, accountancy was
already closely associated with the law and the term 'writer'
(meaning solicitor), used in different circumstances, could describe an accountant, while several instances are recorded of
members of the Society of Writers to the Signet (Scotland's
leading solicitors' society) practising as accountants. Under the
Scottish bankruptcy statutes of 1696, it became the practice for
courts to remit to an accountant the task of assessing a bankrupt's
accounts and of preparing a scheme of ranking of creditors and
division of assets for submission. As Richard Brown recalled in
1905, 'until comparatively recently much accountants' work was
done in solicitors' offices'.[5] Edinburgh being an administrative
more than a commercial centre, when compared with Glasgow,
produced a characteristic distinction in the context of much accountancy work.

In Glasgow, by comparison, accountants, although subject to
the same laws, were much more closely associated with the commercial community, and if they had a second occupation, it was
often as a merchant or financial consultant. The situation commonly occurred in reverse and when bankruptcies were declared
leading Glaswegian merchants found themselves appointed as
trustees for the creditors. Some who acquired a reputation for this
work, entitled themselves 'merchant and accountant', Walter
Ewing Maclae of Cathkin giving up his merchant's business to
devote himself entirely to accountancy.[6] He performed the
winding up of the Glasgow Arms Bank in 1793 with such skill
that it was eventually able to meet all its liabilities and continue in
business. The formation of Scottish life assurance companies in
the early part of the nineteenth century had largely been organ-

ized by Glasgow accountants. Alexander Chambers, a leading excise accountant, helped to found the Ministers' Widows Funds,[7] the first four managers of the Scottish Widows Fund (William Witherspoon, John McKean, Samuel Raleigh, C.A., and John McKenzie) and the original managers of the Scottish Equitable all started life as accountants. Glasgow accountants working for the city's numerous assurance companies developed a considerable expertise in the calculation of premium incomes for life expectancy and hence included mention of their actuarial work in the Institute's title. In addition, Professor Checkland demonstrated how closely Glasgow accountants were connected with the city's banks in the first half of the nineteenth century.[8]

An advertisement from the *Glasgow Mercury* declared in 1784 that[9]

John Gibson and Richard Smellie ... Bring forward the books and accompts of noblemen, gentlemen, merchants and mechanics. They accept arbitrations and determine them speedily, according to the principles of equity and the practice of merchants.... They also act as Factors on estates and subjects under the management of executors and creditors. They collect debts....

Gibson had, in fact, begun as a merchant but, finding himself unsuited to its demands, became an accountant. A detailed survey of Victorian Scottish chartered accountants has shown that, although their fathers were of a varied but mainly middle-class background, the largest percentages in Glasgow were merchants (17%) and businessmen (8%), while those in Edinburgh were the sons of lawyers (16%) and other professional men (10%).[10]

One of the best known general statements on Scottish accountancy was uttered by Sir Walter Scott in 1820. Writing to his brother, himself a paymaster in the 70th Regiment, to suggest a suitable profession for his son, he argued,[11]

... if my nephew is steady, cautious, fond of a sedentary life and quiet pursuits, and at the same time proficient in arithmetic with a disposition towards the prosecution of the highest branches, he cannot follow a better line than that of an accountant. It is highly respectable and is one in which, with attention and skill, aided by such opportunities as I may be able to procure for him, he must ultimately succeed. I say ultimately because the harvest is small and the labours numerous in this as in other branches of our legal practice.

Possibly the key to understanding the early recognition of the Scottish profession lies with Scott's last sentence, where he described accountancy as a branch of legal practice. Many of the tasks performed in England by Masters in Chancery or attorneys and solicitors were undertaken by accountants in Scotland. The Scottish legal system placed responsibility for the estates of bankrupts, pupils (minors) and incapacitated persons firmly in the hands of accountants. In 1824 James McClelland, a Glasgow accountant, included the following tasks among his duties:[12]

Factor and trustee on sequestrated estates,
Trustee or factor for trustees or creditors acting under trust deeds,
Factor for trustees acting for the heirs of persons deceased,
Factor for gentlemen residing in the country for the management of heritable or
    other property,
Agent for houses in England and Scotland. . . .

Curiously liquidations fell towards the end of his list together with 'the keeping and balancing of all account-books belonging to merchants, manufacturers, shopkeepers, etc' – a significantly different order of priorities from a representative English accountancy firm.

Scottish accountants, in contrast to their English counterparts, formed a trusted and integral part of the legal and commercial establishment in the first half of the nineteenth century. Demonstrating the esteem in which the accountant was held in Edinburgh, Robert Balfour wrote to a friend in 1840 to try to persuade him to abandon the Bar for accountancy, arguing that:[13]

It is certainly more varied than that of a lawyer, and I believe it to be certainly not less dignified. It embraces the extensive field of insurance . . . banking . . . finance, whether it be the bankruptcy of a nation or . . . of a private individual, and then, on the other hand, there are arbitrations where conflicting parties voluntarily entrust him [the accountant] with the arrangement of their disputes. And then . . . there are the details of general business in which most of us to some extent engage. It is here that the profession is little more than an infant one. . . .

English accountants, mainly as a result of the different legal and educational system, still sought to establish themselves in a commercial or professional context in the 1850s. English solicitors, in some senses the counterpart of Scottish accountants, had already been granted professional recognition (after much argument earlier in the eighteenth century) when the Law Society received its Royal Charter in 1831.[14] It should not be forgotten, however, that in both Edinburgh and Glasgow, accountants were heavily involved in insolvencies and it has been suggested that the proposed changes in Scotland's bankruptcy laws, which would have relieved them of much lucrative work, were responsible for the timing of their societies' formation.

Making the first moves, in January 1853, to form a professional body in Scotland, Alexander Weir Robertson issued the following circular to fourteen practising accountants: 'several gentlemen connected with our profession have resolved to bring about some definite arrangement for uniting the professional accountants in Edinburgh....'[15] They argued that, since accountants were increasingly being called upon to perform responsible work, it was essential that a society be formed to regulate members' conduct and to protect the public against the unscrupulous. In May 1854 they petitioned Queen Victoria for a charter of incorporation, in a document which underlined the connection between accountancy and the law.[16]

... the business of an accountant in Edinburgh is varied and extensive [ran the text], embracing all matters of account and requiring for its proper execution ... an intimate acquaintance with the general principles of the law, particularly the law of Scotland; and more especially with those branches of it which have relation to the law of merchant, to insolvency and bankruptcy and to all rights concerned with property....

No comparable reference to law followed in the English petition of 1880, or in the Irish one of 1885. The Edinburgh Society's request was successful and a Royal Charter granted in October 1854.

The Institute of Accountants and Actuaries in Glasgow, formed a year earlier, petitioned the Queen in the same year but were not granted a Royal Charter until March 1855. Arguing along a similar path, their petition observed that the 'rapidly increasing' number of accountants performed a range of responsible tasks, which required 'a considerable acquaintance with the general principles of law and a knowledge in particular of the law of Scotland....'[17] In March 1867 the Aberdeen Society became the third and last regional Scottish accountancy body to be granted a Royal Charter. According to Aberdeen directories, there had been six accountants in 1837 and eight of them ten years later. It too, however, had been an early centre for accountants. Malcolm Alexander, a 'teacher of mathematics at Aberdeen' and author of *A Treatise of Book-Keeping, or Merchants Accounts; in the Italian Method of Debtor and Creditor*, wrote a text book based on his personal dealings with merchants, 'retailers and private concerns ... gentlemen of landed estates and their stewards or factors'.[18] As in Aberdeen, the Dundee accountant was closely associated with the solicitor, though five of Dundee's twelve accountants in 1845 worked for banks.[19]

The recurring connection between Scottish accountancy and

the law was, in turn, responsible for the close co-operation with the universities. Because the English accountant had not the same degree of involvement in legal matters, links with colleges came late and mostly concerned the technical aspects of their duties (see p. 118). From the grant of the Edinburgh Society's Charter in 1854 and the introduction of entrance examinations, apprentices were compelled to attend a year's course at a university to study the legal background to the profession's duties.[20] Accordingly, the universities of Edinburgh, Glasgow and Aberdeen set up accountancy departments to cope with the influx of apprentices. Later practising accountants were appointed as tutors. In this continuing tradition, for example, Professor D. S. Anderson, senior partner of Wallace & Somerville,* was appointed to the chair of accounting at Edinburgh and from 1967-68 served as President of the merged Institute of Chartered Accountants of Scotland, while A. D. Paton, a partner in the Glasgow firm of Reid & Mair, was both a senior lecturer in accountancy at Glasgow University and Director of Studies of that city's professional Institute. In 1892 the three bodies had agreed to set common entrance examinations and in 1905 Brown reported that 'for a considerable number of years the Edinburgh and Glasgow Societies, in conjunction with the Institute of Bankers in Scotland, have arranged courses of lectures on subjects [including] ... partnership trust, commercial banking and company law'.[21] This legal connection with Scottish accountancy persisted well into the twentieth century, but only really emerged in England in the 1900s when a knowledge of increasingly complex taxation law became important.

As we have seen, one of the significant features of early English accountancy was the close connection with Non-conformist sects. Such a relationship was absent from the Scottish story. Although legal restrictions existed for chapel-goers, these dissenters from the Presbyterian Church were not excluded from participation in civil roles. A greater degree of religious toleration meant that there was no particular reason why dissenters should be channelled into commercial occupations.

The advanced state of Scottish education together with this small country's limited opportunities encouraged large numbers of well-qualified professional men (doctors, engineers, architects, accountants and so forth), as well as entrepreneurs, to emigrate

* Wallace & Somerville, founded in 1871, amalgamated with Henry Lessels & Son in 1942 and then with Whinney Murray in 1969.

throughout the world in the search for work. The drift of Scottish chartered accountants south, in part following Scottish businesses, was particularly noticeable in the inter-war period, when for instance Brown, Fleming & Murray and Thomson McLintock & Co opened London offices that later outgrew their Glasgow parents (see p. 168).

Although the firm of Brown, Fleming & Murray was not among the first generation of Scottish accountancy practices, it certainly fell within the second. The firm was formed in 1889 when R. A. Murray joined Brown & Fleming, a practice dating from January 1880. The original partners were William Stewart Brown [1851-1888], who had trained with Auld & Guild, being admitted to the Glasgow Institute in 1877, and J. Gibson Fleming, who had been apprenticed with McClelland, McKinnon & Blyth and qualified at Glasgow in 1880.[22] Fleming's father (also John Gibson), a distinguished doctor, was the medical adviser to the Scottish Amicable Life Assurance Society. It may have been significant, in view of his son's choice of profession, that his ancestors had been merchant burgesses of Glasgow since 1643, reflecting the strong connection between commerce and accountancy there.[23] Matthew Tarbett Fleming, J. Gibson's brother, proved to be of great value to Brown, Fleming & Murray later on, as will be seen (see p. 87). However, Brown had died in 1888 not long before Murray joined the practice, and Fleming's death in 1895 left Murray in sole charge until James Herbert Wilson (son of the manager of the Clydesdale Bank, a client then as now) was admitted to the partnership in 1898. In 1904 the firm, having first moved to 163 West George Street, where several accountancy practices had settled, then transferred to larger premises at No. 175 (a splendid red sandstone commercial alcazar designed by John Campbell in 1902), and where they remained until 1981.

Generally, there had been little audit work in the 1850s and 1860s, so that recurrent annual fees were exceptional.[24] The character of Brown, Fleming & Murray's work in the nineteenth century differed considerably from today. Most accountants derived most of their work from the courts (particularly bankruptcy) or other legal connections but, as in England, they tended to have more than one occupation. In Glasgow a particularly close association was built up with the city's Stock Exchange and for a while the Institute was housed in the same building. For example, Robert Aitken [1806-1890], senior partner in Aitken,

Mackenzie & Clapperton (a firm which amalgamated with Brown, Fleming & Murray in 1948), the son of a Glasgow banker, was a member of the Stock Exchange Association as well as being an original Council member of the Glasgow Institute and a local director of the Life Association of Scotland.[25] In turn, his son R. Easton Aitken, having studied at Glasgow University, was assumed a partner in the firm but was better known as a stockbroker, becoming a member of the Association and three times serving as its chairman.

Robert Reid and Robert Alexander Mair (founders in 1871 of the firm Reid & Mair, which merged in 1978 with Turquands Barton Mayhew) also practised as 'house factors and insurance agents'. However, as the nineteenth century drew to a close, accountants steadily dropped their outside commitments, partly because of Institute prohibitions and partly as a result of the growing importance of accountancy work: insolvencies, auditing and later taxation. Thomson McLintock [1851-1920], who had established his Glasgow practice in 1877 at 88 Vincent Street, made a reputation in insolvency work (and derived considerable fees) from his handling of the City of Glasgow Bank crash in 1878.[26] Initially he, too, had followed a second occupation, doubling as a house factor and insurance agent.

As in England, audit work grew steadily in importance so that by the 1890s Brown, Fleming & Murray had a long list of companies demanding an annual examination of their books. Reports were sent to over twenty clients in 1892.[27] These companies covered a broad range of activity, although most fell within an industrial or commercial context, while the practice also undertook many personal commissions, a few being for landowners. Glasgow's function as a port and financial centre is illustrated or reflected by a number of audit clients including the Ardrossan Harbour Company, Gorval Rope & Sail Company, New York Packing & Building Company, Glasgow South Africa Gold Syndicate, Transvaal Chemical Company and the Yuma Syndicate, while others were more locally orientated, such as E. B. Robb's Factory, Carfin Colliery, Aberfoyle Slate Quarries and the Arundel Society.[28] In 1887 Fleming was auditor of the Strathendrick & Aberfoyle Railway of which a James Murray was a director. Brown, Fleming & Murray also audited two local authorities, the Calder Parochial Board and the Drymen Parochial Board. By 1898 the following clients had been added to the audit lists: the

Clyde Navigation Trust, Clan Line, British Gold Mines of Mexico, Cordoba Silver Lead Mines Company, Mining Development Syndicate (of Colorado), Fraser's Trust, Fleming Gibson Trust, Harvey's Distillery, Scottish Grains Company, Shamrock Gold Mines and Poorman Silver Mines.[29]

The prospective, speculative or overseas nature of some of these clients, financed from Glasgow, is also to be seen in the firm's most important audit, the Burmah Oil Company registered in 1886. A predecessor, the Rangoon Oil Company, had been formed in 1871 to prospect for oil in Burmah and in 1876 appointed Finlay Fleming, a firm of managing agents, to look after its business organization in Rangoon.[30] Later Matthew Tarbett Fleming (J. Gibson's brother), the managing agent, recommended that Brown, Fleming & Murray replace Kidston, Goff & Co as the auditors of the Glasgow end of the company.[31] Burmah Oil's first Minute Book records in March 1889 that R. A. Murray of Brown, Fleming & Murray was appointed as the company's auditor, a task which he continued to perform for thirty years.[32] As the chairman, Sir John Cargill, reported in 1937 on Murray's death, 'it was in his capacity as auditor that I first made contact with him, when I returned to Glasgow from Rangoon in 1893 and formed intimate business relations and a close friendship which was to cover a period of over forty years'.* In 1920 on resigning the auditorship of the company, Murray was offered a seat on the Burmah board. The social and business intimacy to which Cargill referred had doubtless been heightened by geographical proximity as in 1903 Burmah Oil moved from 45 Renfield Street to an office building shortly to be shared with Brown, Fleming & Murray at 175 West George Street (not the only co-residence which was to affect the future of the firm, see pp. 163, 170).

Although much of Burmah's organization remained overseas, control of the company's financial dealings ultimately rested in Glasgow, as the 1892 auditor's report demonstrates:[33]

... as previously the foreign accounts have been audited and certified as correct by an accountant in Rangoon, before being sent home, and have been properly incorporated in the books here...

---

* Burmah Oil Company Minute Book, 28 April 1937. On that date J. H. Wilson, a partner, resigned as auditor and on 14 May the firm of Brown, Fleming & Murray, rather than one of its members, were officially appointed in his place.

This was no simple audit because both sets of accounts, home and overseas, had to be checked and notice taken of the depreciation of machinery and the gradual exhaustion of the oil wells, while reserve and insurance funds had also been set up.[34]

The Burmah Oil Company not only formed an important source of fees in itself, but through the establishment of its subsidiaries and associates provided Brown, Fleming & Murray with an additional group of clients. In the Edwardian period Burmah Oil became increasingly interested in the Middle East as a source of oil, first setting up the Concessions Syndicate Ltd (of which John Cargill and James Hamilton, both directors of Burmah at 175 West George Street, were appointed to the board, the accounts being audited by William Auld from its formation in 1905 until the voluntary liquidation in 1915) and then the First Exploitation Company. The latter, in turn, set up the Anglo-Persian Oil Company in July 1909, appointing Brown, Fleming & Murray as its auditors from the outset, who from December 1909 also became auditors of the First Exploitation Company.[35] In July 1910 it was agreed that 'the rate of remuneration to Messrs Brown, Fleming & Murray for the year ending 31 March 1910 was discussed and it was resolved that it should be £75.0.0.'[36] Although it transferred the accounts department from Glasgow to London in 1915, Anglo-Persian retained Brown, Fleming & Murray as accountants, doubtless keen to draw on their experience in the oil business.[37] Anglo-Persian grew to such a size that it opened a new London office (Winchester House, Old Broad Street) and, so closely were Brown, Fleming & Murray involved, that in 1919 they had to follow in their client's footsteps and open a London office themselves (see p. 170).

In October 1922 Price's Patent Candles, from 1919 a subsidiary of Lever Brothers, became part of a newly formed group, Candles Limited, in which Anglo-Persian Oil, Burmah Oil and Shell, all interested in diversifying to secure a market for their paraffin wax, had acquired a significant shareholding. As auditors of both Anglo-Persian and Burmah, it was natural that Brown, Fleming & Murray should be offered the audit first of Candles Limited and then in 1923 that of their subsidiary Price's Patent Candles. However, the latter, a company without limited liability, had been formed by local Act of Parliament in 1848, section xxvi of which stipulated that 'the present auditors ... shall continue until the first ordinary meeting ... when they shall retire and two auditors shall be elected in their place', each being eligible for re-relection and having to hold at least one share in the company.[38] Hence, when Ivan Spens and Robert Murray were elected as auditors in September 1923, they had to comply with this nineteenth-century requirement.[39] Today, although shareholding is discouraged among accountants where they have a professional connection with a company, the two members of Ernst & Whinney (it remains a personal appointment) who audit Price's Patent Candles are still required to own a qualifying share each in the business.

Not as sizeable as Brown, Fleming & Murray, Reid & Mair had been founded by Robert Reid [1843-1907], who had originally trained in the legal department of the City of Glasgow Bank but then served an apprenticeship to become a Glasgow chartered accountant in 1875, his parents being associated with the grocery trade in Kirkintilloch. This legal and commercial background equipped him particularly well to deal with insolvency work, in which he later specialized, and at the time of the City of Glasgow Bank crash kept the firm busy on sequestrations and liquidations. R. A. Mair [1847-1898] became a Glasgow chartered accountant in 1871, having taken articles with Moore & Brown.[40] The mercantile connection was strong on this side, too, as his father, John Mair, had been a Glasgow lace merchant.[41] R. A. Mair later served as secretary to the Vale of Clyde and the Greenock, Port Glasgow & Gourock Tramway Companies.

Reid & Mair was in many ways a typical Glaswegian practice dealing with small businesses from a wide variety of trades. The largest audit clients included John G. Stein & Co, ironmasters, L. Sterne & Co, refrigerating engineers, Robert Melville & Co, sawmillers in Falkirk, and R. & J. Dick Ltd, a retail footwear concern, later manufacturers of machine drives and conveyors. As clients they were in a way too successful, all four prospering only to be taken over by larger companies. Like Brown, Fleming & Murray, Reid & Mair also audited local authorities, but that aspect of their work had disappeared by 1918.

Ernst & Whinney's present Edinburgh practice is the product of a number of amalgamations involving two principal firms, Wallace & Somerville★ (who merged with Whinney Murray in 1969) and Davidson Smith, Wighton & Crawford (who had

★ Wallace & Somerville had merged with William Bishop in 1968, who in 1962–63 had been President of the Institute of Cost and Works Accountants.

joined Turquands Barton Mayhew in 1978). Both firms had strong connections with the Edinburgh Society, D. E. Wallace being an early member, while Sir John Somerville served as President of the Scottish Institute in its centenary year, 1954–55*. Having been apprenticed to Kenneth Mackenzie, Adam Davidson Smith became a chartered accountant in 1872 and served as a Council member from 1888 to 1892.[42] Practising on his own until 1906 when joined by his son Charles, A. Davidson Smith gained a number of clients when his former employer's only remaining partner, John Turnbull Smith, retired; these included the Niddrie & Benhar Coal Company.

Wallace & Somerville developed a considerable expertise in the audit of local authority accounts. Auditors were first appointed to small districts, often parish councils, where they could gain experience of this type of work in the hope of being promoted to successively larger councils, each post then being a personal appointment. During the inter-war period John Somerville had worked his way up the local authority ladder to audit several large counties, East Lothian, Fife, Perth and Roxburgh, while John Lessels had the largest and most prestigious of them all, the Edinburgh Corporation. Somerville was also secretary of the local government auditors' commission. This system presents a further contrast to England where the audit was normally performed by government accountants, the specialized nature of the work encouraging them to form their own professional body – the Institute of Municipal Treasurers and Accountants. Only a few accountants in private practice succeeded in gaining access to this type of work in England (see p. 110). Similarly the Glasgow practice, Fraser, Lawson & Laing, founded in 1922, though initially specializing in insolvency work, built up a reputation for local government auditing, reaching a peak in the early 1960s when R. G. Laing was appointed auditor of Ayr County Council – then fifth in the Scottish Local Authority League Table – and of ten associated district councils.†

The other specialism developed largely in the inter-war period by Wallace & Somerville in Edinburgh was the preparation and

---

* Somerville's full period of office was from 1953 to 1955. Although Brown, Fleming & Murray as a firm did not take a major part in the Glasgow Institute's affairs, a partner, A. I. Mackenzie, was elected President of the merged body from 1972–73.

† Fraser, Lawson & Laing merged with Whinney Murray in Glasgow in 1975.

audit of farm or small estate accounts. The connection had been stimulated by John Somerville's service on the Crofters' Commission and his work for the Farmers Trade Association. The same was also true in Edinburgh of Davidson Smith, Wighton & Crawford, who had built up a considerable agricultural practice opening small offices at Cupar, Leven and Kirkcaldy to deal with the business provided by owner-occupier farms and a few landed estates. The attraction of Edinburgh accountants, rather than a more locally based accountancy firm, lay in their established reputations but more particularly in their legal expertise, important in times of complex tax regulations and high death duties.

Both Edinburgh firms remained small practices in the nineteenth and early years of the twentieth centuries, without close connections with the 'high finance' world of Edinburgh and the other east coast towns, preparing accounts or auditing for the most part family businesses. As has been argued, the links with the legal profession were much stronger in Edinburgh than in Glasgow, where trade and finance exercised a greater influence. The emphasis on family involvement and continuity, so clear in England, was also a salient feature of Scottish practices. 'Almost the majority [of Glasgow chartered accountants]', wrote Cairncross in 1937, 'are the children of a tiny fraction of business and professional people. As in other professions, wealth and influence are as important in shaping the opportunities and interests of children as the ability with which they are endowed.'[43] Although neither of the Edinburgh firms operated within the inner financial circles, family relationships, the various accountancy societies and the universities provided the social and professional introductions from which their work derived.

References

1 *History of Chartered Accountants of Scotland, From the Earliest Times until 1954*, Edinburgh (1954), p. 3.
2 William Perry, *The Man of Business and Gentleman's Assistant ... Book-Keeping by Single and Double Entry ... Adapted to the Use of Gentlemen, Merchants, Traders and Schools*, Edinburgh (1774).
3 Richard Brown, *A History of Accounting and Accountants*, Edinburgh (1905), p. 183.
4 James C. Stewart, *Pioneers of a Profession, Chartered Accountants to 1879*, Edinburgh (1977), pp. 5-6.

5 Brown, *op. cit.*, p. 182.

6 *History of the Chartered Accountants of Scotland, op. cit.*, p. 5.

7 Brown, *op. cit.*, p. 185.

8 S. G. Checkland, *Scottish Banking, A History 1695-1975*, Glasgow (1975), pp. 380-1.

9 *History of the Chartered Accountants of Scotland, op. cit.*, p. 12.

10 M. J. M. Kedslie, 'Social Origins of Scottish Chartered Accountants 1854-1904', Paper Presented at the Third International Congress of Accounting Historians, London, 1980, Table II.

11 Letter written to Thomas Scott, 23 July 1820, quoted from Brown, *op. cit.*, p. 197. In fact the boy joined the army as a soldier and rapidly rose to be a general.

12 *Ibid*, p. 201.

13 *History of the Chartered Accountants of Scotland, op. cit.*, pp. 17-18.

14 Reader, *Professional Men, op. cit.*, p. 54.

15 Quoted from Stacey, *op. cit.*, p. 20.

16 Brown, *op. cit.*, p. 207.

17 *Ibid*, p. 210.

18 Alexander Malcolm, *A Treatise of Book-keeping, or Merchants Accounts; in the Italian Method of Debtor and Creditor*, London (1731).

19 Brown, *op. cit.*, p. 202.

20 Stacey, *op. cit.*, p. 21.

21 Brown, *op. cit.*, pp. 214-15.

22 Stewart, *op. cit.*, p. 57; Partnership Deed between W. S. Brown and J. G. Fleming, dated 10 March 1880, for five years from January.

23 *One Hundred Glasgow Men*, p. 135 (copy in Mitchell Library, Glasgow).

24 Stewart, *op. cit.*, p. 14.

25 *Ibid*, p. 42.

26 R. Winsbury, *Thomson McLintock & Co - The First Hundred Years*, London (1977), pp. 11, 15.

27 Brown, Fleming & Murray's Statement Book, No. 2 (1890-1892).

28 *Ibid*.

29 Statement Book, No. 6 (1898).

30 T. A. B. Corley, Communications, Entrepreneurship and the Managing Agent System: Burmah Oil Company 1886-1928, unpublished research paper (1979), pp. 5, 6.

31 *Official Directory of Chartered Accountants of Scotland*, Edinburgh (1896), pp. 55-6, records Kidston, Goff & Co at 102 Hope Street, Glasgow.

32 Burmah Oil Company Directors' Minute Book 1886-1889, 6 March 1889, pp. 11, 15.

33 Brown, Fleming & Murray Statement Book, No. 2 (1890-1892), p. 338.

34 *Ibid*.

35 *Anglo-Persian Oil Company Report*, 26 July 1909, Brown, Fleming & Murray appointed auditors, p. 8. First Exploitation Company Minute Book 1909–27, 20 December 1909, Brown, Fleming & Murray appointed as auditors, p. 2.

36 Information supplied by the BP Group Historian, Dr R. Ferrier: Anglo-Persian Oil Company Board Minutes, 25 July 1910.

37 *Ibid*, 23 January 1915.

38 11 & 12 Victoriae c. 10 (1848), An Act for the Incorporation, Establishment and Regulation of 'Price's Patent Candle Company', pp. 205, 217.

39 Ref. 135, Price's Patent Candles, General Minute Book, 18 September 1923, p. 112.

40 Stewart, *op. cit.*, p. 142.

41 *Ibid*, p. 106.

42 *Ibid*, p. 175.

43 *The Accountant*, No. 3276, 18 September 1937, Alexander Cairncross, 'The Social Origins of Accountants', p. 374.

✿✿✿ CHAPTER 4 ✿✿✿

Edwardian Accountancy

The Edwardian period has often retrospectively been regarded as a 'golden age' in English history; a time without major wars, when the economy produced steady growth and when the Empire reached the limits of its might. In a sense this is a false image and also, it is fair to say, one very rarely adopted by the Edwardians themselves. There were damaging strikes throughout 1911-12 (miners, seamen, dockers, railwaymen and others) raising fears of revolution, the American and German economies in fact grew much faster than Britain's, the Irish Home Rule campaign and the Suffragettes added to the disruption, while in foreign affairs war threatened to break out on several occasions prior to 1914.[1] Although a time of conflicting fortunes, the Edwardian period provided great and growing employment for accountants, just as the 1840s had been critical in the Victorian era. McAuliffe, Davis & Hope, founded in 1895, flourished particularly overseas where they extended their operations throughout South East Asia and South America before the outbreak of war. Barton, Mayhew in London, C. Herbert Smith & Russell in Birmingham, Woolley & Waldron in Southampton, Buckley, Hall, Devin & Co in Hull and Howell & Hanbidge in Sheffield were all established within these thirteen years. However, it would be wrong to argue from this evidence alone that a distinct phase occurred in the creation of accountancy firms, as this group does not constitute a sufficiently representative sample. But the fact of their foundation combined with the unchecked growth of Turquand, Youngs and Whinney, Smith & Whinney suggests that a number of English Edwardian accountants found this a profitable period before the holocaust of 1914-18.

The firm of Barton, Mayhew & Co was established in December 1907 when Harold Barton [1882-1962] and Basil Mayhew [1884-1966] left their employers Price Waterhouse to set up practice on the third floor of 26 Great St Helens, London EC3. Barton, the son of Major Bernard Barton, owner of a Hull seed crushing mill, originally articled to George Gale, a chartered accountant in Hull, qualified in September 1904, while Mayhew, articled to his father Edgar, a chartered accountant in Ipswich, became an A.C.A. in 1906. They had both joined Price Waterhouse in 1905, but deciding to set up on their own, were each allowed to take one client with them - Barton retaining the audit of Griffiths & Co, a building contractors, and Mayhew that of the retailing subsidiaries of Van den Berghs, the margarine manufacturers, including Meadow Dairy. The latter, as an expanding and successful business, proved to be a fortunate acquisition for Barton, Mayhew. In 1909, when Meadow Dairy took over the Keeloma Dairy, Van den Berghs considered it prudent to appoint another director to the former's board to safeguard their increased holding; they selected Basil Mayhew.[2] Meadow's growth, financed by Van den Berghs, had been too fast for its own good and Mayhew was entrusted with representing preference shareholders' capital. His financial advice was clearly appreciated as in December 1913 the board of Van den Berghs, dissatisfied with the management of another subsidiary, Pearks, also consulted him in the revitalization of this ailing company.[3] Mayhew's business acumen, as will be seen, was much in demand in the inter-war period, particularly by Bowaters and the Colman family.

It seems to have been a common pattern in small but growing Edwardian practices for one partner to concentrate on acquiring new clients, while the other organized and performed the accountancy work in the office; a particularly successful combination when it was endorsed by the respective personalities of the partners. Basil Mayhew, a man of distinguished appearance and gregarious character, took much responsibility for getting fresh business and entertaining clients; Harold Barton, a more purposeful man, ensured that the work was performed efficiently and expertly. Although this distinction is not a perfect one (Barton through his membership of the Society of Yorkshiremen in London and various dining and debating clubs secured much new work, while Mayhew developed an expertise in family estates and personal accounts), it does characterize many small partnership arrangements. The same was also said to have been true of Shuttleworth & Haworth in Manchester, where George Haworth, being an extrovert, was the business-getter and of C. Herbert Smith & Russell in Birmingham, where H. H. Russell as a technician organized and performed most of the accounting work.

Barton's Yorkshire origins soon proved valuable in the acquisition of the Eucryl (toothpaste manufacturers) audit, as the company had their works in Hull, Barton's home town. To secure the audit they opened a so-called Hull office, which was in fact simply an arrangement with Barton's brother, who had his solicitor's chambers in The Land of Green Ginger and allowed them to use his rooms. Once the audit had been established, the deal terminated and Barton, Mayhew's City telegraphic address, devised with the Hull office in mind, 'Usually London', lost its real meaning.

By contrast, Whinney, Smith & Whinney, as an established City practice, faced the task of maintaining their reputation while expanding in an increasingly competitive context. The graph of real fee income (Fig. 2), reveals that the firm reached a high point in 1902 with a slightly lower peak in 1904. This pattern, with its trough in 1903, also reflected in Turquand, Youngs' fees, probably resulted from the aftermath of the Boer War. The end of hostilities in 1902 and the sudden influx of demobilized soldiers produced a short depression before the economy could adjust to peacetime conditions. Subsequently Whinney, Smith & Whinney's fee income declined in the 1904-07 period, rising again between 1909 and 1910. The miners' strikes and general disruption of 1911-12 appear to be the cause of the temporary fall in income then, which was more serious in real terms than the cash figures revealed. There then followed a steady rise until the outbreak of war in August 1914. In fact, as Table II shows, the 1905-10 period produced a general business recovery which suggests that the firm's low income largely resulted from falling insolvency fees – only 17.2% of total income, yielding £2,161 in 1905. Audit income continued to grow in monetary terms, rising from £7,365 in 1905 to £10,018 in 1910. However, the recovery exhibited by Whinney, Smith & Whinney's fees in 1909-10 corresponded with widespread difficulties in the economy. The monetary contribution of audit fees, though up, represented a percentage fall (from 58.6% in 1905 to 35.4% in 1910) as insolvency work picked up to 53.0% or £15,010. The Edwardian period, therefore, marks a transitory phase in accountancy when neither auditing nor insolvency was of overwhelming importance. Although auditing contributed the largest single source of fees, the firm still did best in times of depression or financial crisis when insolvency fees boosted their income to its greatest heights. By the 1920s and

Figure 2 Predecessor Firms' Fee Income 1900–1920

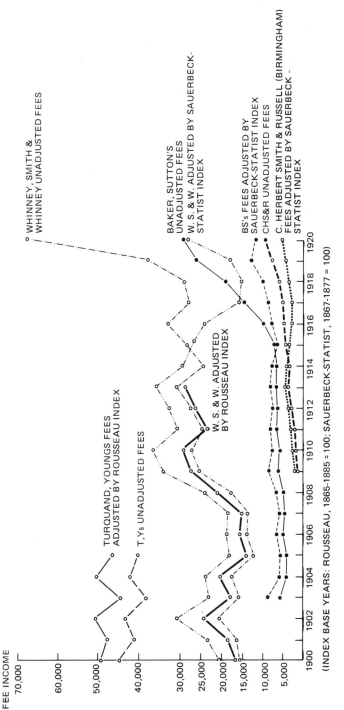

(INDEX BASE YEARS: ROUSSEAU, 1865-1885 = 100; SAUERBECK-STATIST, 1867-1877 = 100)

1930s, as will be seen, this was no longer the case and accountants, along with everybody else, fared badly in times of recession.

The most important trend revealed by Table II was the continued growth of audit work so that it is to these client companies that we must now turn our attention. Whinney, Smith & Whinney consolidated or built up a further group of specialisms in the Edwardian period, principally in brewing and the audit of large estates. Having bought public houses at over-inflated prices in the tied-house race, a number of breweries fell into serious financial difficulties in 1906. Arthur Whinney, who was by then well known in the City (and possibly because Whinney, Smith & Whinney had audited the Meux Brewery between 1891 and 1904), helped to reconstruct both Ind Coope and Allsops, the latter jointly with Turquand, Youngs, the auditors of Guinness. In 1914 Whinney, Smith & Whinney became auditors of Ind Coope and their subsidiaries, also gaining the audit of Strettons Derby Brewery in the same year. Arthur Whinney earned a considerable reputation for company reconstructions following this brewery work, which in the inter-war period led to his appointment by the Austin Motor Company and later by the Dunlop Rubber Company.

In addition, Whinney, Smith & Whinney had developed an expertise in estate accounting, two of their largest clients dating from the earliest days: the Earl of Scarbrough's various English lands (from 1861) and the Duke of Wellington's Spanish and Belgian estates (1866), one of their first tasks having been for Sir William Erle, the preparation 'of your farm accounts from September 1849 to September 1854'. To these were added Lord Tredegar's estates (1891), Lord Penrhyn's slate quarries in North Wales, principally at Bangor (1889), Lord Rendlesham's estate (c. 1910) and the personal affairs of Lord Rowallan (1917). At about the same time Edwin Waterhouse recalled how he had been called by the Duke of Bedford to modernize his estate accounting.[4] The imposition of death duties and supertax were not the only inducements for aristocratic landowners to tighten up their administration; heightened competition from overseas, including American grain and the first imports of refrigerated meat, added to the pressures for efficient estate management.

The steady growth in audit work, rated top of an accountant's duties in a 1906 text book, in part reflected increasingly restrictive legislation.[5] The 1900 Companies Act re-introduced the compul-

Table II The Percentage Composition of Whinney, Smith and Whinney's Fee Income
(For an explanation of the 'Total' figures see p. 78)

YEAR	Accounting		Auditing		Insolvency		Government Work		Taxation		Trustee & Executorship		Special Work		TOTAL
	%	£	%	£	%	£	%	£	%	£	%	£	%	£	£
1905	13.0	1,630	58.6	7,365	17.2	2,161	–	–	0.1	17	5.4	682	5.6	705	12,560
1910	3.9	1,091	35.4	10,018	53.0	15,010	–	–	0.6	158	3.4	953	3.8	1,087	28,317
1915	9.2	2,569	44.6	12,482	30.6	8,565	6.0	1,019	1.4	393	6.8	1,903	1.3	377	27,308
1918	7.7	2,091	48.1	13,078	31.4	8,542	1.7	463	2.5	685	1.8	499	6.7	1,810	27,168
1920	9.5	6,146	38.3	24,868	45.1	29,321	0.5	310	2.0	1,319	1.4	920	3.2	2,076	64,960
1925	8.0	6,123	48.5	37,093	26.8	20,449	–	–	4.9	3,719	7.4	5,633	4.5	3,421	76,438
1930	11.0	6,681	67.4	40,708	6.2	3,733	–	–	5.9	3,570	3.2	1,944	6.2	3,774	60,410
1935	16.0	7,531	67.2	31,614	1.9	891	–	–	6.0	2,831	2.3	1,078	6.5	3,078	47,023
1939	10.2	5,929	73.3	42,765	2.7	1,580	–	–	6.3	3,702	1.5	862	6.0	3,503	58,341
1941	8.1	3,949	73.9	35,922	3.7	1,820	2.3	1,097	6.2	3,026	1.7	806	4.1	2,015	48,635
1945	9.2	8,272	62.9	56,632	3.2	2,896	10.5	9,437	7.5	6,733	2.3	2,101	4.3	3,895	89,966
1950	7.4	11,272	63.8	97,284	4.3	6,577	6.9	10,572	11.2	17,040	1.4	2,129	5.1	7,726	152,600
1955	4.5	8,816	69.6	137,876	0.7	1,328	1.2	2,334	14.2	28,058	1.8	3,566	8.1	16,073	198,051
1960	8.4	29,006	59.7	206,025	0.2	736	3.3	11,464	11.0	38,009	2.4	8,384	14.8	51,320	344,944

sory external audit for all registered companies and provided for the auditor's remuneration – the 1844 Joint Stock Act had required an external audit but this was negated by the 1856 legislation – although the auditor still did not need to hold defined professional qualifications.[6] In requiring that the audited annual balance sheet, which was to contain a limited summary of share capital, liabilities and assets, be filed with the Registrar of Companies (thereby opening it to public inspection), the 1907 Companies Act placed a little extra pressure on businesses to see that their accounts were properly prepared and audited.[7] It did, however, distinguish between private and public companies; the former being, in general, small family businesses with a maximum of fifty shareholders, the shares not saleable to the public, were exempted from these provisions.

'The publication of the balance sheets of private banks', wrote Waterhouse in 1890, 'was followed by a series of amalgamations between them and the joint stock banks competing with them.'[8] This late nineteenth-century merger movement in many ways foreshadowed that of the accountants themselves in the 1960s and 1970s. It also produced a great deal of extra audit work for a few fortunate practices. In this way the Midland Bank's progressive expansion through amalgamation brought much additional work to Whinney, Smith & Whinney, as their auditors. In 1890 the bank had only forty-five branches but by merging with regional banks increased the number to 280 by 1900.[9] In every case the Midland replaced the local bank's auditors on take-over. An examination of the reports of the various provincial and City banks, that merged with the Midland, has demonstrated how various auditors were employed prior to incorporation but on amalgamation how they were replaced and the custom concentrated into the hands of the Midland's auditors alone: the Central Bank of London (John Young and Edward Hunter 1869-90, Alexander Young and two others 1891), the Oldham Joint Stock Bank (David Smith of Manchester 1880-97), the Huddersfield Banking Company (Welton, Jones & Co 1889-96), the Yorkshire Banking Co (H.W. & J. Blackburn 1877-1901), the City Bank (various individuals 1856-81) and the London Joint Stock Bank (John Griffiths and Thomas Welton 1888-92).[10]

Banking, like accountancy, is a service industry and the motives underlying the medium-size bank's desire for amalgamation in the late nineteenth century were echoed by those of the intermediate-sized accountancy practice of the 1960s and 1970s (see p. 225). The Leeds and County Bank, which was taken over by the Midland in 1890, recognized that the significant increase in the needs of its business customers could not be accommodated locally: 'the formation of large and powerful combinations', admitted the Leeds Bank's chairman, 'had almost become a necessity to meet the calls now made upon them by mercantile and manufacturing firms.'[11]

Following the pattern established in the 1890s, the Midland Bank's earliest amalgamations in the early twentieth century concentrated upon joint stock banks in regions where it was poorly represented or not at all.[12] The large branch networks of the Leicester Banking Company (in 1900), the Nottingham Joint Stock Bank (1905), the Yorkshire Banking Company (1901) and the Sheffield Union Banking Company (1901) all joined the Midland's network. The amalgamations of the first two decades of the century focused on banks which had already conducted vigorous expansion programmes of their own, such as the North & South Wales Bank taken over in 1908 and the Metropolitan Bank in 1914, whose auditors must have been particularly upset, having seen their client grow rapidly but then disappear altogether.[13] The geographical motivation behind the Midland's expansion is reflected by that of the largest accountancy firms in the 1960s as they too merged with established regional practices in areas where their clients demanded national services.

Meanwhile Turquand, Youngs, which had long been one of the City's leading accountancy practices, continued to occupy a pre-eminent position within the profession. Unfortunately nothing further has been discovered of the character and development of their clients during the Edwardian period because the bulk of the firm's records were destroyed by fire in the early 1970s. Their rising fee income, however, tells its own tale of success. An indication of their expansion is provided by the move to progressively larger premises. Initially William Turquand had occupied rooms at 13 Old Jewry Chambers, moving in *c.* 1860 to 16 Tokenhouse Yard, Lothbury, where the firm remained until *c.* 1880.[14] Continued growth required the removal to 41 Coleman Street, when again the need for space prompted the move to 19 Coleman Street where Turquand, Youngs shared accommodation with the Equitable Life Assurance Company. Having moved to a new site at 4 Coleman Street in 1968, they made their final relocation in 1972 to Lynton House, Tavistock Square, following the merger with Barton, Mayhew. Whinney, Smith & Whinney exhibited a similar pattern. Moving from 8 Old Jewry in 1899 to occupy larger premises at No. 32, further growth necessitated the transfer in 1910 to a late Victorian office block at 4b Frederick's Place.

Henry McAuliffe entered public practice sometime in 1895 at 23 Billiter Buildings before he was joined by Alfred Davis in 1897, the two moving to Threadneedle House, 28-31 Bishopsgate Street Within, early in 1901. The move to Threadneedle House, also occupied by the Bank of Scotland, like Whinney, Smith & Whinney's move to rooms in the Yorkshire Penny Bank at Leeds or Buckley & Hall's early premises in the Union of London & Smith's Bank, Hull, proved fortunate. Although the first and last banks never became audit clients themselves, they did all constitute sources of investigation and insolvency work with regard to other businesses and doubtless on occasion recommended these accountancy practices to their own clients when the need arose. McAuliffe and Davis, admitted Francis Hope to the partnership in 1903 and in the following year opened their first overseas office at Baku in South Russia.[15] It was principally designed to deal with the audit of the neighbouring oilfields and the St Petersburg Land Mortgage Company, but was forced to close precipitately in 1917 when the British community fled from the Bolshevik Revolution. The first South American office, set up by David Bell at Rio in 1908 under the style McAuliffe, Davis, Bell & Co, was designed to facilitate the audit of the Brazilian operating branches of the Barcelona Traction Light & Power Company, then a major client of the firm. Both the Barcelona and Brazilian companies were Canadian owned and based in Toronto, the former having a City office which McAuliffe, Davis & Hope audited. By 1914 the firm had extended its operations to the Far East, establishing offices in Penang (1909), Singapore (1912), and Kota Bahru (1915) to deal with accountancy work arising from the Duff Development Company and Soerabaya in Java (1918) largely for estate audits, while a further Latin American office had been opened in Mexico City. Other offices in the Dutch East Indies, Medan, Sumatra (1919) and Batavia, Java (1921), followed.

The Far Eastern connection arose from the audit of London-based agents such as Harrisons & Crosfield, which encouraged McAuliffe, Davis & Hope to expand overseas in an attempt to secure the audit of their clients, various rubber and tea companies. Much later, in 1935, a merger with Derrick & Co, a Singapore-based firm, greatly strengthened their position there. Founded by G. A. Derrick, an unqualified accountant who had set up in practice in 1889 after working in Singapore first as an operator for the Telegraphic Company and then as a clerk with the accountants A. G. Gunn & Co, the firm then spread throughout the Far East, acquiring a number of prestigious audits including the Straits Trading Company and from 1901 Fraser & Neave. In 1904 they were appointed secretaries of Singapore Cold Storage and by 1909 performed secretarial work for a number of rubber companies, including Alor Gajah, Ayer Panas, Pajam, Pantal and Balgowrie, while Derrick became chairman of Great Eastern Life and a director of McAlister & Co. By the Edwardian period the long acceptance of limited liability combined with continued economic growth meant that this kind of accountancy specialism was common. In London the practice of Russell Limebeer, for example, earned an audit specialism in rubber estate companies together with shipping and trading groups with extensive Middle East interests.[16]

At this early stage, work in the Far Eastern and South American offices was performed mainly by chartered accountants recruited in the U.K. and contracted for tours of four years. Being an accountant in those far distant parts of the world more accurately resembled the lifestyle of an explorer rather than a financial expert. As will be seen when Whinney Murray set up their Middle Eastern practice, the accountant's duties were less defined and often more wide ranging than at home. Accountants had on occasion to take responsibility for the actual running of their clients' affairs in the absence of British managers. A. D. Knox, a partner in McAuliffe's South American firm, recalled how, in the 1930s, the journey from Para up river to Porto Velho to audit the Madeira Mamore Railway took twenty-two days and a further twelve to return. Basic problems of travel, accommodation and health assumed giant proportions, always threatening to overcome accountancy work. In time, however, as conditions improved and local accountants became more expert and experienced, recruitment from the U.K. for South America dwindled and virtually ceased in the 1950s.

Baker, Sutton & Co's story began with John Baker (son of the Town Clerk of Islington), who had served his articles under Mr

Littlejohn, working with him (Ernest Littlejohn, elected an annual subscriber of Lloyds in 1892) 'for eight or nine years during which he had much experience in business with Lloyds'.[17] Setting up on his own in 1893, Baker was joined by T. G. Haward in the following year and, when Haward and another partner, Ernest Watson, left in 1903, *The Accountant* announced that Baker had 'taken into partnership Mr Percy John Sutton, A.C.A., many years with Messrs Chatteris, Nichols & Co and that the firm's business ... will be continued at Chiswell House, Finsbury Pavement, and 19 George Street, Croydon, under the style of Baker, Sutton & Co.'[18] In 1904 Baker, Sutton moved to Eldon Street House and closed their Croydon office in 1909. It is not known for what reason the latter was established, though it might have had some connection with the furniture trade for which the firm did much work (see p. 64) and encouraged the opening of their High Wycombe office in 1907, a town much concerned with furniture production and where John Baker lived.

Following his connection with Ernest Littlejohn, Baker built up a specialism in insurance work, auditing a number of individual brokers and Glanvill & Enthoven, together with the Excelsior Permanent Building Society[19] and from 1916 Cornhill Insurance and Lloyd's Brokers Association.[20] In September 1971 Baker, Sutton merged with Gérard Van de Linde & Son, a practice which had developed similar specialisms from the late nineteenth century, being *inter-alia* auditors to Coutts & Company, bankers, the Corporation of Lloyds and Lloyds Register of Shipping.

A number of Ernst & Whinney's provincial predecessor firms were established in the Edwardian period. The Birmingham practice, C. Herbert Smith & Russell (though having origins which may be traced through Powell, Jerome & Co to J. S. James & Son, Accountants and General Dealers, first mentioned in 1821), began as such in December 1908 in rooms at Phoenix Buildings, 82-84 Colmore Row.[21] A typical Birmingham practice with clients situated at various benches in the workshop of the world, their audit and accounting work included metal bedsteads, brass fittings and hollow-ware companies. One of their earliest clients, for example, Best & Lloyd, was a manufacturer of gas light fittings.

Other provincial practices founded in the Edwardian period included Buckley & Hall in Hull (1903), Woolley & Waldron in Southampton (1905) and Howell & Hanbidge in Sheffield (1914).

The first was established by E. W. Buckley and W. G. Hall – both incorporated accountants* who had started their careers with Hodgson, Harris & Co, a large practice based in Hull – in Victoria Chambers, Bowlalley Lane, but soon moved to the more spacious and newly erected premises of the Union of London & Smith's Bank at the corner of Silver Street and The Land of Green Ginger, which became a source of work sponsoring investigations and liquidations. Their largest client was T. J. Smith & Nephew, manufacturers of surgical dressings, the outcome of a close friendship between Buckley and H. N. Smith (T. J.'s nephew); a business destined to expand considerably in the course of the 1914–18 War.

Woolley & Waldron was founded in 1905 at Southampton by Frederick Woolley, another incorporated accountant, when he left Hamilton & Rowland, an established Southampton practice, to set up on his own. Ernest Waldron joined the firm as an office junior in 1907 and having qualified as an incorporated accountant was admitted to the partnership in 1925. Although their clientele mostly constituted small family businesses, they had also attracted a number of audit clients including Welsh & Co, brewers, later taken over by Coopers Brewery and then by Watneys, G. P. Wilson & Son, ironfounders, at Northam and F. A. Hendy & Co, bicycle assemblers and retailers, who, like William Morris, moved into the car business, becoming agents for Ford: Frederick Woolley's son, Eric, later became their secretary and later still a director. In 1912 Woolley was appointed secretary to the local committee administering the *Titanic* disaster fund. As a result of his professional standing in the town, he also secured the secretaryship of the Society of Motor Manufacturers and Traders, the Southern Counties Federation of Building Trades Employers, the Southampton Chamber of Commerce, the Southern Flour Millers Association and the Southern Association of Wholesale Fruit and Potato Merchants. As a consequence of this work, which developed into a minor specialism for some accountants, Woolley created a separate secretarial department.

The Sheffield practice established in 1914 by Douglas Howell and Charles Hanbidge, both newly qualified chartered accountants, was upset by the outbreak of war in August when Hanbidge

---

* That is a qualified member of the Incorporated Society of Accountants and Auditors.

left to join the forces. After being severely wounded, he retired from the partnership, the firm meantime developing as a small general practice with a cross-section of clients from the Sheffield trades. Although the other three provincial firms are quite distinct, they have one important feature in common: each reflected in microcosm the economic structure of its home town, whether Southampton as an entrepôt and market town, Birmingham as a centre for small- and medium-sized manufacturing businesses, or Hull as an agricultural and fish-processing port.

More generally the Edwardian period was the time when links with the United States were first established or consolidated. In 1912 S. B. Murray, Joint General Manager of the Midland Bank, suggested to Arthur Whinney, their auditor, that Whinney, Smith & Whinney might 'enter into an agency arrangement with MacPherson & Co of New York and Philadelphia' as the Midland themselves were extending their operations to America. However, the view prevailed 'that this would not be desirable but that they [Whinney, Smith & Whinney] should themselves establish an office in America'.[22] A list of City bankers and financiers, each with strong transatlantic connections, survives amongst Whinney, Smith & Whinney's records. Each in 1913 had been asked their views on the projected opening of a New York office. Stephen Baker, President of the Manhattan Bank's City branch, argued 'against opening more than two branches [in North America]' and thought that they would have 'a tough job getting going'.[23] He recommended that a partner be on the spot all the time but added that they 'might do better amalgamating' with an established American firm. Others were prepared to send letters of introduction, while Gilbert Thorne, Vice President of the National Park Bank, thought that 'the bulk of the business must come from London for some years as local prejudice must be overcome'. Nevertheless, in 1914 Whinney, Smith & Whinney opened an office at 64 Wall Street on their own account. However, little time remained to test the perception of these comments as the office closed in 1917 following America's entry into the war. Arthur Whinney discouraged his staff from taking American citizenship, a requirement if they were to remain in New York during the hostilities.

Although the New York office had been opened to service the Midland Bank, early signs indicated that a struggle lay ahead. Charles Palmour, the resident partner, wrote that 'everything here is at present absolutely stagnant. The most annoying thing to my mind is that most of the big things which the L.C. & M. [London, City & Midland] are likely to be interested in already have accountants and it will be difficult to break in....'[24] With the signing of peace in 1918, Whinney, Smith & Whinney asked Ernst & Ernst (a Cleveland-based accountancy firm, founded in 1903, with a New York office) to act on their behalf rather than re-open the New York office. It had been thought that Ernst & Ernst had first approached Whinney, Smith & Whinney in 1923 when Colonel Blyth and Sir Arthur Whinney discussed the possibility of the latter becoming their British and Continental correspondents – an arrangement which was confirmed by A. C. Ernst and C. J. G. Palmour in the following year.[25] However, both Sir Arthur Whinney, in a speech, and later E. F. G. Whinney refer to Whinney, Smith & Whinney approaching Ernst & Ernst in 1918 to act for them in New York following the closure of their American office. From this small beginning (and it is not known why Whinney, Smith & Whinney should have chosen this particular American practice) collaboration developed leading to various correspondent arrangements, cross-partnerships and finally, in 1979, to a more formal association, joint name and international partnership.

Price Waterhouse had been among the very first British accountancy firms to establish American connections, opening in 1890 an office in New York. A partner, George Sneath, had made several visits to the country to evaluate enterprises seeking funding in the City, being called in 1889 to supervise the investigation of a group of breweries prior to their amalgamation and subsequent flotation on the London market. This was a period when the American economy was growing very fast and the London partners of Price Waterhouse wisely concluded that they should set up a permanent base in New York to deal with this flood of work. Two years later they opened their next office in Chicago, America's second financial centre.[26] In fact the American side of Price Waterhouse proved so successful that in 1895 its resident partners, L. D. Jones and W. J. Caesar, negotiated a separation from the London partnership, retaining the name but acting for London on agency terms, though later ties were strengthened by the conclusion of a cross-partnership arrangement. Given Price Waterhouse's clear success, it remains an interesting, but unanswerable question, as to what might have happened to Whinney,

Smith & Whinney's American operation had there been no First
World War.

Elsewhere accountancy firms were equally enterprising. Russia's backward but slowly industrializing economy and strong
political and social links with Britain provided opportunities for
accountants in the latter part of the nineteenth century. Harding
had travelled to Russia via Constantinople on business in 1875,
though its precise nature remains a mystery. Ernest Cooper recalled how 'business journies have taken my firm to all five
continents . . . my brother, William, in the early 1860s, paid a long
visit on business to Russia', principally to Moscow and St Petersburg. The work mostly involved acting for English companies
with widespread overseas interests.[27] Deloittes opened an office in
St Petersburg in 1913, Price Waterhouse following suit in 1916.[28]
The latter, like Barton, Mayhew which had established an office
at Montreal in 1914, also opened a Canadian office in 1907, in
the same year forming an Egyptian partnership, and set up an
Argentinian base in 1912. Of course the First World War cut short
many of these overseas operations, but they form good evidence that English accountancy firms had already developed
international horizons. In this, as always, they were following a
parallel path to the evolution of the businesses which they served.

The Edwardian era witnessed the beginnings of an important
new area of accountancy work – taxation. Although this formed
the first period in which taxation exercised an important influence
on accountancy, it was not the first time that direct taxes had
troubled clients. Pitt the Younger had originally been responsible
for devising a system of income tax in 1799, but on proving
unsuccessful, it was revised by Addington in 1803, who established the schedules which have survived to the present. At this
stage, income tax had been viewed merely as a temporary expe-
dient, a means of raising extra revenue during the French Revolu-
tionary and Napoleonic Wars. Not until the 1840s did income tax
become a regular source of peacetime revenue. In his 1842 and
1845 budgets, Sir Robert Peel switched from customs and excise
duties to income tax as the principal means of collecting the state's
revenue, thereby creating the reality of a free trade system. However, as the government's requirements were not then great, the
rate could be set at seven old pence in the pound (2.9%). This fact,
together with the simple collection and assessment procedures,
meant that accountants did not find themselves being asked to

deal with complex tax problems. The early Day Books of Whinney, Smith & Whinney make no mention of revenue matters until the Edwardian period.

By 1900 it was becoming accepted that the government had a duty to intervene in society, not only to encourage the efficient operation of the economy, but also to correct the more obvious social injustices which existed. The introduction of such benefits as old age pensions, unemployment payments, compensation for injuries sustained at work and better hospitals all cost money. As well as promoting these measures, Asquith's Liberal government of 1902–14 also argued that the great disparities in incomes ought to be reduced. For the first time the government acted not simply to raise money for public expenditure (which itself always had social consequences), but with the deliberate intention of redistributing wealth. They chose income tax and estate duties as their method. Estate or death duties, first introduced in 1894, increased in severity following Lloyd George's 1909 budget. In the meantime, the cost of the Boer War had brought a further rise in the basic rate of income tax to 1s 3d (6.25p) in the pound, though in 1902 it was reduced to 11d (4.6p) on the cessation of hostilities.[29] The 1909 budget also introduced supertax, fixed at a low rate, and estimated to bring in (from incomes of £3,000 and above) a total of half a million pounds.[30] Hence, the whole question of personal taxation for the rich was becoming more important and increasingly complex. An accountant's professional advice could make all the difference to a client's liability to taxation through a carefully considered strategy to minimize payments.

The Finance Act of 1903 had reiterated the right of a solicitor, barrister or accountant to plead the defendant's cause in a case concerning tax,[31] accountants being defined as members of 'an incorporated society'. Ernest Whinney recalled how tax problems had first been brought to Whinney, Smith & Whinney before the First World War, though they did not become significant until the 1920s. The firm's Audit Book for 1910 lists a number of substantial landowners who would have been liable for supertax during their lives and for death duties afterwards, while a 'Nichols, E. M.', is specifically noted as being a supertax client.[32]

Although the imposition of death duties in 1894 resulted in the first reference in Whinney, Smith & Whinney's Day Books to taxation matters ('W. E. Johnson, allowed by Taxing Master'),[33] this did not produce any appreciable increase in tax work for accountants. Fees directly attributable to taxation advice were negligible even as late as 1910. It is possible that the growth in trustee and executorship work (from £606 in 1890 to £953 in 1910) reflected a greater concern with inheritance, though here, too, there are no dramatic developments. Even Lloyd George's 1909 budget appears not to have stimulated tax work greatly. Indeed, even in 1915 when the introduction of Excess Profits Duty encouraged businessmen to entrust their tax forms to an accountant's care, tax fees only generated 1.4% of fees. In 1925 when contemporary reports are full of the crushing burdens of taxation and when accountants themselves have spoken of their involvement in tax matters, fees from this work merely produced 4.9% of Whinney, Smith & Whinney's income, some £3,719. Steadying at around 6% throughout the 1930s and war years, taxation really only began to make a substantial contribution to the firm's total fee income after 1945 (Table II).[34]

Because the state intervened more actively in the economy and took a greater role in society throughout the Edwardian period, governments found it necessary to control and order their growing finances more efficiently. The progressive extension of public services in the nineteenth century necessitated the adoption of a comprehensive system of book-keeping to allow governments to audit their rising expenditure. Suprisingly it was not until 1830 with the 'reception of the French budget-system', a national system of double-entry replacing the older method of unconnected accounts, that the Exchequer could obtain an overall picture of spending. The introduction was followed in 1834 by the creation of a post, the Comptroller and Auditor General, designed to survey past expenditure at the annual audit.[35] The Poor Law Amendment Act of 1834 had resulted in the employment of district auditors to regulate the flow of monies destined for poor relief.[36] Although the 1879 District Auditors' Act revised procedures, not until 1890 did local authorities receive permission to engage professional accountants rather than the district auditors.[37] In that year the Accrington Municipal Corporation secured Parliamentary consent to call in a chartered accountant. They argued that the professional qualification of an independent accountant could provide the council with superior skill and experience because the district auditors, like the early shareholder auditors, were simply interested councillors of no particular expertise. Such pressures had prompted the formation of the Institute of Munici-

pal Treasurers and Accountants in 1885 and encouraged individual authorities to incorporate in their private bills powers to
appoint professional auditors, the first being the West Brom-
wich Act (1889), which was limited to chartered and incorporated
accountants.

As well as being involved in local government, eminent accountants increasingly attended Parliamentary committees and inquiries. J. G. Griffiths of Deloitte, Plender & Griffiths investigated
the Egyptian debt problem in 1882, Edwin Waterhouse was appointed to the 1900 Companies Act committee, William Plender
acted for the Metropolitan Water Board in 1903, while Frederick
Whinney reported on the Ordnance Department's accounts.[38] At
a dinner given by the Council of the English Institute in 1894,
Lord Randolph Churchill noted that it had taken only four
months to complete the last investigation and that all the recommendations in the 'lucid and valuable report' had been adopted.

The Edwardian period also corresponded with a major development in cost accounting; it was, however, a technical advance whose application firms of chartered accountants largely
ignored until the Second World War. The following is partly an
explanation of the introduction of cost accounting methods but
also a suggestion as to why it failed to be adopted on a significant
scale by British business in contrast to the United States, and why
accountancy practices were so little involved in its evolution.

In the early stages of the Industrial Revolution manufacturing
units remained relatively small and their production processes,
though often perplexing in accounting terms for entrepreneurs,
did not demand detailed financial analysis for their practical success. Although managers produced haphazard or misleading
accounts, they could happily rely on their instincts and experience
to make decisions because they were intimately involved in the
running of the business. Even as late as the 1860s, the managers of
the Dowlais Iron Company, a profitable concern, made important decisions with little or no accounting data, while such costings as they did perform were rudimentary and did not form the
basis for fixing prices.[39] The continued refinement and extension
of machinery, with the need to compete with a growing number
of neighbours, encouraged in the 1830s the construction of large
factories employing hundreds of workers each performing separate functions within a complex chain of production. A few contemporaries realized that *ad hoc* accounting methods could no

longer cope with the situation. For example, Charles Babbage, Professor of Mathematics at Cambridge, wrote in 1835 that[40]

the great competition introduced by machinery and the application of the principle of the sub-division of labour render it necessary for each producer to be continually on the watch to discover improved methods by which the cost of the article he manufactures may be reduced; and, with this view, it is of great importance to know the precise expense of every process, as well as the wear and tear of machinery which is due to it.

Nevertheless, Babbage's statement remained a forlorn cry in an unresponsive atmosphere, while such advances as were made in the 1840s and 1850s came from France.[41] Entrepreneurs and accountants alike neglected the problem in mid-Victorian Britain. It is to America in the 1870s that we have to turn to see his points being taken up in an attempt to devise practical solutions.

In the late 1860s Albert Fink, not an accountant but a civil engineer and bridge builder, superintendent and later senior Vice President of the Louisville & Nashville Railway, decided to determine much more accurately the basic measure of unit costs on his railway, the ton mile.[42] This entailed reorganizing the existing accounts according to the nature of their costs rather than according to the departments in which the functions were carried out. Wishing to discover the railway's economic characteristics in greater detail, he analysed the network by its separate lines to find the reasons for the differences in costs. Such investigation revealed, for example, that lines frequently used by goods trains required much maintenance and that if these lay through mountainous terrain then costs rose further as the locomotive's appetite for coal grew, which in turn had important repercussions for freight rates per ton mile. These had never before been properly quantified. Such information, and a constant review of current financial and operating costs, permitted him to evaluate the performance of different railway divisions and their operating executives, in much the same way that one might examine the various processes of manufacture or compare the output of two similar factories. Finally, offering a certain justice for the consumer, Fink used these data to set his railway's charges, basing them more fairly on detailed costings rather than a vague perception of the company's needs.

These methods, perfected in the 1860s and 1870s, were swiftly adopted by America's first large industrial enterprises and remained the basic cost accounting techniques until well into the twentieth century. Textile manufacturers had been among the first to modify these procedures in an attempt to analyse their unit costs.[43] Then, as with the railroads, these cost data became a managerial tool. Information was used to rationalize internal operations, check the productivity of workers, control the receipt and use of cotton and check the efficiency of modifications in machinery or plant design. When Andrew Carnegie set out to reorganize the Edgar Thomson Steel Works in Pittsburg, he recruited William Shinn from the Pennsylvania Railroad as his chief executive to implement costing systems that then guided Carnegie's management decisions.[44]

The next critical phase in the development of modern industrial accounting was pioneered at the E. I. Du Pont de Nemours Powder Company by Pierre du Pont, a graduate not in accounting but management studies from the Massachusetts Institute of Technology.[45] He and his team succeeded in ending 'the long separation between cost, capital and financial accounting'.[46] After carefully defining costs, du Pont and his managers devised a more precise definition of profit with more specific criteria for evaluating financial performance. By effectively combining and consolidating the three basic types of accounting, they laid the basis for 'modern asset accounting', and had done this by about 1910. Through their concept of turnover, the Du Pont managers were able to account specifically, and for the first time, for that part of the contribution made by modern management to profitability and productivity. Many sceptics thought that large companies such as Du Pont would topple from the weight of internal inefficiency or would pass on the costs of their overladen bureaucracies to the consumer and finally go bankrupt from lack of competitiveness. In fact, their system lowered the cost of integrating each department's activities, provided routine data for daily operating decisions and long-term information about the return on investments.[47] Subsequently these techniques of industrial management developed by the largest American businesses – principally by Du Pont, General Electric and General Motors – spread rapidly throughout the manufacturing giants of the United States.

By contrast Britain failed to produce any significant advances in costing techniques, nor, more seriously, did British managers or accountants seek to implement these American discoveries. This lack of imagination and enterprise must be seen in conjunction with the nation's relatively poor economic performance in

the late nineteenth and early twentieth centuries when her traditional supremacy in manufacturing and commerce was seriously
challenged by both the United States and Germany. One of the
major debates in English economic history surrounds the 'climac-
teric' of the 1870s and subsequent so-called Great Depression
(as the 1875–95 period was dubbed before the 1930s).[48] A wide
variety of explanations have been put forward to explain the
country's failing performance, ranging from a lack of investment
due to the calls of Empire, cyclical fluctuations in trade, to the
natural maturing of the oldest industrial nation. The failure to
follow the American lead in management accounting and organization was certainly a major omission and could perhaps have
been of critical importance.

   The first book on accounting for management, and a fairly
basic one at that, to be published in England was Garcke and
Fells's *Factory Accounts*, first edition 1887.[49] Although the authors
discussed important questions of capital and financial accounting
(depreciation, reserve funds, taxation, stock valuation and the
various methods of keeping ledgers and journals), there is in fact
only the briefest reference to cost accounting. Garcke was an
electrical engineer while Fells was an incorporated accountant
employed in industry as assistant secretary of the Brush Electric
Light Corporation, where Garcke had once been employed
too.[50] Their study, based on personal practical experience and the
needs of British industry, received a rather curious assessment in
The Accountant where a reviewer described it as 'more of a theoretical than a practical work' and 'in the nature of a work on
political economy than an ordinary everyday business treatise'.[51]
Similarly Slater Lewis's *The Commercial Organization of Factories*
(1896) is as much an argument to convince managers of the value
of accounting as a demonstration of its method, but it was also
confined to a discussion of financial and capital accounting, leaving cost accounting untouched.[52] Such practical costing exercises
as took place were of a limited nature. The Birmingham iron
bedstead trade in the 1890s offers the first example of the application of fairly simple cost accounting. By forming the New Trades
Combination Movement, E. J. Smith succeeded in spreading cost
techniques that he had pioneered in his own business, throughout
the industry.[53] Yet he did not attempt to raise the efficiency of
manufacture, being concerned to fix a fair selling price to guarantee
reasonable profits for the owners without cheating the consumer.

Why then were British managers and accountants so unresponsive to methods which had earned such dividends in America? Accounting methods are in the main a dependent variable, responsive to need, despite the growing professionalization of this function in the late nineteenth century.[54] The failure to adopt and develop cost accountancy, therefore, largely resulted from business's lack of demand rather than an essential lack of expertise among accountants. As L. R. Dicksee, Professor of Accounting at the L.S.E., bemoaned in 1915, 'in general, a knowledge of accounts is not considered any part of the necessary education of a business officer, who accordingly is often quite ignorant of the uses that accountants have for him. On the contrary, he is usually obsessed with the fixed idea that accounts are a necessary evil, that money spent on them is a sheer waste.'[55] Dicksee was here referring to capital and financial accounting; cost accounting appeared not even to be on the brink of recognition for managers – an example, therefore, of the profession responding passively to the needs of the business community rather than taking the initiative.

The timing of Garcke and Fells's book is significant. Until the last quarter of the nineteenth century British manufacturers' superiority meant that they had little need to pay attention to costing methods. The emergent industrial nations, like America and Germany, which had to be on their mettle to break into established markets, were the ones concerned to make their growing businesses as efficient and modern as possible. By the 1880s, when the force of their competition made itself felt, British business began to look, rather half-heartedly, at cost accounting – the period when the first English publications appeared.[56] This also explains why its earliest exponents were not accountants in private practice but engineers or accountants in industry, men closest to the problems and particularly anxious to improve their organization and output.

The case is further supported by the example of the North Eastern Railway in the latter part of the nineteenth century. Until about 1900 its managers had relied on competition from the roads and coastal shipping to govern the level of their freight rates, with marginal and essentially intuitive adjustments for specific commodities and distances.[57] When farmers complained in the 1880s that imported foodstuffs were carried more cheaply than home produce, the N.E.R. replied that the former, being collected in bulk from the ports, were simpler to handle. However, the dispute raged as the railway possessed no statistics to confirm their argument. Indeed, it was not until the turn of the century that they even thought it necessary to devise a costing framework for freight charges. The company then pioneered the systematic use of ton-mile statistics in Britain and by 1914 was able to use them to shed the first clear light on the whole question of undue preference which had plagued relations between farmers, port authorities and railways. Average train loads for specific lines were calculated and the figures used to determine rates. This led to a greater flexibility in charges with the creation of special rates in place of a strict price charge varying directly with distance.[58]

Thus, although Britain lagged behind America in the adoption and diffusion of management accounting techniques, evidence exists to show that some companies were receptive to new approaches and ready to innovate. Pilkington Brothers, the glass makers at St Helens, while a modest family business, had engaged the London chartered accountants, Wenham, Angus & Co, in 1872 to put 'the accounts upon the best commercial footing' and thereby started a tradition of financial adventurousness.[59] In 1913, aware of the need for greater efficiencies, the company devised a system of costing, setting up a separate department and purchasing only the second Hollerith machine to be manufactured.[60]

More generally it is informative to look at accountants in industry and the regard with which directors held their auditors and financial advisers. As the Dicksee quotation implies, accountants had still to persuade Edwardian businessmen of their value in the running of companies. Internal accounts departments were a rule 'indifferently staffed' and their heads ranked in comparison with other sections 'somewhere on a level with a colour sergeant, or possibly a sergeant major, the nearest approach to an "officer" being the professional auditor – who, of course, is not one of the regular staff at all'.[61] Yet even this situation represented an improvement on the nineteenth century when insolvencies and book-keeping formed the basis of their reputations. 'Many accountant's clerks are successful', wrote Witty in 1906, 'in obtaining appointments as accountants and secretaries to companies and other commercial concerns.... Indeed there has during the past few years grown up a big demand for qualified accountants to fill every kind of important position in the mercantile world.'[62] An early example of this type of recruitment was Samuel Swarbrick's appointment as General Manager of the Great Eastern Railway in

1868, having previously served first as the Lancashire & Yorkshire and then Midland Railway's accountant.[63] However, promotions such as these were rare when made to positions of importance and had a significance for the future rather than during the Edwardian period.

Naturally the auditor's relationship with the board of directors reflected these general attitudes. The apocryphal story which relates of an auditor being told to keep his opinions to himself by the chairman at a large textile company's board meeting as 'Thow's nowt but scorer' represented a commonly held view amongst management. Edwin Waterhouse recalled how he, as auditor of the L.N.W.R., had to battle to maintain the *status quo* when in 1905 a proposal had been made 'with regard to a matter of account affecting the locomotive department, which seemed to me to mix up capital and revenue in a matter likely to lead to error'.[64] His arguments produced laughter from some directors while others discounted his advice; it was probably only because of his strength of character and the fact that he had been their auditor for about thirty years that he succeeded in preventing the proposal from being accepted. Such an outcome was by no means typical. For example, in 1903 Edward Holden, Managing Director of the Midland Bank, recorded in his diary that he had seen 'Mr Whinney Senior who came in to discuss with me the question of depreciation of investments. He said he thought the proper course would be for the bank to take a sum off their reserve fund, corresponding to the depreciation, but I [Holden] pointed out that there was no necessity for us to do that.'[65]

Auditors, as the shareholders' representatives, were often regarded with suspicion and felt to be a nuisance when safeguarding their interests, but because the management, in effect, controlled their appointment and supplied the figures, it meant that the auditor was not placed in a position of strength to argue a case. His was an ambiguous and ill-defined situation. A conscientious accountant, while performing the role of auditor, might, if the directors of his client companies so conspired, find himself with a dwindling practice. However, as will be seen, in the inter-war period, as the attention paid by the legislature to auditing increased and as accountants earned a sound reputation as financial advisers, their opinions were more widely acknowledged.

Despite the failure to come to grips with cost accounting, any assessment of the state of the accountancy profession on the outbreak of war in 1914 must begin with the satisfying conclusion that their business future seemed very secure. Accountants had captured a broad range of work in key areas of the economy. Although they may have resented it, managers found it increasingly difficult to organize their businesses' vast and increasing resources without the accountant's particular expertise. The steady growth in demand for these services meant that some accountants specialized either in particular types of audit work or in liquidations, trustee and secretarial work, investigations and the formation of public companies.[66] As the scale of business expanded, in a context of more complex financial organization, greater public awareness and higher taxation, it could be predicted that accountants would continue to prosper.

In addition, the formal recognition of the profession, by the 1880 Royal Charter, had gone a long way to raising accountants in the public esteem, thereby endorsing their functional utility. Galsworthy, an astute observer of middle-class life, made Aunt Hester suggest that Nicholas Forsyte's son should become an accountant rather than be sent to serve as an officer in the Royal Navy. An admiral, she argued, was paid a 'pittance', while 'an accountant had many more chances, but let him be put with a good firm where there was no risk at starting'.[67] This recognition was reflected in the numbers joining the profession. The censuses for England and Wales reveal 4,974 accountants for 1841 and 11,517 in 1881. The apparent fall in numbers to 7,930 in 1891 is explained by stricter rules of definition following the formation of recognized accountancy bodies. Within these new terms of reference growth continued from 7,930 in 1891 to 9,499 in 1911, as reflected in the membership of the English Institute of Chartered Accountants, which grew from 1,766 in 1891 to 3,177 by 1904.[68]

The rise in the level of expertise and professional status of accountancy induced, at long last, a reluctant recognition by the universities. In 1901 Birmingham University established a faculty of Commerce with a lecturer in accountancy;[69] similar posts followed at London, Manchester and Liverpool Universities in the Edwardian period. Unlike the legal and medical professions, accountancy was not welcomed in the ancient seats of learning and it had been something of a struggle to secure academic recognition in England and Wales, Scotland – as so often in the university world – being slightly different. Indeed, Oxford, Cambridge and some of the older English universities still do not offer courses in accountancy. In America, by contrast, over 100 universities offered options in accountancy to over 3,500 students annually as early as 1914.[70]

References

1 Donald Read, *Edwardian England*, London (1972), p. 3, *passim*.
2 Peter Mathias, *Retailing Revolution, A History of Multiple Retailing in the Food Trades based upon the Allied Suppliers Group of Companies*, London (1967), p. 156.
3 *Ibid*, p. 151.
4 Edwin Waterhouse's Diary, 1890, p. 400.
5 Richard A. Witty, *How to Become a Qualified Accountant*, London (1906), p. 92.
6 Leonard W. Hein, *The British Companies Acts and the Practice of Accountancy 1844-1962*, New York (1978), p. 347.
7 Marriner, *op. cit.*, p. 245.
8 Waterhouse, *op. cit.*, 1890, p. 398.
9 Edwin Green, *op. cit.*, p. 7.
10 Midland Bank Archives, Reports of the respective banking companies.
11 Quoted from Green, *op. cit.*, pp. 13-14.
12 *Ibid*, p. 17.
13 *Ibid*, p. 18.
14 *Post Office Directories*, London (1852), p. 1035, (1860), p. 901, and (1880), p. 1299.
15 *Institute of Chartered Accountants in England and Wales Yearbooks*.
16 *Russell Limebeer, A London Firm of Chartered Accountants*, London (1978), p. 18.
17 Charles Welch, *London at the Opening of the 20th Century*, London (1905), W. T. Pike's Contemporary Biographies, Accountants, pp. 606, 635.
18 *The Accountant*, No. 1466, 10 January 1903, p. 64.
19 Baker, Sutton & Co Fee Book No. I, pp. 1-7.
20 *Ibid*, p. 86.
21 Although much of Ernst & Whinney's Birmingham practice owes itself to the merger with C. Herbert Smith & Russell in 1962, Whinney, Smith & Whinney had already opened an office in the city when, in 1956, they amalgamated with a local firm Harold E. Clarke & Co, which had a pedigree dating back to F. Charlton & Co, established in 1854.
22 M.B.A., S. B. Murray's Diary 1911-1916, 18 November 1912, p. 289.
23 Typewritten list, entitled New York, dated 1913.
24 Typewritten notes, undated and unsigned.

25 *Ernst & Ernst 1903-1960, A History of the Firm*, Cleveland (1960), p. 74.
26 G. E. Richards, Price Waterhouse, History of the Firm, the first fifty years 1850-1900 (typescript, 1950), pp. 8-9.
27 Ernest Cooper, *op. cit.*, p. 52.
28 *Deloittes, op. cit.*, p. 91. They also opened an office at Cincinnati in 1905.
29 Garratt, *op. cit.*, p. 47.
30 Sir Robert Ensor, *England 1870-1914*, Oxford (1936), p. 414.
31 Stacey, *op. cit.*, p. 70.
32 Whinney, Smith & Whinney Audit Book 1910.
33 Day Book 1894-1902, 1895, p. 50.
34 Table II.
35 Ernest Barker, *The Development of Public Services in Western Europe 1660-1930*, Oxford (1944), p. 63.
36 Stacey, *op. cit.*, p. 44.
37 *Ibid*, p. 46.
38 *History of the English Institute, op. cit.*, p. 45.
39 Edwards and Baker, *op. cit.*, pp. 147-8.
40 Charles Babbage, *On the Economy of Machinery and Manufactures*, London (1835), p. 203.
41 David Solomons, *Studies in Costing*, London (1952), p. 8.
42 Alfred D. Chandler, *The Visible Hand, The Managerial Revolution in American Business*, Harvard (1977), pp. 116-17.
43 *Ibid*, p. 247.
44 *Ibid*, p. 267.
45 Yamey, *Historical Development of Accounting, op. cit.*, H. Thomas Johnson, 'Management Accounting in an Early Integrated Industrial: E.I. Du Pont de Nemours Powder Company 1903-1912', p. 184.
46 Chandler, *op. cit.*, pp. 445-7.
47 Thomas Johnson, *op. cit.*, pp. 203-4.
48 Mathias, *First Industrial Nation, op. cit.*, p. 395.
49 Emile Garcke and J. M. Fells, *Factory Accounts, Their Principles and Practice, A Handbook for Accountants and Manufacturers*, London (1887).
50 Kitchen and Parker, *Six English Pioneers, op. cit.*, pp. 62-3.
51 *The Accountant*, No. 700, 5 May 1888, p. 278.
52 J. Slater Lewis, *The Commercial Organization of Factories, A Handbook for the Use of Manufacturers, Directors, Auditors, Engineers, Managers, Secretaries, Accountants . . .*, London (1896), pp. xxv, xxix, 12-30, 206-7, 388, 390, 396.
53 Solomons, *op. cit.*, p. 51.
54 Harold F. Williamson (Editor), *Evolution of Internal Management Structures*, Delaware (1975), Peter Mathias, 'Conflicts of Function in the Rise of Big Business: The British Experience', p. 45.

55 Lawrence R. Dicksee, *Business Methods and the War*, Cambridge (1915), p. 19.

56 Kitchen and Parker, *op. cit.*, p. 38, and R. H. Parker, *Management Accounting: An Historical Perspective*, London (1969), pp. 19-20.

57 R. J. Irving. *The North Eastern Railway Company 1870-1914, An Economic History*, Leicester (1976), pp. 123-5.

58 *Ibid*, p. 126.

59 T. C. Barker, *Pilkington Brothers and the Glass Industry*, London (1960), p. 170.

60 T. C. Barker, *The Glassmakers, Pilkington*, London (1977), pp. 234-5.

61 Dicksee, *Business Methods, op. cit.*, pp. 19, 49.

62 Witty, *op. cit.*, p. 80.

63 Robert Thorne, *Liverpool Street Station*, London (1978), pp. 24-5.

64 Waterhouse, *op. cit.*, 1905, pp. 778-9.

65 M.B.A., Edward Holden's Diary, Vol. V (1903-1905), p. 9.

66 Stacey, *op. cit.*, p. 55, and Brown, *op. cit.*, p. 314.

67 Galsworthy, *Man of Property, op. cit.*, p. 243.

68 Brown, *op. cit.*, p. 237. See also Appendix II (B).

69 Stacey, *op. cit.*, p. 64.

70 *Ibid*, p. 66.

CHAPTER 5

The First World War

On 4 August 1914 Britain declared war on Germany and embarked on the four bloodiest years of its history. This conflict, which eventually was to draw the whole nation into its orbit, gave a new and often terrible significance to the expression 'total war'. Accountants were involved in two very different ways, either as soldiers – not simply as paymasters but as troops in battle – or as professional advisers concerned with the smooth running of the economy. The distinction not only concerns the historian but at the same time caused individuals much heartsearching. Young accountants, swept up by the call to duty and honour, sought to serve their country in the fighting forces and volunteered in their thousands.[1] However, it soon became clear that their professional financial skills were desperately needed at home to order and control the production of war material and later the distribution of food itself. Harold Barton's experience illustrates the accountant's divided loyalties in wartime. Having enlisted in the Artists' Rifles, Barton attended officer training but on advice decided to serve as an accountant, travelling to India and Mesopotamia to standardize the Red Cross's system of accounts there.[2] But after being stabbed on board a troopship by a sepoy who had run amuck, Barton returned home and was again considering military service when he received a letter from the Colonel of the East Riding Territorial Force based at Hull, who argued that, 'I know what your desire is, but I really do think that you are doing as good work for your country in the position in which you are now placed....'[3] As a result he compromised and transferred to the Ministry of Munitions to deal with the costing of aircraft production.[4] He was then promoted to Assistant Controller of Aircraft Accounts. Hence, following the dual wartime experience of so many accountants, this chapter is divided into two parts: the first devoted to those accountants who served in the trenches and on ships as soldiers and sailors, and the second to the remainder who stayed in Britain to work for the government in a professional capacity or continued in private practice.

By 1914 accountants had, in fact, already built up a tradition of military service. The Edinburgh Society had been closely involved in the Volunteer Rifle movement of 1859 following the shock of the Indian Mutiny.[5] Number 6 (Accountants') Company of the Queen's Rifle Volunteer Brigade, the Royal Scots, was composed of Edinburgh members, funds to arm and equip the unit being supplied by subscriptions from chartered accountants. By 1860 membership of the company had risen to seventy, expanding to 140 by 1900.[6] The 17th Company of the 1st Lanarkshire Regiment of the Rifle Volunteers was similarly established by the Glasgow Institute, also founded in 1859.[7] Accountants joined special units during the Boer War when volunteer regiments were allowed to go on active service and many members fought in South Africa.[8]

In England accountants often became keen members of the militia. Robert Mayo,* President of the Birmingham Institute of Chartered Accountants in 1882, had, for example, been an ardent volunteer, serving as Quartermaster of the 1st South Staffordshire Volunteers, a regiment he had joined on its formation.[9] Frederick Whinney rose to the rank of Major in the 3rd Volunteer Battalion of the Middlesex Regiment and was awarded the Volunteer Decoration for long service. His son, Harold, recalled an evocative episode when the family travelled to a special parade in an open landau presenting 'a colourful picture of a very large, rather fierce looking officer in full dress, packed in tight by numerous children. It made a stir along the whole route of cheers, catcalls, whistles ever to be remembered.' Arthur Whinney followed in his father's footsteps, though he joined the 20th Middlesex (Artists') Rifles. In fact Whinney, Smith & Whinney had secured the audit of the London Rifle Brigade in 1860 when they had been called in to investigate 'the defalcations of the late secretary' and perform the basic accounting.[10] The picture was similar overseas. G. A. Derrick, who had enrolled in the Singapore Volunteer Artillery in 1888, rose to the rank of Colonel, was awarded the Volunteer Decoration and on the outbreak of war became full-time Commandant of the Singapore Voluntary forces, retiring from the partnership of Derrick & Co shortly afterwards. Another partner,

---

* The firm of Mayo, Powell & Co, which later became Powell, Jerome & Co, was taken over by C. Herbert Smith & Russell in 1927.

D. J. Ward, took leave of absence to serve in the army in Europe, where he rose to command a battalion of the Gloucester Regiment, having won an M.C. The strong connection between professional men and volunteer regiments is similarly mirrored in the 1930s when many young accountants joined Territorial units (see p. 186).

Once it had become clear that the First World War was not going to be a short sharp conflict, over by Christmas, but a European-wide stalemate, Kitchener set about enlisting men in their millions, using established loyalties as the basis for his recruitment campaign. Men from the countryside and provincial towns were recruited on a county basis. The Gloucester Regiment, for example, eventually raised twenty-four battalions from the farmers, labourers and townsfolk of the shire. As men died so new units were formed, trained and sent into the fray with the survivors of earlier engagements. In towns the same principle applied; men were encouraged to join the army by appeals to their established work loyalties. Commercial battalions were set up in Liverpool and Manchester to recruit clerks from shipping lines, insurance offices and the cotton exchanges, accountancy firms, banks and merchant houses, who enlisted in their thousands.[11] The King's Regiment in Liverpool raised twenty-two battalions in the First World War, of which four (17th–20th) were 'Pals', composed of groups of workers or friends who wished to serve together rather than be split up by recruitment or training schemes. In addition, Reserve, Works, Docks, Garrison and Home Service battalions were formed. The phrase 'Old Pals', therefore, had a very real meaning. The men who came forward in these waves chose their own titles for their units (which included the North East Railway, 1st Public Works, and Arts and Crafts), in some instances even being organized around their own offices. In almost every case they joined their work comrades – a spontaneous and genuinely popular mass movement. The London Regiment included a G.P.O. battalion drawn from the capital's postal workers. In the City, Foster & Braithwaite, members of the Stock Exchange, urged their younger staff to fight, declaring that 'the firm expects all the unmarried staff under 35 years of age will join Earl Kitchener's army at once ... the firm will endeavour to do their best for their dependents and will recognise their prior claim to reinstatement'.[12] Young accountants and their clerks volunteered by the score, inspired by patriotism – so many to be slaughtered in the mud of France.

To sustain the spirit of battle and sacrifice, many businesses began publishing special magazines for members of their staff serving in the forces – such was the strength of corporate patriotism. Price Waterhouse, for example, produced a *Staff War Bulletin* from February 1915, while Turquand, Youngs started the *Forty-Ones' Bulletin* in 1914 (the firm's offices were then situated at 41 Coleman Street), which was sent to staff at the front. News from home mixed with stories from soldiers, while those killed or decorated in action were suitably commemorated. By May 1915 twenty-one members of Turquand, Youngs were serving in the forces, nine as officers and twelve as N.C.O.s, and a further seven were in the National Guard under Adam Turquand-Young, their platoon commander.[13] The peace number of the magazine in February 1919 recorded that of the thirty-six who had served in the armed forces, four had been awarded the Military Cross for bravery and one made a Chevalier de la Légion d'Honneur. Seven had been killed in action. Curiously only one of the Turquand, Youngs' staff was a paymaster, but as a naval paymaster on board a cruiser, he too had been exposed to the dangers of war.[14] Sixteen members of Barton, Mayhew had seen active service, of whom five had enlisted under Lord Derby's system in late 1915, by which men of military age 'attested' their willingness to serve in an attempt to avoid conscription.

It was a similar story elsewhere. Fifty-nine members of Cooper Brothers served and nine were killed, including Harold Cooper, a partner who died on the Somme in 1916,[15] while 148 members of Price Waterhouse past and present saw action. Arthur Whinney's son Jack was killed and another son Ernest Whinney, who had spent a brief period in the Royal Army Service Corps, survived the war to become a partner in 1928. Like the Pay Corps, the R.A.S.C., which performed an important logistics function, recruited large numbers of accountants to regulate and administer the broad range of supplies needed by troops in many theatres of war. Charles Palmour, later to become senior partner of Whinney, Smith & Whinney, became a Major in the R.A.S.C. If a practice consisted of just two partners, it was often agreed that one would volunteer and the other remain to run the firm. Hence, Harold Barton enlisted while Basil Mayhew stayed in London, Charles Hanbidge of Howell & Hanbidge and R. E.

Ware of Ware, Ward joined the army, the last being seconded to government duties after a period of military service.[16] In Scotland 171 members and 228 apprentices of the Edinburgh Society, 212 members and 734 apprentices of the Glasgow Institute and eight members and 27 apprentices of the Aberdeen Society saw service in the forces.[17] While conscription never applied in Ireland, many accountants and their clerks volunteered, 128 being on active service by 1918.[18]

The acute demand for fresh troops in 1916 resulted in the introduction of conscription, but accountants, because they were often required professionally to perform tasks for government, became a certified occupation excused from military service at 31 if married and 41 if single. *The Accountant* in May 1916 recorded with approval that[19]

skilled technical labour has been recognized as of more value to the State employed on technical work than when used in the firing line, and we are pleased to note from recent indications that the professional knowledge and training of qualified accountants is, to some extent, beginning to receive similar recognition. Members of the profession with experience of costing are, we understand ... in request for certain branches of war work, although ... only ineligible men, or married men over 30 years of age with families can receive consideration.

Writing to the firm's New York office in March 1917, Arthur Whinney reported 'my two remaining partners and I have been considering the general position having regard to the National Call. Tullock will probably go ... for military service in July, but Campling and I are over age. Work we have been doing for the government will I think slack off now, so we are freer to undertake other duties. It seems to me that we might be of considerable assistance to ... the new costing department, which I expect will develop considerably....' In October 1917 *The Forty-Ones' Bulletin* noted that, '... nine members of our staff have, on the application of the firm, been exempted from service in the army till January next year. They are, every one of them, engaged from time to time upon government work, directly occasioned by the war and their services are on that account rightly regarded as indispensable....'[20] It might be added, however, that public criticism of the inclusion of accountants within the certified category was such that they were omitted from the second list (a measure of popular ignorance of their value) but were reinstated due to government demand in the third list of 1917.

Although the sacrifices made by accountants as soldiers were in many cases invaluable, it probably remains true that the profession's contribution to the war effort was most effective in the field of costing and administration. The onset of war had produced a crop of emergency legislation, including the first Alien's Registration Act (5 August 1914), which required that enemy aliens of military age be interned and others repatriated.[21] Because of London's central positon in the world money market, a number of German banks and financial institutions operated in the City. Under the Trading with the Enemy Act, senior accountants were appointed to take over the running of these companies. Deloittes liquidated the Laender and Dresdner Banks,[22] McLintocks managed or wound up a number of German businesses,[23] Cooper Brothers supervised the affairs of the Deutsche Bank,[24] while Sir William Plender was appointed as overall controller of German, Austrian and Turkish banks.[25] Although Whinney, Smith & Whinney were not involved in this initial reorganization, in 1915 they took control of a group of businesses including the Odol Chemical Works, Brash & Rothenstein, Elkan & Co and Bunge & Co, owned by Germans but based in Britain. Barton, Mayhew similarly supervised a number of German enterprises – Nitsche & Gunther, the Pera Cigarette Co and two merchant banks.

At the outset most politicians and generals believed that the war would be a swift mobile campaign brought to a decisive conclusion by Christmas. The slogan 'business as usual' (first displayed in Harrods) was widely adopted not only to quell panic but as a genuine response to this assumed short-term war.[26] Government intervention remained as yet sporadic and reluctant. Although public control had been established over the railways, shipping and other vital areas of the economy, under the wide-ranging Defence of the Realm Act ('D.O.R.A.'), the government actually did very little. Controls existed if necessary but were still considered inappropriate.

It was the unforeseen character of the war itself which upset this desultory 'business as usual' policy, although the slogan continued in use long after it had lost its appropriateness. Stanley Young, for example, made recourse to the phrase in *The Forty-Ones' Bulletin* for 1916 to describe Turquand, Youngs' position and to cheer those at the front.[27] By the winter of 1914 the war had stabilized, trenches had been dug from the Alps to the English Channel and movement had come to an end. British arsenals, whose output for the moment remained at peacetime levels, did not manufacture sufficient quantities of shells and explosives, so that the country's entire munitions works in 1914 had not the capacity to sustain a major artillery barrage.[28] By 1915 it was obvious that long-term planning was needed to reorganize the country for a war of an entirely unexpected and wide ranging character. Accordingly as part of this strategy, the government steadily recruited accountants to serve at critical points throughout the economy.

In May 1915 the Ministry of Munitions, recently founded by Lloyd George, closed the era of 'business as usual' by taking responsibility for the management of important sectors of the economy – the phrase henceforth being invoked merely as propaganda.[29] To try to ensure that supplies were used efficiently and that the state was not hoodwinked by profiteers, the government assumed an increasingly interventionist role and, in the nature of the case, accountancy techniques became the major instruments of control. Thus, eminent City accountants were appointed to senior positions in the revitalized ministries. In 1915, for instance, Arthur Whinney became Adviser on Costs of Production at the Admiralty and later Assistant Accountant General to the Navy.[30] Charles McLintock performed costing work for the Ministry of Munitions' factories, while towards the end of 1916 William McLintock [1873-1947] was consulted over the merger of various explosives companies headed by Nobel Explosives.[31] S. H. Lever as Costing Accountant to the Railways, Gilbert Garnsey as Deputy Director of Munitions Accounts, H. Peat as Financial Secretary and Accounting Officer to the Ministry of Food and Nicholas Waterhouse as Director of Costings and later Financial Adviser to the War Office were all practising accountants seconded for government work.[32]

In the first year of the war there had been scandalously little provision for the payment of pensions and allowances to the dependents of men in the services. The only official body in August 1914 for the handling of allowances, in fact, was the Royal Hospital for Soldiers at Chelsea whose rates had remained unaltered since the Boer War. Any supplement came from the National Relief Fund or the Soldiers' and Sailors' Families Association.[33] Even when allowances were granted, there remained outrageously long delays before payment was made. So great was the outcry against the muddle, that voluntary societies felt compelled to investigate, followed by Parliament's own select

1 A Victorian engraving of William Turquand (1819–1894), the first President of the Institute of Chartered Accountants in England and Wales, 1880–82

2 A bust of Sir Robert Palmer Harding (1821–1893) by Sir Edgar Boehm. Harding followed Turquand as the English Institute's President and was one of the founders of Whinney, Smith & Whinney

3 *Right* Oil portrait of Frederick Whinney (1829–1916) by Sir William Llewellyn

62, St Vincent Street,
Glasgow, 3rd July, 1871.

The Subscribers have commenced business as Accountants, House Factors, and Insurance Agents, at the above address, under the firm of Reid & Mair.

The following have kindly permitted themselves to be named as References.—

Alexander Stronach Esq., Manager, City of Glasgow Bank.
Robert Gourlay Esq., Sub-Manager, Bank of Scotland, Glasgow.
James S. Fleming Esq., Writer, Glasgow; and
Messrs. Moore & Brown, Chartered Accountants & Stock Brokers, Glasgow.

Robert Reid

Formerly Law Secretary's Assistant in City of Glasgow Bank.

Rob. A. Mair

Formerly with Messrs. Moore & Brown, Chartered Accountants & Stock Brokers, Glasgow.

Agents for
Scottish Widows' Fund Life Assurance Society,
Scottish Provincial Assurance Company.

4 A Victorian advertisement for the Glasgow accountants Reid & Mair indicating the range of tasks which they then performed

5 *Right* A mid-Victorian photograph of J. Townley Trotter, a founder member of the English Institute of Chartered Accountants and leading Manchester accountant

J. Ambler

7 Market St MANCHESTER.
and 44 WELLINGTON Rd ECCLES.

Harding & Pullein.
Accountants,
16, Gresham Street,
London.

HARDING, WHINNEY, GIBBONS & Cº

Accountants.

8, Old Jewry.

WHINNEY, HURLBATT & SMITH.

Chartered Accountants.

8, Old Jewry. E.C.
London.

F. J. G. Whinney
Partner

Ernst & Whinney
Lynton House
7 Tavistock Square
London WC1H 9LS

01 387 0966
Telex 28674

6 Four visiting cards (the top three Victorian) to illustrate the change of style from Harding & Pullein in 1848 to Ernst & Whinney in 1979

BROWN, FLEMING & MURRAY,
CHARTERED ACCOUNTANTS.

J. IVAN SPENS.
G. F. R. BAGULEY.
R. N. GOOCH.
G. H. GARBUTT.
J. S. WILSON.
A. I. MACKENZIE.
T. W. MACDONALD.
F. R. WILLIAMS.

4B, FREDERICK'S PLACE,
OLD JEWRY,
LONDON, E.C.2._____19___

GLASGOW:	175, WEST GEORGE STREET.
PARIS:	21, AVENUE MONTAIGNE.
ANTWERP:	14, PLACE DE MEIR.
BERLIN:	FRIEDRICHSTRASSE 103.
HAMBURG:	ESPLANADE 6.
WARSAW:	PLAC NAPOLEONA 9.
BASRA:	POST BOX 44.
BAGHDAD:	POST BOX 108.
HAIFA:	POST BOX 482.

TELEGRAMS "YARRUMCA" (STOCK) LONDON.

TELEPHONE: MONARCH 2865.

Codes { WESTERN UNION.
{ BENTLEY'S.
{ A.B.C. 5TH EDITION.

DEAR SIR,

WHINNEY, SMITH & WHINNEY,
CHARTERED ACCOUNTANTS

S. H. MEARNS.   F. W. BAILEY.
E. F. G. WHINNEY.   W. D. MONTGOMERY.
D. H. WHINNEY.   H. P. PATTERSON.
W. S. CARRINGTON.   E. W. G. JOICEY-CECIL.
R. L. LATIMER.   G. W. WILKS.

LEEDS . . . . CENTRAL BANK CHAMBERS.
MANCHESTER · · PRINCE'S CHAMBERS, 26, PALL MALL.
JOHANNESBURG P.O. BOX 7983
PARIS . . . . 21, AVENUE MONTAIGNE (VIIIe)
ANTWERP . . . 14, PLACE DE MEIR.
BASRA . . . . 39, STRAND, ASHAR.
BAGHDAD . . . P.O. BOX 108.
HAIFA . . . . P.O. BOX 482.

Correspondents :
AUSTRALIA · DAVID FELL & CO., SYDNEY, AND BRANCHES.
CANADA · · EDWARDS, MORGAN & CO., TORONTO, ONT. AND BRANCHES.
N. ZEALAND · ERNEST HUNT, TURNER & CO., WELLINGTON.
JAMAICA · · CARMAN & BRUCE, 20, DUKE STREET, KINGSTON.
U.S.A. · · · · ERNST & ERNST, 19, RECTOR STREET, NEW YORK · AND BRANCHES.

4B, FREDERICK'S PLACE,
OLD JEWRY, LONDON, E.C.2.

TELEPHONE NOS. { LONDON · MONARCH 6526 (5 LINES)
{ LEEDS · 31117 (2 LINES).
{ MANCHESTER · DEANSGATE 6336 (2 LINES)
{ JOHANNESBURG · 33-1236.

TELEGRAPHIC ADDRESSES:-

"WHINNIES." · · { LONDON.
{ LEEDS.

"ACCREDIT," · · MANCHESTER.

{ JOHANNESBURG.
{ PARIS.
"DEMONSTRAT." { ANTWERP.
{ BASRA.
{ BAGHDAD.
{ HAIFA.

CODES { WESTERN UNION.
{ BENTLEY'S.
{ A.B.C. 5TH EDITION.

WHINNEY, SMITH & WHINNEY,

C. J. G. PALMOUR.
S. H. MEARNS.   F. W. BAILEY.
E. F. G. WHINNEY.   W. S. CARRINGTON.
D. H. WHINNEY.   H. G. C. FENTON.
R. L. LATIMER.   H. P. PATTERSON.

LEEDS . . . . CENTRAL BANK CHAMBERS.
MANCHESTER · · PRINCE'S CHAMBERS, 26, PALL MALL.
JOHANNESBURG · P.O. BOX 7983.
PARIS . . . . 21, AVENUE MONTAIGNE (VIIIe).
ANTWERP . . . 14, PLACE DE MEIR.
BASRA . . . . 39, STRAND ASHAR.
BAGHDAD . . . P.O. BOX 108.
HAIFA . . . . P.O. BOX 482.

Correspondents:
Australia -David Fell & Co. Sydney- and Branches.
Canada   -Edwards Morgan & Co. Toronto, Ont- and Branches.
N.Zealand -Ernest Hunt, Turner & Heslop. Wellington.
Jamaica   -Carman & Bruce, 20, Duke Street, Kingston.
U.S.A   - Ernst & Ernst, 19, Rector Street, New York- and Branches.

4B FREDERICK'S PLACE,
OLD JEWRY, LONDON, E.C.2.

TELEPHONE NOS { LONDON - MONARCH 6526 (5 LINES)
{ LEEDS - 31117 (2 LINES).
{ MANCHESTER - BLACKFRIARS 7423 (2 LINES).
{ JOHANNESBURG - 33-1236.

TELEGRAPHIC ADDRESSES:-
"WHINNIES." - { LONDON.
{ LEEDS.
"ACCREDIT", - - MANCHESTER.
{ JOHANNESBURG.
{ PARIS.
"DEMONSTRAT" { ANTWERP.
{ BASRA.
{ BAGHDAD.
{ HAIFA.

Codes: { WESTERN UNION.
{ BENTLEY'S.
{ A.B.C. 5TH EDITION.

WHINNEY, SMITH & WHINNEY.

SIR ARTHUR WHINNEY, K.B.E.
C. J. G. PALMOUR.
CHARLES F. CAPE.
S. H. MEARNS.
R. L. LATIMER.
F. W. BAILEY.

LEEDS · · CENTRAL BANK CHAMBERS.
PARIS · · 7, RUE RICHEPANSE (VIIIe).
ANTWERP · 14, PLACE DE MEIR.
BERLIN · · FRIEDRICHSTRASSE 103.
HAMBURG · ESPLANADE 6.
BASRA · · 39, STRAND, ASHAR.
BAGHDAD · 22/240, BANK STREET.

Correspondents:
Australia - David Fell & Co, Sydney- and Branches.
Canada. - Edwards, Morgan & Co. Toronto, Ont- and Branches.
S.Africa. - Douglas Low & Co. Johannesburg- and Branches.
N.Zealand - George Ross, Wellington.
U.S.A. - - Ernst & Ernst 27, Cedar Street, New York - and Branches.

4B, FREDERICK'S PLACE,
OLD JEWRY, LONDON, E.C.2.

_____192___

TELEPHONE NOS. LONDON - CENTRAL 6889 (5 LINES).
LEEDS - 22159.

TELEGRAPHIC ADDRESSES:-
"WHINNIES" { LONDON.
{ LEEDS.

{ PARIS.
{ ANTWERP.
"DEMONSTRAT" { BERLIN.
{ HAMBURG.
{ BASRA.
{ BAGHDAD.

Codes { WESTERN UNION.
{ BENTLEY'S.
{ A.B.C. 5TH EDITION.

---

7 Four letterheads, the bottom three showing the changing partnership and territorial growth of Whinney, Smith & Whinney between the 1920s and early 1950s. The Brown, Fleming & Murray letter dates from 1948

8 *Top* The London brass plates of Whinney, Smith & Whinney and Brown, Fleming & Murray from 4b Frederick's Place. The top left plate was originally part of a set which read 'Harding, Whinney, Gibbons & Co'. When the firm became Whinney, Smith & Whinney in 1894 the earlier right-hand plate was replaced by the existing one and the name 'Harding' was scored out. These solid brass plates were symbols of confident Victorian respectability and were much prized as the heavy polishing witnesses

9 A reconstruction of a Victorian accountant's office (re-created for the English Institute's Centenary Exhibition in 1980), which features Frederick Whinney's candlesticks and a number of Whinney, Smith & Whinney ledgers on the high desk

10 Nos 35–36 Waterloo Street, Birmingham, a finely restored Classical office building, occupied in 1833 by a predecessor firm of C. Herbert Smith & Russell, and the premises also of V. W. Houghton, a chartered accountant who audited the Midland Bank before Harding, Whinney & Co acquired the assignment on Houghton's retirement

12 R. A. Murray, who in 1889 joined the Glasgow practice of Brown &
Fleming and six years later became the senior partner

11 *Left* A late Victorian photograph of Frederick's Place that shows Dauntsey
House at the end, displaying an impressive bank of brass plates

13 Princes's Chambers, 26 Pall Mall, Manchester, a typical late-Victorian office block, occupied in part by Sir Thomas Smethurst and from 1928 by Whinney, Smethurst & Co

14 Eldon Street House (1904), a purpose-built Edwardian office block, designed by the London architect George Sherrin and occupied by Baker, Sutton & Co

15 Harold Barton (left) in military uniform on board a troopship bound for India where he was to work on the Red Cross's accounts, *c.* 1916

16 Three Baker, Sutton partners pose in front of a cricket pavilion: Jeffrey Baker, Sydney Baker and Harry Keasley (first two from left and far right) with W. J. McArthur, Company Secretary of John Walker & Sons, the whisky distillers, their client. They are gathered for a Saturday afternoon match in 1929 and hence Sydney Baker is still in his office clothes, while Keasley has changed into an attire more suited to a country outing

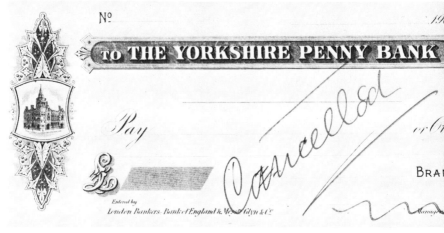

17 *Top* A Yorkshire Penny Bank cheque with *above* a vignette of
their head office (designed by Henry Perkin), where Whinney,
Smith & Whinney opened their Leeds office in 1926

18 Sir Arthur Whinney (1865–1927) portrayed by Sir William Llewellyn. He was President of the English Institute of Chartered Accountants in 1926–27 and senior partner of Whinney, Smith & Whinney from 1905

19 Sir Basil Mayhew (1884-1966) painted here in later life after he had left Barton, Mayhew to become a director of Colmans.

20 Players in a golf match organized in 1955 between Brown, Fleming & Murray's London office and BP executives. Ivan Spens, the former's senior partner, is third from the right in the middle row; Lord Strathalmond of BP is on his right

committee. Eventually the government took reluctant responsibility for the payment of war pensions. Sir William Plender of Deloittes served on the Civil Liabilities Commission appointed to sort out the mess.[34] Nevertheless, charities continued, in the absence of a comprehensive state service, to perform much valuable work, Basil Mayhew acting as Secretary to the Joint Financial Committee of the British Red Cross and Order of St John.

The Ministry of Munitions, by contrast, was an upstart and aggressive body from its inception, less set in its ways than the older departments, which made it, at the design of its creator Lloyd George, an ideal instrument for direct government action.[35] The new ministry took responsibilities beyond its title and original brief, eventually including such related fields as aircraft production (where Harold Barton was Assistant Controller of Accounts), the development of agricultural machinery and the production and use of sulphuric acid.

As the government pursued an increasingly interventionist policy, so accountants were drawn more closely into its working to revise and develop techniques to deal more effectively with wartime problems of supply, distribution and production. The major advance in accountancy practice under this stimulus came in the field of costing. Industry had to be regulated to obtain maximum output at fair prices – prices which would offer a reasonable rate of return and hence provide incentives for higher productivity (controlled businesses were still operating in the market place rather than as government departments or nationalized industries) while not exploiting the prevailing circumstances of imperative demand and shortages of supply to produce extortionate profits. To determine the median of reasonable charges, independent checks on costs were undertaken by professional accountants.[36] Lord Selborne pointed a finger at profiteers, arguing that it was vital to discover 'the weak points in all existing contracts and protect ourselves against extravagance in the future, at the same time controlling the elaborate system of cost accounting' and in addition, to exercise a check on 'the capital expenditure which is made [by] the various works [munitions factories and so forth], which are constructed at the national expense'.[37] Hence, S. H. Lever, as an accountant who had acquired costing skills whilst working in America, was recalled from New York to fill the post of Assistant Financial Secretary to the Ministry of Munitions and later became Financial Secretary to the Treasury.[38] His brief was to see that efficient costing techniques and controls were applied internally and that cost-effective agreements should take the place of competitive contracts for the supply of munitions. Armament companies which had previously been unaware of the advantages of costing methods had, of necessity, to install costing systems and began at last to appreciate their value.

As was to be the case in the Second World War, contracts for military supplies were organized on a 'cost-plus' basis. The Army Contracts Department, which dealt with all supplies other than those arranged by the Ministry of Munitions, attempted to settle fair prices for requisitioned commodities. Previous notions of 'fair price' devised in 1915 following D.O.R.A. Regulation 7, which gave the government powers to order manufacturers to produce certain goods, initially led to difficulties. In 1916 the situation was clarified when the definition was sharpened to mean costs rather than market prices, which had soared due to profiteering.[39] This, in turn, led to the development of a major organization designed to establish actual costs – the cost-plus method of payment first being used by the Ministry of Munitions in September 1915 for certain metals and by the War Office itself in June 1916 when buying up the whole of the domestic wool clip. Powers to examine companies' books of account were obtained in February 1916 and became not only the basis for a system of output and price control but also resulted in the improvement of outmoded or inadequate accounting methods.

By 1918 a Select Committee accepted that 'the importance of this accountancy work cannot be overestimated; it is not merely essential that the accounts should be on a proper basis for the purpose of accurate payment and the prevention of waste. It is also important from an administrative point of view....'[40] Indeed, many accountants who had become engaged in cost accounting, either in ministries or in factories, remained so occupied after the war and, to further the aims and techniques of their specialized art, in 1919 founded the Institute of Cost and Works Accountants. Yet the English Institute of Chartered Accountants still remained unimpressed by their work and scorned their request for a charter of incorporation, adding that 'such persons are not engaged in professional work, but are employed in the service of traders'[41] – a curiously insular and unimaginative attitude which must, in part, be related to the poor performance of British business between the wars (see p. 171). However, as with advances in science, so with accountancy: war could be a means of accelerating peace-time progress in business techniques and financial control.

As both sides became increasingly war-weary, so their respective governments adopted more fiercely interventionist policies. By 1917 Britain was considerably weakened, conscription having further depleted the workforce, and armies, severly mauled by the Somme offensive, demanded fresh recruits. In the face of labour shortages and a growing disenchantment with the war, the government moved more actively into the organization of the economy. By October 1917 it had established 143 National Factories, British mines had been taken over in September and placed under a Coal Controller, metal refining was directly ordered by the Ministry of Munitions, while Cotton and Woollen Boards of Control had been set up.[42]

From the spring of 1917 food rationing also became a reality. In April the Ministry of Food had announced an 'educational campaign to concentrate public attention on the necessity of reducing the consumption of bread and flour'.[43] One of the most complicated schemes of control related to meat as it had to cover imports and home-produced livestock for both civilian and military use, the government taking responsibility for its slaughtering, purchasing, pricing and distribution. A Public Meals Order restricted the quantities of food which could be served at restaurants, hotels and boarding houses. Accounts were to be kept on a weekly basis and a food register had to follow a prescribed order for regular inspection.[44] On 25 April it was announced that 'the Food Controller would take control from next Monday of all the larger flour mills in the United Kingdom' to determine price and distribution.[45] An entry in Baker, Sutton's Fee Journal records that in March 1919 they assisted Turquand, Youngs in their work for the Ministry of Food and themselves were employed by the Sterilized Milk Company which had contracts to supply the Ministry and was liable to Excess Profits Duty, on which Baker, Sutton advised them.[46] Price Waterhouse, as auditors of Van den Berghs, the Dutch margarine manufacturers, were prompted to expand as a result of their client's wartime contracts with the government and their establishment of factories in Great Britain. Pre-war, Van den Berghs supplied much of Britain's margarine from Holland and in view of the importance of this import trade requested that Price Waterhouse send a representative to Rotterdam in 1914 to exercise financial control over exports to the U.K. The volume of work increased to such an extent that an office was formally established there in 1919. As the war increasingly assumed a total character in these ways, so the role of the accountant, fulfilling the essential function of monitoring public regulation, grew in importance.

Although some accountancy firms did gain a certain amount of government work (it generated 6.0% of Whinney, Smith & Whinney's fees in 1915), this never assumed significant proportions and did not compensate for the general disruption in economic activity caused by the war. As Fig. 2 shows Whinney, Smith & Whinney's and C. Herbert Smith & Russell's fees mirrored the fortunes of the country as a whole. The former's income grew in cash terms from £24,953 in 1914 to £29,082 in 1918 with a peak of £33,041 in 1916. However, when these are adjusted by the Sauerbeck–Statist price index (1867-77 = 100) to take account of inflation caused by wartime shortages, the picture is reversed, the firm's fees falling in real terms from £29,356 in 1914 to £15,147 in 1918. Despite the fact that staff were away in the forces or seconded to government duties, Table II reveals that fees from auditing grew and occupied an increasing percentage of the firm's business, rising from 35.4% in 1910 to 44.6% in 1915 and 48.1% in 1918. Insolvency work, as might be expected in a tightly controlled economy where under-production was the major problem, was much reduced – declining to 30% and contributing a mere £8,500 per annum, the smallest total in the 1910-25 period. While C. Herbert Smith & Russell's real fees exhibit a decline from 1914 to 1917, Baker, Sutton grew so rapidly in cash terms that this translated itself into an expansion in real income. Both firm's level of fee income was much lower than Whinney, Smith & Whinney's (a much older established practice) and the range of fluctuations (generated by special jobs such as insolvencies, investigations, prospectus issues) was much more limited as Baker, Sutton and C. Herbert Smith & Russell relied on regular accounting, auditing and tax work for the bulk of their income. Accordingly the graphs of their fees are much smoother than either Turquand, Youngs' or Whinney, Smith & Whinney's, who as well-known City firms periodically attracted important special commissions.

However, one wartime feature worked against the general downward trend in fee incomes – the imposition of special taxes. Wars, of necessity involving the diversion of resources from productive to wasteful ends, have always been burdensome affairs. Raising general taxes from the outset, in November 1914 Lloyd George's budget doubled the ninepenny rate of income tax, increased tea duty to eight pence in the pound and raised the tax on beer by one penny a pint.[47] Subsequently the basic rate of income tax rose steadily throughout the war, reaching five shillings in the pound in 1917 and six shillings in 1919. The number of those liable to pay supertax also grew. Predictably, demands for accountants to deal with tax problems rose accordingly. In 1910 taxation had only generated 0.6% of Whinney, Smith & Whinney's fees (£158), but by 1915 it had reached 1.4% (£393) and in 1918 2.5% (£685). Although these figures remained relatively insignificant they represented an important trend for the future. They were boosted not only by lower personal tax thresholds and increasing numbers requiring professional advice, but also by the imposition of an Excess Profits Duty. This was a levy introduced to prevent fortunately placed businesses (such as armaments manufacturers or suppliers of military equipment) from making excessive profits from the urgent needs of a nation at war. Companies with contracts to supply the government were required to demonstrate their level of peacetime profits, any gains in excess of that figure being subject from 1915 to an Excess Profits Duty of 50% that rose to 80% in 1917.[48] The rules were complex: businesses could select any three-year period from their previous ten years' operation as the basis for the profits figure. Accordingly accountants received many commissions to delve back into their clients' books to determine the most favourable period of business, a pattern which was repeated in the Second World War with the imposition of a tougher Excess Profits Tax (see p. 195). Public regulations and higher rates of tax, rules which became ever more complex, thus demanded professional expertise on both sides of the transaction: public and private sector, government and governed, tax gatherer and tax payer, regulator and regulated.

Events shaped in a similar fashion in America. Preparations for war in 1916–17 resulted in substantial new taxes with their 'own mass of special regulations, particularly for companies directly involved in government production', which generated additional work for accountants.[49] An Excess Profits Tax brought further fees. Robert Montgomery, a distinguished American tax accountant, recalled in his memoirs how his expertise brought him into the army, swift promotion to Colonel and command of the

War Department Board of Appraisers, with a seat on the Price Fixing Committee of the War Industries Board.[50] Later he was sent to France to 'inaugurate an appraisal and cost-accounting system as a basis for billing between the Allied governments arising from exchange facilities. . . .'[51]

As in America, British accountancy practices received fees for government work. However, this, like taxation, never assumed significant proportions, earning a maximum of 6.0% of fee income for Whinney, Smith & Whinney, £1,019 in 1915. This partly resulted from the general spirit of patriotism and self-sacrifice which prompted accountancy firms to perform much of this work for very low fees. Those accountants who audited munitions works or factories with government contracts could do disproportionately well. In Hull, for instance, Smith & Nephew, the manufacturers of surgical dressings audited by Buckley & Hall, greatly increased their output on the outbreak of war to prepare for the coming battle. W. B. Hall, son of the founder partner and later himself to become senior partner, recalled a car tour of Hull with his father and H. N. Smith on 5 August 1914 as the latter rented warehouse accommodation for the impending expansion in the production of field dressings. Although Smith & Nephew prospered during the war years, they had entered into what turned out to be a somewhat onerous contract with the French government, allowing them to curtail orders on the cessation of hostilities. When the fighting stopped Smith & Nephew were left with large stocks and contracts for further purchases of cotton from their Lancashire suppliers. It was largely because Ernest Buckley succeeded in re-negotiating these contracts that Smith & Nephew survived this tight financial predicament.

One of the First World War's major social effects was to admit women into general employment.[52] In the spring of 1915 the militant suffragettes had staged a final demonstration under Christabel Pankhurst, marching on Whitehall with the slogan 'we demand the right to work'.[53] Thousands of women were subsequently recruited to replace men now in the forces working in arsenals, factories and offices. Jobs for which they had previously been considered totally unsuited were now theirs for the asking – such was the hypocrisy of Edwardian man. With clerks, messengers and young accountants away at the front, practices were desperately short-staffed. Pride was swallowed; women became employed as typists, telephonists, clerks – even as auditors. Whinney, Smith & Whinney took on their first woman in 1914 when Miss C. Claydon, a secretary, was employed, remaining with the firm after the peace and the next war until her death in 1960.

As the statistics show, clerical and commercial employment for women expanded critically in 1915 setting it apart from almost all other jobs where comparable developments did not follow until the introduction of universal male conscription in May 1916.[54] As a letter to *The Accountant* recorded,[55]

... having lost every unmarried audit clerk of military age by enlistment, we, in May 1915, began to approach those of our clients whom we thought would have no objection to their work being checked by women. In each case we received permission to 'go ahead' and this we have continued to do ever since – with advantage to ourselves, in that we have been enabled to undertake an enormous amount of Government work in addition to our usual business.

Certainly the introduction of women workers into traditional male areas of work was initially greatest in genteel clerical employment. The National Provincial and Union Bank of England took on their first woman teller in September 1914, while the Atlas Insurance Company declared that 'ladies were employed ... for many years before the war as typists only. Their engagement to replace our permanent staff on active service commenced in November 1914.'[56] Although women had now, if only temporarily, been admitted to the broad sweep of employment, they were always paid less than men, even where they performed the same tasks.

Before the war the English Institute of Chartered Accountants had been totally opposed to the employment of women. With a certain aplomb, the Council declared, 'we have no desire to say anything that might tend to encourage women to embark on accountancy, for although women might make excellent bookkeepers, there is much in accountancy proper that is, we think, unsuitable for them'.[57] They gave no reasons for their prejudice. Only the London Association of Accountants admitted women before the First World War – in 1909.[58] In this general refusal the accountants were in line with the other professions. There had, for example, been a move to admit women to the Architectural Association as early as 1893, but it had been soundly defeated by 78 votes to 37, although by 1908 two women had completed their articles and passed the qualifying examinations set by the

Royal Institute of British Architects.[59] In 1888 Miss Harris Smith of London, in practice since 1878, first approached the Society of Incorporated Accountants for membership but, despite her obvious skills and experience, was refused admittance until 1919.[60] The Sex Disqualification (Removal) Act of 1919 opened chartered accountancy and the legal profession to women. Miss H. M. Claridge, who had joined a Bradford firm during the war, qualified as the Incorporated Society's first female member in 1920; doubtless prejudice had been swayed to some extent by the fact that her father was its President that year.[61] The English Institute of Chartered Accountants did not, however, admit its first woman member, Miss E. Watts, until 1924,[62] the Irish Institute having been the first chartered accountancy body to open its doors to women, in May 1919.[63] The Scottish societies were the last to admit women, Glasgow's first being Miss Isabel Guthrie in 1923 and Edinburgh's Miss Helen Somerville in 1925.[64]

The return of troops in 1919 resulted in most women accountants and clerks losing their jobs, though this was not the case at Whinney, Smith & Whinney where their excellent work encouraged the firm to keep them on. In Britain generally, only a few female typists, telephonists and secretaries could be fairly sure of retaining their posts and by 1920 almost two-thirds of those who had entered employment during the war had left it again.[65] By 1921 with the onset of protracted depression, the figure for women's employment was not much higher than it had been in 1914. The First World War's influence on women's access to professional careers was short-lived, although better here than in other areas of work. Even so, only 43 women could achieve membership of all the accountancy bodies in 1921 and 119 by 1931;[66] not until 1945 were they able to occupy a full place in the accountant's world.

As well as extending the accountant's range of duties, the 1914-18 War demonstrated to a wide audience that the profession had an important contribution to make to the economy. The recognition of those accountants who had been involved in vital government work raised them further in the public's estimation. Arthur Whinney was knighted in 1919 for his work on naval accounts, though it might be mentioned that he had been offered a title by Asquith in 1915 but declined, adding, '... if my business experience and organizing capacity could be utilized for the benefit of the country, I should be only too happy....'[67] Basil Mayhew was knighted, not as an eminent accountant *per se*, but for his work with the Red Cross, while William McLintock, who had performed a number of government jobs, received a knighthood in the early 1920s, having overhauled the finances of the Royal Household.[68] From Price Waterhouse & Co, Wyon, Halsey, Waterhouse, Garnsey and Dickinson were all knighted for a variety of governmental work.

Until 1914 only Sir William Plender and Sir R. P. Harding of all the past Presidents of the English Institute had received such an honour. It was usually the second generation of eminent accountants who were awarded titles: Arthur Whinney rather than Frederick, William McLintock rather than Thomson, Francis D'Arcy Cooper rather than Arthur, Nicholas Waterhouse rather than Edwin, and John Mann Junior rather than John Mann Senior.[69] It was not simply that accountants had become respectable in the eyes of the public; this recognition also reflected the subtle influence of social elevation. As Pixley deduced in 1897, 'those who have been articled to our members since the date of the charter come from the same class as do those who are now at Woolwich, Sandhurst and the Inns of Court. They have been educated at the same class of schools....'[70] Fathers may have been of humble or lower middle-class origins, but their sons, benefitting from their wealth, went to public schools or university and made friends and contacts in more elevated circles, later bringing them more closely into contact with government. The process of formal social advancement did much to raise the standing of the profession, making accountancy a valued as well as a valuable occupation.

References

1 Arthur Marwick, *The Deluge, British Society in the First World War*, London (1965), pp. 35, 47.
2 Newspaper cutting, *c.* 1916.
3 Letter to Harold Barton from an unnamed Colonel at Hull, 20 July 1917.
4 Letter from the Ministry of Munitions, 8 August 1917.
5 Brown, *op. cit.*, p. 218.
6 *Ibid*, p. 219.
7 *Ibid*, p. 228.
8 *A History of the Chartered Accountants of Scotland, from the earliest times to 1954*, Edinburgh (1954), p. 40.
9 *Aris's Gazette*, Obituary, 17 August 1903.

10 Day Book 1859-1864, 1860, p. 41; Day Book 1867-1871, 1867, p. 10.

11 John Keegan, *The Face of Battle*, London (1976), pp. 217-19.

12 W. J. Reader, *A House in the City*, London (1979), p. 130.

13 *The Forty-Ones' Bulletin*, Vol. I, No. 4, 29 May 1915.

14 *Ibid*, Vol. II, No. 1, 10 January 1916, p. 12.

15 *Cooper Brothers, op. cit.*, pp. 10, 11.

16 History of Ware, Ward, *op. cit.*, p. 6.

17 *History of the Chartered Accountants of Scotland, op. cit.*, p. 58.

18 Robinson, *op. cit.*, pp. 167-8.

19 *The Accountant*, No. 2163, 20 May 1916, p. 583.

20 *The Forty-Ones' Bulletin*, Vol. II, No. 7, 16 October 1917, p. 4.

21 Marwick, *The Deluge, op. cit.*, pp. 37-8.

22 *Deloittes, op. cit.*, p. 100.

23 Winsbury, *op. cit.*, p. 31.

24 *Cooper Brothers. op. cit.*, p. 12.

25 *History of the English Institute, op. cit.*, p. 59.

26 *History of the First World War*, Vol. II (1970), Arthur Marwick, 'The War at Home', p. 573.

27 *The Forty-Ones' Bulletin*, Vol. II, No. 1, 10 January 1916, p. 11.

28 *History of the First World War*, Vol. II (1970), Alan Milward, 'Industry at War: the Allies', p. 671.

29 A. J. P. Taylor, *The First World War*, London (1963), p. 86.

30 *The Times*, Obituary, 31 May 1927; *The Accountant*, No. 2739, 4 June 1927, p. 840.

31 Winsbury, *op. cit.*, pp. 30-1.

32 *History of the English Institute, op. cit.*, p. 59.

33 Marwick, *War at Home, op. cit.*, pp. 574-5.

34 *Deloittes, op. cit.*, p. 104.

35 Marwick, *The Deluge, op. cit.*, p. 250.

36 Stacey, *op. cit.*, pp. 91-2.

37 *Hansard, House of Lords*, 11 November 1915.

38 Robinson, *op. cit.*, p. 229.

39 Sidney Pollard, *The Development of the British Economy 1914-1967*, London (1969), p. 50.

40 *First Report of the Select Committee on National Expenditure on the Ministry of Munitions*, quoted from Garratt, *op. cit.*, p. 107.

41 *The Accountant*, No. 2526, 5 May 1923, quoting the English Institute's annual report, p. 683.

42 Marwick, *The Deluge, op. cit.*, pp. 250-1.

43 *Parliamentary Debates, The House of Commons*, Vol. 92, No. 40 (1917), p. 1654.

44 *The Daily Chronicle*, 14 April 1917, p. 3.

45 *Ibid*, 15 April 1917, p. 5.

46 Baker, Sutton & Co Fee Ledger (1903-1926), pp. 113, 121.

47 Milward, *op. cit.*, p. 573.
48 Stacey, *op. cit.*, 93.
49 *Ernst & Ernst*, *op. cit.*, pp. 23–4.
50 Robert H. Montgomery, *Fifty Years of Accountancy*, New York (1939), pp. 183, 186.
51 *Ibid*, p. 187.
52 Arthur Marwick, *Women at War 1914-1918*, London (1977), p. 12.
53 Taylor, *The First World War*, *op. cit.*, p. 87.
54 Marwick, *Women at War*, *op. cit.*, p. 48.
54 *The Accountant*, No. 2163, 20 May 1916, p. 581.
56 Marwick, *Women at War*, *op. cit.*, p. 48.
57 *The Accountant*, No. 1971, 14 September 1912, p. 341.
58 Stacey, *op. cit.*, p. 95. The London Association of Accountants (founded in 1904), which absorbed the Corporation of Accountants in 1939, then became the Association of Certified and Corporate Accountants.
59 Alastair Service, *Edwardian Architecture*, London (1977), p. 128.
60 Robinson, *op. cit.*, p. 179.
61 Garratt, *op. cit.*, pp. 121–2.
62 *History of the English Institute*, *op. cit.*, pp. 65–6.
63 Robinson, *op. cit.*, p. 180.
64 *History of the Chartered Accountants of Scotland*, *op. cit.*, p. 63.
65 Marwick, *Women at War*, *op. cit.*, p. 162.
66 *Ibid*, p. 167.
67 Letter from Arthur Whinney to H. H. Asquith, 31 May 1915.
68 Winsbury, *op. cit.*, pp. 37–8.
69 R. H. Parker, *British Accountants*, *op. cit.*, pp. 10–11.
70 F. W. Pixley, *The Profession of a Chartered Accountant*, London (1897), p. 128.

❀❀❀ CHAPTER 6 ❀❀❀

The Inter-War Years

Part I: At Home

The inter-war years are characterized by a striking and tragic paradox. Mostly they are remembered for unemployment, poverty and decline in the coal, textile and shipbuilding industries; the intense privation and suffering endured in the traditional manufacturing and mining centres being graphically depicted by such authors as George Orwell, Walter Greenwood and J. B. Priestley. The number of registered unemployed (in fact much less than the number of those actually out of work) rose from 1.7 million in January 1930 to 2.5 million by December and at its peak neared 3 million, when it represented 22% of Britain's working population.[1] However, the other side of the coin is not so well documented. In fact, national income grew in real terms by 37.5% (per capita by 23%), between 1913 and 1937, which was faster than in the so-called 'Golden Age' before the First World War.[2] The explanation for this contradictory situation lies in the intensely regional nature of decline and the depression. While Scotland, South Wales, Lancashire, Yorkshire and Tyneside with their concentration on coal, textiles or shipbuilding were hit hard by world recession and stiff competition, the Midlands and the South East prospered, where the development of light industry (principally car manufacture and electrical goods of all kinds) together with the continued growth of the service sector – accountancy included – ensured that Britain was a country of two nations; 'rich and poor', as Disraeli had suggested, but with the division between the two depending on occupation and geographical location. As George Orwell observed, 'to study unemployment and its effects you have got to go to the industrial areas. In the South unemployment exists, but it is scattered and queerly unobtrusive. . .'[3]

More specifically, the present chapter seeks, against this background of contrast, to trace and evaluate the growth of certain accountancy practices – Whinney, Smith & Whinney and Turquand, Youngs in the City and C. Herbert Smith & Russell in Birmingham, both areas of general prosperity. Paradoxically these successful London firms extended their activities into the depressed areas. For example, Whinney, Smith & Whinney opened offices in Leeds and Manchester in 1926 and 1928, while between 1919 and 1929 Barton, Mayhew amalgamated with H. W. & J. Blackburn, a firm based in Bradford and Leeds. Conversely and more understandably, practices in depressed regions extended their operations to more prosperous territory. A number of Glasgow firms, including Brown, Fleming & Murray (p. 168) and Thomson McLintock, established offices in the City, while many newly qualified Scottish accountants migrated south to find employment in growing English practices. Hence, the main theme underlying this inter-war period of accountancy history is not blanket economic decline and social disaster, but one of sharp regional contrast, which makes the privation and suffering that more poignant.

It was often said that accountants prosper in times of adversity. As has been seen, this was certainly true of the nineteenth century when the bulk of their work came from insolvencies, but by the 1920s the emphasis had shifted from bankruptcy to audit work as the principal form of business – in 1925, for example, Whinney, Smith & Whinney earned 56.5% of their fee income from accounting and auditing as against 26.8% from insolvencies.[4] Adversity, therefore, certainly brought some short-term gains from windings-up, but meant in the long term the loss of a potential audit client and a regular income. The inter-war period was not a bad time for City accountants (as will be seen, they did rather well), but like most others in the business world, or directly dependent upon it, they suffered, or did less well, in times of recession.

The annual fee incomes (in real and cash terms) for Whinney, Smith & Whinney, Baker, Sutton and C. Herbert Smith & Russell have been expressed in graph form on Fig. 3. The former's cash income declined from peaks in 1921 (£83,564) and 1923 (£83,464) – the collapse of the post-war boom at the end of 1920 brought much bankruptcy work, insolvencies contributing 45.1% of Whinney, Smith & Whinney's fees even in 1920 – to a low point in 1932 of £58,047, almost exactly corresponding with the 1929-31 recession. Recovery followed, reaching another peak

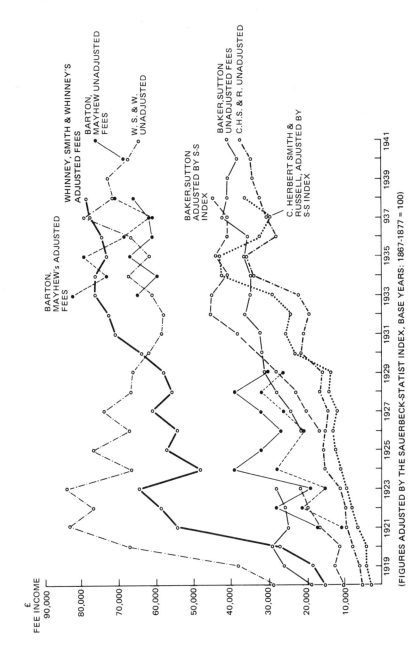

Figure 3 Predecessor's Firms' Fee Income 1918–1941

in 1937 (£79,482), again paralleling the nation's economic revival before the Second World War. The sharp drop clear from both Whinney, Smith & Whinney's and C. Herbert Smith & Russell's fees for 1926 evidently resulted from the disruption caused to business by the General Strike. Hence, in cash terms, these firms' receipts (with the curious exception of the immediate post-war collapse) mirror the overall fortunes of the country, falling in times of adversity and rising during recovery, which is in contrast to the nineteenth century when their insolvency-based fee incomes rose dramatically in times of crisis.

However, when the three firms' fee incomes are expressed in real terms, taking account of falling price levels during these years, their fortunes appear in a very different guise. The 1924 and 1926 troughs remain, but it becomes clear that they each experienced slow but continuous growth from 1926 to 1938, Whinney, Smith & Whinney's real fee income rising from £53,578 to £78,155. National wages and prices fell faster than their fees. In essence this expansion was founded upon a growing audit practice: in 1920 only 38.3% of Whinney, Smith & Whinney's income derived from auditing (£24,868), rising to 48.5% by 1925 (£37,093). In 1930 67.4% (£40,708) and in 1939 73.3% (£42,765) of fees were earned by auditing. Accounting, taxation, trustee and executorship work remained fairly constant throughout the period in terms of generating cash and their percentage contribureal fall was in insolvency work, which plummeted from 45.1% in 1920 to 1.9% in 1935 when it earned a mere £891. It was not until the secondary banking crisis of 1973–74 that insolvencies again became a significant part of the practice.

C. Herbert Smith & Russell, the smaller Birmingham practice, like Baker, Sutton in London, experienced steady growth with few dramatic fluctuations over the inter-war period. The former's cash fees rose from £15,336 to £32,946 between 1929 and 1938, which when translated into real terms grew slightly more dramatically from £13,336 to £36,204. The greater range evident in the fluctuations of Whinney, Smith & Whinney's graph result, as before, from special assignments (insolvencies, prospectus issues or investigations) which boosted fees dramatically for short periods of time. C. Herbert Smith & Russell and Baker, Sutton, being smaller firms with a greater reliance upon accounting and audit work generally for smaller clients, were not subject to these violent distortions in their fee incomes.

Unfortunately there are two gaps in Barton, Mayhew's fee run (1929-33 and 1938-40). However, the figures serve to illustrate the end of the post-war boom and the putative influence of the General Strike and subsequent depression in 1929, while the higher levels which they had achieved in the mid 1930s must betray something of the widespread recovery.

Having seen that Whinney, Smith & Whinney's rising fortunes in the inter-war period were based upon an expansion in the audit side of their activities, it remains to discover more about their clients and the services which they came to demand. The firm's Audit Books reveal that their clients grew in number from 218 in 1910 to 436 in 1933[5] and became more diverse in character. The following important companies were new audits: Dunlop Rubber (1924), Imperial Airways (1924), Chrysler Motors (1924), Bass & Co (1926), Worthington & Co (1926), Aerograph (1932), Dodge Brothers (1930), Magnesium Elektron (1936), Thorn Electrical Industries (1937) and Remington Rand (1939). Chrysler Motors, Aerograph, Dodge Brothers and Remington Rand, companies, which represented 'new' industrial growth, were American based and had been introduced to Whinney, Smith & Whinney by Ernst & Ernst to deal with their British outlets. As will be seen, the Dunlop audit followed an investigation conducted by Sir Arthur Whinney, which, in turn, led to Whinney, Smith & Whinney's appointment as auditors of Imperial Airways, while the Bass and Worthington audits came after Sir Arthur Whinney's assistance in the negotiations that brought about their merger in 1926. The firm were appointed joint auditors of Thorn Electrical Industries when the company went public, Whinney, Smith & Whinney having been responsible for the accountants' report in a prospectus published in December 1936. The audits of Ellis & Goldstein (1937) and Arnott & Harrison, toolmakers (1937), were acquired in a similar fashion.

We have already seen that Whinney, Smith & Whinney, not then a firm with a strong industrial practice, had built up a considerable expertise in banking, financial institutions and estate accounting. In these areas they consolidated their position, acquiring the following clients in the inter-war period: the Bank of New South Wales, London Office (1918), Provident Accident & Whitecross Insurance Co (1919), Lloyds Syndicate Survey Department (1920), Yorkshire Penny Bank (1922), Pall Mall Trust (1925), Charterhouse Investment Trust (1926), Save and Prosper group (1934) and Aviation & General Insurance (1936); and in the last category: the Earl of Plymouth's Estates (1922), Duke of Buccleuch's Boughton and Furness Estates (1924), Earl of Pembroke's Wilton Estate (1925), Duke of Portland's Welbeck Estates (1926) and the Earl of Harewood's Estates (1926). In addition London's traditional trades were well represented among their recent acquisitions: publishers, Associated Illife Press and numerous subsidiaries (1923); printers, Charles Skipper & East (1923), Fanfold (1929); clothing, G. Glanfield & Sons (1923), A. Rosset Silks (1923), Rodier (1927), E. Mayer Fabrics (1927), D.M.C. Thread Co (1932) and Fashion Silk & Rayon Weavers (1933); and furniture, Austin Veneer & Panel Co (1937).

It is also clear that as Whinney, Smith & Whinney's audit practice grew in size, not only did they extend their specialism, but the overall character of their clients diversified. For example, the following industrial audit clients were added: MacDonald & McCorquodale, civil engineers, one of whose assignments was to heighten the Aswan Dam (1922), United Anthracite Collieries, nine collieries in South Wales (1923), Dunstable Portland Cement Co (1925), Poldi Steel Co (1925), British Timken (1930), Henry Meadows, engineers at Wolverhampton (1936). Other important audit clients included the South Essex Waterworks Co (1920), Mazawattee Tea Company (1921) and Bell & Howell (1932).

In the immediate post-war years Whinney, Smith & Whinney, in common with many other accountancy firms, suffered from a shortage of experienced partners; elderly men who had remained during the war now took their overdue retirement, while younger men who would normally have risen to take their places had either been killed when serving in the forces or lacked the necessary accumulated skills. It was partly for these reasons that Whinney, Smith & Whinney took over the practice of Charles Cape, a joint auditor of the English Institute, whose small and largely locally based business clientele was absorbed, Cape becoming a partner in Whinney, Smith & Whinney.

Although established as late as 1907, Barton, Mayhew had also built up an impressive clientele by 1930. They audited several small banks (British Mutual Bank, and the Property & General Finance Corporation), Allied Steel Makers, Dalziel Foundry and had a number of medical or charitable bodies among their clients, a connection which had arisen from Sir Basil Mayhew's first marriage to the daughter of Stephen Paget, a Consultant Surgeon at the Middlesex Hospital. These included the British Red Cross Society, Order of St John, Croydon Nursing Homes, United Nursing Services Club, R.A.F. Benevolent Fund, Queen Alexandra's Hospital and the Royal College of Nursing.[6] In the 1930s Sir Basil Mayhew's links with the National Farmers' Union brought the audit of the first agricultural marketing boards: the Hops Marketing Board (1931), Pigs (1933), Milk (1933) and Potato (1934). In 1932 Mayhew was appointed receiver and ger of Southern Roadways and this later led to the audit of British Road Services.

It was in this period that Bowaters, already a substantial family enterprise, undertook a rapid expansion programme in their paper-making business. By such rapid growth Bowaters became an important and highly valued client for Barton, Mayhew in the same way that Imperial Airways had enhanced the business of Whinney, Smith & Whinney, Hanson Trust that of Buckley, Hall, Devin, or Lucas Industries that of C. Herbert Smith & Russell – all young and fast-growing enterprises.

In the inter-war period the structure of British industry was characterized by a number of significant amalgamations, which in retrospect may be seen to have formed a prelude to the nationalization statutes of the 1940s and 1950s. In 1923 the railways grouped into four major companies (the largest of which, the L.M.S., employed 250,000), later forming the basis for British Railway's regional divisions. Turquand, Youngs, who audited several smaller railway companies, understandably lost this work as the few specialist railway accountants secured the audits of the four new giants. In 1933 a Conservative-dominated National Government recommended that the various bus, tram and railway companies operating in the capital be amalgamated to form the London Passenger Transport Board, which was then audited by Deloittes, Sir William McLintock having been responsible for the complex financial negotiations that preceded the reorganization.[7]

Also in 1923, a government committee under Sir Herbert Hambling recommended that the existing air companies (Instone Air Line, Daimler Airways, Handley Page Transport and British Marine Air Navigation Co) be merged to form a single airline to fly Empire mail routes – Imperial Airways. Sir Eric Geddes and Sir George Beharrell, both directors of Dunlop Rubber, joined the board of the newly created company, the former as its chairman, and it was on their suggestion that Whinney, Smith & Whinney, who had performed the investigations of the merged companies, were appointed auditors of Imperial Airways. In addition, public utilities were also slowly taken over by government and local authorities and in 1926, with the creation of the Central Electricity Board, the National Grid became responsible for the wholesale supply of power. Some accountancy firms were exceptionally fortunate in securing the audit of these much enlarged organizations; others, less fortunate, lost a number of smaller clients. The increasing scale and complexity required corresponding increases in accountancy firms' size and range of expertise, if they wished to retain such audits.

The merger movement of the early 1920s, as mirrored in private enterprise, was in part a product of the collapse of the post-war boom. The immediate recession reached its worst in 1921 when it assumed catastrophic proportions (Whinney, Smith & Whinney gained eight insolvency cases in 1921-22, including the Trade & General Insurance Co, Austin Motor Co, Belsize Motor Co and the Sun Fuel Co) and threw $2\frac{1}{2}$ million into unemployment,[8] almost 25% of the workforce. These difficulties caused many substantial businesses to rationalize their operation and structure in the following years. A wave of mergers swept together British companies on a scale not to be witnessed again until the 1960s, creating *inter alia* amongst the largest I.C.I., Unilever and later English Electric.[9] Just as a wave of mergers had swept through the United States in the 1880s, Britain now followed suit so that by the mid 1920s the 100 largest U.K. companies accounted for about 22% of manufacturing value, a percentage attained by American businesses in 1909,[10] although British companies in the inter-war period tended to be of smaller scale than their American counterparts. Much of the growth evident in the largest 100 U.K. businesses had been achieved by amalgamation, which meant, as in the public sector, that fortunate auditors could, by keeping pace with their expanding clients, gain a considerable amount of new work.

Practical examples of the way in which companies, that had got into difficulties in 1921 and were saved by financial reorganization, are provided by the cases of the Austin Motor and Dunlop Rubber Companies. Having been heavily involved in the production of munitions, Austin had been hit particularly hard by Excess Profits Duty, the payment of which in 1919 severely exacerbated their cash flow problems.[11] Against the advice of the Midland Bank, Sir Herbert Austin made a fresh issue of £3.35 million in ordinary shares. However, by January 1920 80% of the stock remained with the brokers, and when Austins failed to pay off their overdraft from the recent capital issue and as matters deteriorated further, in April 1921 the Midland Bank filed a petition for their bankruptcy.[12] Sir Arthur Whinney was installed as receiver and manager of the Austin Motor Company. Happily both confidence and a fresh injection of working capital were forthcoming after a change in the composition of the board. On the recommendation of the Midland, a new works director, Carl Engelbach, was appointed who then proceeded to reorganize the company's internal operation.[13] Although the receiver left Longbridge in April 1923, Sir Arthur Whinney remained involved until 1926, when the Midland were satisfied that the new board and fresh capital together with the production of two fine cars – the Austin 12 and the famous Austin 7 – had ensured the business's future prosperity.

The second example concerns the Dunlop Rubber Company, which had got into serious financial difficulties through a mixture of ill-luck (principally a dramatic fall in the value of their rubber stocks) and bad management. The company made a huge loss of £8.3 million in 1921 and at the annual general meeting in December 1922 the shareholders suggested that a committee of inquiry be set up. On 24 February it was reported that Sir Arthur Whinney had agreed to conduct the investigation.[14] Under his chairmanship the committee's report was completed in September 1923 but never made public, the major result being a restructuring of the board of directors as the du Cros family were ousted from power and replaced by professional managers; Sir Eric Geddes became the new chairman, with Sir George Beharrell as managing director. Because of their close involvement in the reorganization and their standing as professional accountants, it was recommended in the Directors' Report for May 1924 that Whinney, Smith & Whinney be appointed as joint auditors[15] with Stokes Bros & Pim, the Dublin firm that had been associated with Dunlops since its foundation in 1896.[16]

Important operational and managerial changes followed. The Directors' Report for 1925 opened on a confident note: 'the business of the company throughout the year 1924 has shown a great expansion.... The concentration of manufacture at Fort

Dunlop [Birmingham] ... is practically completed with the resultant economies ... it has been necessary to increase capacity at Fort Dunlop',[17] while the sales, manufacturing and accounting departments had been reorganized and more successfully integrated.

That Whinney, Smith & Whinney should have secured the audit of Imperial Airways shortly afterwards was not very suprising. Besides the fact that Sir Eric Geddes and Sir George Beharrell were directors of the two companies and Sir Eric chairman of both, Dunlops had long maintained a connection with Imperial Airways and the aeronautical industry in general. From 1912 Dunlop Rubber manufactured aircraft fabrics, diversifying into parts including wheels, tyres, brakes, cables, hoses, valves, engine and instrument mountings.[18] In 1924 the directors of Imperial Airways held their early meetings in Dunlops' boardroom, so in many ways it was quite natural that Whinney, Smith & Whinney should be recommended as their auditors, a post which they continued to hold until 1939 when they became auditors of its successor, B.O.A.C. (see p. 206).

The trend in the 1920s towards larger organizations with their sophisticated internal management structures also demanded new accounting techniques. The most common approach then adopted was the holding company–subsidiary arrangement,[19] by which the principal company held the stocks or shares of another and, while controlling its major undertakings, left it free to run its daily transactions. Accounts were needed in a form which would satisfy two distinct parties: the investor who required a clear picture of the earnings of the whole group to judge its overall viability and 'the holding company which needed safeguards against disclosures that might help [more secretive] competitors'.[20] Although the publication of audited profit and loss accounts did not become a statutory requirement until 1948, the 1929 Companies Act began to develop the concept of minimum disclosure.[21] However, its requirements remained limited (company balance sheets were required to distinguish between fixed floating assets, to show balances for several named intangible and fictitious assets, to provide a small amount of information concerning subsidiaries) and called for the inclusion of the directors' report but did not compel consolidated accounts. As a result company accounts remained, in general, exceptionally vague throughout the 1920s and 1930s. For example, in order to conceal

information contained in the directors' report one device commonly followed was to paste the printed accounts on to the
annual return so that only the side containing the balance sheet
and the audit report could be seen.[22] The words 'Not for Publication' were often printed on the accounts sent to the Stock Exchange. In addition, there are numerous examples where directors
filed less information with the Registrar of Companies than they
had presented to the shareholders, all of which suggests that certain businessmen wished to restrict the amount of financial information available to the public.[23] What is suprising, therefore, is
not that the Royal Mail Steam Packet Company should have
been prosecuted in 1931 in a case which centred on the issue of
disclosure, but that many other businesses should not have been
taken to court as well. In a sense the Royal Mail offenders were
selected as an example to encourage the others.

In fact the Hatry affair in 1929, which preceded the Royal Mail
case, had provided an earlier reminder that legislation was needed
to improve company reporting. In 1929 Clarence Hatry had attempted to buy the United Steel Company for £5 million but,
on failing to raise all the capital by fair means, he issued forged
local authority securities retaining the money so obtained.[24] He
was forced to confess when the banks got nervous and refused to
lend further funds to Austin Friars Trust, a key company in the
Hatry group, which had delayed publication of its annual report
before the collapse to conceal its grave financial position from the
investing public.[25] The case, in which Sir Basil Mayhew appeared
as an expert witness for the defence, simply highlighted the inadequacies of government controls and Stock Exchange rules for
enforcing deadlines for the publication of reports to shareholders
and what was to be contained within them. Hatry himself was
sentenced to fourteen years imprisonment for forgery and fraud.
Sir Gilbert Garnsey of Price Waterhouse, to whom he had con-
fessed, was given the difficult task of sorting out the financial
labyrinth that he left behind.

However, the major legal case of the inter-war period that
turned on questions of accounting concerned the Royal Mail
Steam Packet Company. The shipping line had fallen into difficulties in the late 1920s inevitably as a result of the depression in
world trade but also because the Hatry collapse had made the City
nervous of similarly structured financial groupings, amongst
which Lord Kylsant's vast shipping interests provided a prime

example.[26] The group had been assembled and maintained by a complex system of cross-shareholdings and inter-company loans, such that few could really be sure of the strength or stability of the empire. In order to try to buttress failing confidence in the company, the directors established an advisory committee of eminent City men a few weeks before the 1929 annual general meeting. It included F. Hyde, Managing Director of the Midland Bank, and Sir William McLintock representing the Treasury.[27] Although the committee helped to restore some faith in the group, trade continued to deteriorate and its position worsened until Kylsant was summoned in 1931 to face charges of publishing accounts that he knew to be false. After Kylsant's imprisonment, McLintock was entrusted with the unravelling of the group's tangled financial skein in order that it could be reconstructed and set on a sounder footing. Such was McLintock's skill in rearranging the affairs of the shipping line that one of its creditors, the Belfast Bank, then looking for a major City firm of auditors, appointed his practice as such in 1935.[28]

The Royal Mail case was instrumental in publicizing the inadequacies of the 1929 legislation and, as will be seen, prompted many companies to improve their accounting procedures. Briefly, Lord Kylsant, chairman of the shipping line, and the company's auditor, H. J. Morland, a partner in Price Waterhouse, were accused of deliberately misleading shareholders as to the true state of the company's financial position. The line had been doing badly since 1921 and from 1926 Kylsant, with the knowledge of the auditor, had been transferring large sums from undisclosed internal reserves to help pay dividends.[29] Neither the resulting loss of capital nor the company's true trading losses were disclosed in the annual accounts, though Morland had given them an unqualified opinion. Both Kylsant and Morland, charged under the 1861 Larceny Act (the first time such a case had been brought under criminal law and the first time that an auditor had been held responsible for the veracity of published accounts), were accused of preparing statements of account which they knew to be false with the intent to deceive the shareholders. On this count they were both acquitted. Kylsant, however, received a twelve-month prison sentence for preparing a prospectus for a debenture issue which concealed the true position of the company. Under the 1929 Act the auditor was merely required to say whether a balance sheet showed a 'true and correct' view (as distinct from the 'true and fair' view ordered by the 1948 Act), which the Royal Mail accounts satisfied, although they would not have complied with the later requirement.[30]

The real controversy surrounding the case did not concern the actual movement of cash from reserves to pay dividends but whether this transfer should be disclosed. In the Royal Mail accounts Morland, on his own initiative, had added the phrase 'including ... adjustment of taxation reserves' to describe the transfer.[31] Recent research into twelve iron and steel companies has shown that the creation of reserves was a widespread practice and that their secret use was also common.[32] Indeed the Royal Mail's reserve had initially been formed after an over-generous provision for estimated Excess Profits Duty. After the tax had been paid the balance was retained for use in tougher times. It has been argued that this occurrence was so common as to suggest that some managers deliberately overestimated their liability for tax in order later to create a sinking fund or undisclosed reserve.[33]

Whilst Morland was found not guilty, the judgement nevertheless indicated that more was expected from an auditor in his review of published accounts and that he would, in future, be viewed as an independent arbiter to whom the investor could look for protection and guidance. The auditor's importance in a world of increasingly complex accountancy (where the shareholder could not always be expected to understand the arithmetic) was growing and his responsibilities followed accordingly. The Royal Mail case brought an end to the respectability of secret reserves, businesses for the most part apparently disclosing such transfers afterwards.[34] 'Following the Kylsant case', wrote de Paula, 'several companies immediately proceeded to re-design the form and presentation of their accounts ... showing separately any extraneous items which do not represent current earnings or charges.'[35] Although the English Institute argued for a tightening of the 1929 Act, the government failed to respond. The Stock Exchange issued a requirement in 1939 for listed companies to prepare consolidated accounts, but it proved abortive with the declaration of war and it was not until the 1948 Act that adequate provision was made for consolidation and the preparation of meaningful profit and loss accounts.[36]

The Anglo-Persian Oil Company produced some of the earliest consolidated accounts dating from 1929, although they were not included in the published reports until 1948.[37] Even then the problems created by the complexity of the company's overseas operations meant that a partial consolidation (excluding overseas companies' accounts) had to suffice in the short term, although a Group Income Statement was published in 1956. The first form of partially consolidated accounts – comprising the balance sheets of the parent company and its principal subsidiaries – was drawn up by the Anglo-Persian's Management Accounts section in 1929 (possibly with the assistance of the auditors, Brown, Fleming & Murray), being intended simply as an aid to management. Depreciation figures were not quoted until legally required by the 1948 Companies Act. By contrast the Distillers Company reports included depreciation figures from 1931 to 1935 (doubtless added as a result of the Kylsant case) but withdrew them until their disclosure was required by the 1948 Act.[38] Fully consolidated statements were published by Distillers from 1945, three years before they became a legal requirement. Edwards' conclusion from his study of published accounting statements in the iron and steel industry that 'differences between companies were more marked than differences over time' probably reflects British business as a whole in the inter-war period.[39]

The same study of the published accounts of twelve iron and steel companies demonstrated that depreciation charges were by no means always made, a point which caused the auditors, Peat, Marwick, Mitchell, to qualify the accounts of Samuel Fox & Co every year from 1929 to 1939. Several businesses simply charged a proportion of their profits rather than make provision for the needs of their plant.[40] Perhaps the most revealing conclusion from this examination concerns the Wigan Coal & Iron Co's balance sheet, which from 1869 until 1928 was presented in the same format, that recommended in the model articles attached to the 1856 Companies Act.[41] The fact that their balance sheet compared well with those for other businesses suggests a lack of technical development in the published accounts of large areas of British industry.

In Britain, the first known published consolidated balance sheet was produced for December 1920 by Nobel Industries in September 1922. Under Sir Josiah Stamp (who had been a member of Sir Arthur Whinney's Dunlop investigation team) a unified accountancy system was developed at their Central Secretarial Department in 1923 to show the financial results of all companies in the group on a common basis.[42] Indeed, Nobel Industries were novel not only in introducing important accountancy techniques, but also in demonstrating the viability of new management structures for merged businesses. Routine functional responsibilities such as purchasing, personnel, publicity, legal, taxation and investment matters were centralized at Nobel House, while subsidiaries operated largely as autonomous bodies, each having delegate directors who served on the main working committees of the Nobel Board. When I.C.I. took over Nobel Industries in 1926, Nobel's managers occupied strategically important posts and had an influence over I.C.I.'s enlarged management structure.[43] Not surprisingly, therefore, I.C.I. was among those companies that introduced consolidated accounts before they became legally necessary.

Notwithstanding the Nobel example, where consolidation had been confined to the balance sheet, the major step forward in the adoption and publication of consolidated accounts for the shareholders was taken at Dunlop Rubber by F. R. M. de Paula, their Chief Accountant and later Controller of Finance, who extended the principle to the profit and loss account.[44] De Paula, originally a chartered accountant in private practice, had served under Sir Eric Geddes in the Ministry of Munitions during the First World War where George Beharrell had been his immediate superior in the Statistical Section. When Sir Eric Geddes was posted to France as Director-General of Transportation with Beharrell as his second-in-command, de Paula became the latter's Assistant.[45] Returning to his practice, in 1926 he was appointed to the part-time Chair of Accountancy at the London School of Economics. Here de Paula developed his ideas on consolidated accounts, stressing their utility in mitigating the managerial diseconomies of scale sometimes encountered within merged enterprises by securing centralization of control with decentralization of responsibilities.[46] In 1930 Geddes and Beharrell asked him to join Dunlops so that he might put his seminal theories into practical effect. In March 1934, after discussions with Sidney Mearns, Whinney, Smith & Whinney's partner-in-charge of the audit, de Paula submitted Dunlops' 1933 accounts in consolidated form to the board, arguing in the attached memorandum that[47]

the effect of these proposals is that the Company discloses the whole of its reserves and presents the whole of its financial position in as informative a manner as is possible.... These proposals have the entire approval of the Company's auditors.

The method that de Paula drew up in 1934 has been described

as 'a landmark in accountancy history.'[48] Reasoning that, if the principle of consolidation were confined to the balance sheet alone, then a large part of its practical value was lost, he added that 'it is necessary to see on the one hand the earnings and on the other hand the financial position of the whole group . . . [making] it possible to judge whether the aggregate earnings represent a reasonable return upon the total invested in the group'.[49] Accordingly, Dunlop Rubber's profit and loss account for the year ending December 1933 contained a note stating that 'the profits [and losses] of subsidiary companies are included . . . to the extent of dividends declared',[50] while a detailed consolidated statement of assets and liabilities was attached, which had also been reported upon by the auditors. A further innovation in March 1938 was the inclusion of a statement of comparative profits over a period of five years, 1933–37, 'to enable shareholders to obtain a clear view of the main trends in the company's financial position'.[51]

The Dunlop example had an important effect on British business. Writing the third edition of his *Holding Companies and their Published Accounts* in 1936, Sir Gilbert Garnsey noted,[52]

since the first edition of this book [1923] . . . considerable progress had been made in Great Britain in the common appreciation of consolidated statements. . . How far their real merits are realized outside the ranks of accountants, the financial press and finance houses, it is difficult to say, but . . . there is a greater demand for it nowadays.

In fact the New York Stock Exchange in 1919 had encouraged the presentation of either statements of all constituent companies or consolidated accounts, a practice already in evidence.[53] At the initial annual general meeting of the United States Steel Corporation in 1902, Price Waterhouse under Arthur Lowes Dickinson, on being elected as their first auditors, produced the first public consolidated balance sheet in America.[54] This precedence over Britain in accountancy techniques accurately reflected America's earlier merger movement and corresponding introduction of sophisticated management structures to cope with the new multi-unit enterprises.

Other industrial organizations brought additional work to British accountants. The rise of trusts, cartels, trade associations and other business combinations demanded financial control and guidance which increasingly became the responsibility of accountants. For example, in the early 1920s Lever Brothers operated an agreement with Brunner, Mond & Co over the supply of soap to the latter's customer, the Co-operative Wholesale Society. Brunner, Mond's auditors, as neutral professionals, were entrusted with the task of monitoring its observance. Unfortunately Brunner, Mond proved false, preparing bogus invoices to the C.W.S. intended to deceive the auditors so that they could undercut Lever Brothers by rebates on other goods.[55]

F. W. Bailey, who had opened Whinney, Smith & Whinney's Leeds office in 1926, derived a considerable amount of work from his secretaryship of trade associations, including Roadstone, Phenol Producers' Association (1927) and Cresylic Acid Refiners' Association (1945). Similarly Frederick Woolley of Woolley & Waldron in Southampton and W.D. Montgomery of Whinney, Smith & Whinney's Manchester office undertook such tasks. However, the general view, voiced here by Soames Forsyte, that 'unscrupulous trusts and combinations had been cornering the market in goods of all kinds and keeping prices at an artificial height',[56] influenced the government and a committee of inquiry was held to test whether they did in fact act in a monopolistic fashion. The law remained unchanged until long after the Second World War when many trade associations were barred from certain practices by the 1956 Restrictive Trade Practices Act and as a result some accountants lost valuable work, though, as Bailey recalled, the lengthy legal disputes leading to the decision did bring consultancy fees.

Larger and more complicated business organizations, such as those produced by the 1920 merger movement, in turn created a demand for more rigorous methods of financial assessment and management information.[57] Accountants, as independent expert observers having experience denied to most directors and possessing skills now more readily appreciated, were increasingly recruited into the ranks of management. In the nineteenth century they had occasionally been invited to sit on boards, generally in a non-executive capacity, valued simply for their expert knowledge in book-keeping. In 1913 a substantial majority of English accountants were in private practice, but by 1939 over half of them were in the direct employ of business.[58] Even so their potential was not always recognized, as de Paula argued in 1926, 'the chief accountant should not be merely the head book-keeper but he should be the chief financial officer of the concern, being responsible to the general manager for the whole ... finances of the business and its financial control'.[59] Nevertheless the 1920s witnessed some accountants rising to serve in the highest echelons of management. For example, Francis D'Arcy Cooper resigned as a partner in Cooper Brothers to join the board of Levers in 1923, becoming chairman two years later on the founder's death.[60] When the newly merged Unilever was formed in 1929, Cooper initiated a policy of consolidation and rationalization of subsidiaries, at the same time centralizing a number of functions in the London headquarters.[61]

Vickers provide a further case where accountants were called to play a critical role in a company's development. Financial crisis had hit Vickers in the summer of 1925 when orders for new shipping fell, prompting the board to invite Dudley Docker, Reginald McKenna, Chairman of the Midland Bank, and Sir William Plender to advise them on the best course of action, by their prestige and experience convincing the shareholders of its suitability.[62] In 1921-22 a detailed investigation had been undertaken by Mark Webster-Jenkinson, an independent accountant with a special knowledge of armaments production gained during the First World War when employed by the Ministry of Munitions. Webster-Jenkinson's far-reaching recommendations – decentralization of control by splitting the company into four or more groups by product (rolling stock, cars, shipbuilding, armaments) to ascertain the book value of their assets and divide the capital up accordingly – had been ignored but now, three years later, were revived and his advice sought.[63] However, Webster-Jenkinson modified his original plan, suggesting that the company be divided according to function rather than product. In the event, Vickers' situation was such that a merger with Armstrongs was arranged and the detailed financial arrangements fell to a committee of three composed of James Frater Taylor, another accountant with industrial experience who had been investigating Armstrongs, Webster-Jenkinson for Vickers and Sir William Plender representing the Bank of England which provided financial support for the enterprise.[64]

In 1909 F. W. Woolworth, a highly successful American business, decided to extend operations to Britain, opening their first shop in Liverpool, with others following a year later in Preston, Manchester, Leeds and Hull.[65] Having established a successful base, the company moved to London in 1919 and, probably through the firm's solicitors, were introduced to Baker, Sutton, who became their auditors. The latter then helped them to find the necessary finance for their rapid expansion programme (producing by 1929 766 shops in Britain) by recommending F. W. Woolworth to the National Provincial Bank and in 1931 were responsible for the company's floatation on the Stock Exchange. This resulted in the formation of Baker, Sutton's share registration department as the firm was entrusted with the setting up and maintenance of the Woolworth share register.

This growing influence of accountants was probably not explained so much by the fact that directors reconsidered their traditional prejudice against accountants, as that circumstances conspired to compel their employment in strategic points of business where their usefulness was recognized. The unprecedented size and complexity of the merged companies brought new financial problems which were often beyond the grasp of many managers. For instance, when Lord Cozens-Hardy took over the chairmanship of Pilkingtons in 1931, he not only reorganized their managing committees but engaged a number of accountants to introduce a system of budgetary controls.[66] In practice this fell to the company's chief accountant, P. L. Robson, who, having studied the budgetary controls devised by de Paula at Dunlops, brought the proposals to fruition in January 1933. The growing influence of Pilkingtons' accountants was a particular feature of the inter-war period. Robson's standing was especially high for he had just saved the company a considerable amount of unnecessary taxation by altering the existing procedure of charging a fixed annual rate of depreciation on capital assets to charging the actual cost of replacement in a given financial year. The Inland Revenue made allowances for depreciation and there was a large amount of dead wood that could be written off at a stroke.[67]

At I.C.I., on the prompting of their auditor Sir William McLintock, the company began a massive programme of writing off under-used plant – some £22.3 million being written off at their Billingham fertilizer works between 1931 and 1934 because of gross over-capacity.[68] That McLintock was able to persuade the board of its necessity, is a measure of the auditor's growth in influence. Courtaulds provide yet another instance of an accountant playing a major part in long-term planning. R. A. Kinnes, who had left Price Waterhouse to become their Chief Accountant in 1935, raised the possibility of breaking down Courtaulds into a number of subsidiary operating companies linked together by a holding company to control policy and finance.[69] Although the proposal had been rejected in 1938-39, Kinnes persevered and in 1943 asked Price Waterhouse to prepare a report on the proposition. Despite their favourable verdict, the idea was shelved until Kinnes' persistent pressure secured its ultimate approval in January 1947.[70]

There follow three cases of accountants aiding vital management decisions, the first helping a manufacturing company to expand in the face of acute financial difficulties, the second developing various schemes to try to save an insolvent business and the third creating an entirely new enterprise. They serve to illustrate not only the degree to which accountants were involved in business but also the range of tasks which they were asked to perform in the inter-war period.

The first example concerns Sir Basil Mayhew's consultancy work for Bowaters. In response to the growing demand for newsprint, which had stimulated Eric Bowater's desire for expansion, in 1923 the company decided to build a new paper mill at Northfleet.[71] However, delays to its completion combined with Eric Bowater's inexperience in financial matters put the company under great strain, such that in 1925-26 there was no certainty that the business would survive. Of the greatest importance in the long run was the decision to change the auditors.[72] Instead of Messrs Touche, in January 1926 they appointed Blackburns, Barton, Mayhew and by doing so obtained the professional services of Sir Basil Mayhew.[73] One of Bowater's talents was his ability to select proficient advisers so that with Arthur Baker, an engineer, dealing with technical matters and Sir Basil Mayhew guiding financial affairs, the company narrowly pulled through. On the latter's suggestion a new company, W. V. Bowater & Sons (1926) Ltd, was formed to take over the old merchant business and raise fresh preferred capital on the stock market. Given the business's uncertain position this was not easy and it only succeeded when John Keeling (a close friend of Harold Barton, a fellow Yorkshireman) of the London & Yorkshire Trust agreed to underwrite the issue. Mayhew was also instrumental in negotiating with Armstrongs, the mill contractors, the financial arrangements for the much delayed and partially complete buildings. Bowaters' survival depended on both the final sum and the method of payment. Sir Gilbert Garnsey, of Price Waterhouse, had been called in to represent Armstrongs and together they agreed that a further £175,000 should be paid in cash, the remainder in securities.[74] Thus Bowaters were just able to carry on.

In 1926 Sir Basil Mayhew had also been responsible for devising a general reconstruction scheme for Bowaters. It involved the formation of a Committee of Management which, as its first Minute Book recorded, witnessed important changes.[75]

A good deal of re-organization had already taken place, in particular the whole of the accountancy system and records had been centralized and ... the new scheme was working satisfactorily. There now remained the allocation of staff to the various positions outlined in the proposed organization of the Trading and Service Departments as it was to be noted that the Finance and Accounting Section had been re-arranged in accordance with the organization scheme.

In 1928, when looking for a new secretary and chief accountant, it was natural that Bowaters should ask a qualified member of Barton, Mayhew's staff to join them. Although Barton, Mayhew were reluctant to lose him, H. J. Inston was duly appointed from January 1928, also serving as a member of the Committee of Management,[76] and in 1952 becoming Bowater's Director of Finance.

This was not the only example of Barton, Mayhew losing qualified staff to industry. Through Sir Basil Mayhew's friendship with Sir David Milne-Watson, Governor of the Gas Light & Coke Company, the firm came in 1930 to perform a major reorganization of its accounting procedures, while also advising groups of tar distillers and creosote producers on national marketing schemes. A. E. Sylvester, a partner, having been involved in the investigation, left the firm to become the Gas Light & Coke Co's financial Comptroller and its Managing Director in 1942, rising after nationalization to be chairman of the Gas Council. Indeed, Sir Basil Mayhew retired from the practice in 1936 when the Colman family (into which his second marriage had taken him) needed his expert knowledge as a director, having encountered the Colmans through their ownership of two provincial newspapers, the *East Anglian Daily Times* and *Norfolk News*, which Barton, Mayhew audited.

The second example concerned the insolvency of the Belsize Motor Company at Clayton, Manchester, and involved Charles Palmour, a partner in Whinney, Smith & Whinney. The slump in 1921-22, combined with a 'disastrous lock-out during the 14 weeks of the best selling period during the year',[77] had forced the Midland Bank to call in the receivers, Sir Thomas Smethurst (a local Manchester accountant) and C. J. G. Palmour (Whinney, Smith & Whinney were known to the Midland as their auditors) who were jointly appointed in April 1923. The two then prepared a scheme of reconstruction by which Thomas Smethurst & Co would act as the new company's auditors and a chartered accountant, Mark Webster-Jenkinson (an industrial consultant then company secretary to the Electric & Railway Finance Company), as its chairman. Despite their efforts the business did poorly in 1924-25. Outstanding debts were not settled and sales of new cars were down, '... being required to sell fifteen a week ... their sales during the last four weeks were 14, 14, 6 and 11'.[78] Consequently Sir Arthur Whinney was appointed receiver and in 1926 the company was finally wound-up. As the voluminous correspondence reveals, a great deal of work had gone into Belsize's reconstruction, involving detailed discussions with engineers about the viability of its automobiles, the Excess Profits Duty outstanding and the ways in which the business could be reconstituted. It was unfortunate that recovery in the long term could not be effected.

Because Whinney, Smith & Whinney enjoyed this close connection with the Midland Bank, they were repeatedly called upon to perform special tasks for the bank's clients. In 1933, for example, they were asked to assist in devising a scheme for the amalgamation of companies engaged in the cotton industry.[79] In the light of the previous decade of 'extreme depression, owing to the capacity of the industry having exceeded the available trade', Whinney, Smith & Whinney proposed a programme of centralization and rationalization so that a 'controlling or parent company shall be formed to acquire management and control of each of the companies ... to join the amalgamation'. As was usual in such schemes, the holding company would be entitled to the trading profits and make all the policy decisions relating to members of the group. Here, therefore, was another situation unheard of in the nineteenth century, where a firm of accountants was being requested not simply to check a company's books, but to arrange a complete scheme of merger and reorganization which placed them at the very root of managerial decision-making.

The third case concerns the development of an entirely new enterprise and features Ivan Spens [1890-1964], senior partner of Brown, Fleming & Murray in London, and his client, the New Trading Company, founded by Siegmund Warburg in 1934 and later to form the nucleus of S. G. Warburg & Co, established in 1946. The Warburgs, a family of merchant bankers in Hamburg with a history dating back to the late eighteenth century, coming under increasing pressure during the 1930s from the hostile political climate, expanded their activities abroad.[80] While Eric Warburg established a bank in New York,[81] Siegmund emigrated from Germany in 1933. In London he was introduced to Ivan Spens by Dr Hans Schaeffer of the reorganized Kreuger group – with which Spens had been involved (see p. 176). When Siegmund Warburg eventually formed the New Trading Company after consultations with Spens, it was natural that Brown, Fleming & Murray should be appointed as its auditors. Moreover, both Spens and R. N. Gooch also served as personal advisers to its board. When, for instance, Siegmund Warburg sought general business advice he normally went first to Spens and Gooch for their opinions, often arranging in his meetings with the Bank of England to be joined by the former.

Finally a general point ought to be made about accountants and business in the inter-war period. It has recently been suggested that the major reason for Britain's lag behind America (in the timing of mergers, the creation of sophisticated organizations which necessitated the employment of accountants in financial and costing exercises) was the essential difference in the scale and structure of their markets.[82] In a large and industrially young such as America, the visible hand of the manager was needed to create integrated groups if businesses were to operate productively. In Britain, a compact island with efficient and well-developed markets, it was not necessary to erect complex managerial hierarchies. Here suppliers, manufacturers and distributors tended to be sited close together and could operate efficiently, negating the necessity for companies to integrate and diversify as extensively as in the United States. It is an interesting and plausible argument, which could go a long way to explaining Britain's apparent sluggishness to adopt the latest managerial techniques and reluctance to employ accountants in critical areas of industry.

Following the First World War, taxation took an increasing part of accountants' time, initially with the final settlement of Excess Profits Duty claims. As Ernest Whinney recalled, before 1914 tax and death duties 'were of small consequence and clients paid without the need of professional advice'. Since then, their magnitude and complexity had increased, the standard rate being increased from 1/2d in 1914 to 6/- in 1919.[83] Whinney, Smith & Whinney increasingly dealt with personal and business tax clients: in 1918 only 2.5% (£685) of their fee income fell into these categories.[84] Although the volume of personal tax work grew, it remained of minor importance when set beside their audit clients and in 1939 produced a mere 6.3% of fees, £3,702. This small percentage increase is more significant when it is considered that the general level of income tax fell throughout the war period, being brought down from 6 shillings in 1922 to 4 shillings in the pound between 1926 and 1930. Increases in the late 1930s (rising to 5/6 in 1939) were largely to pay for rearmament. In fact, not until after the Second World War did taxation assume substantial proportions in its own right. It ought, however, to be mentioned that the audit category in Table II (see p. 99) did, on occasion, include an element of taxation advice which was not ferentiated in the fees charged, so that the taxation percentages are in fact a slight understatement of the work performed. Whinney, Smith & Whinney, Barton, Mayhew and Brown, Fleming & Murray (in London) all set up separate specialist departments to deal with these matters in the inter-war years, Turquand, Youngs following suit in the 1950s.

These, therefore, were the major reasons why certain City accountancy firms prospered in a period of widespread economic difficulty. This very prosperity encouraged geographical expansion, bringing these practices into some of the most depressed areas of the country, while the continued growth of their largest clients created pressure to open provincial offices to serve them more effectively. Whinney, Smith & Whinney's first regional office was opened by F. W. Bailey, who had been articled with Charles F. Cape & Co, at Leeds in May 1926, occupying rooms on the second floor of the Yorkshire Penny Bank Head Office in Infirmary Street. In 1922, on the recommendation of the Midland Bank, who were among its leading shareholders, Whinney, Smith & Whinney had been appointed joint auditors of the Yorkshire Penny Bank with Smithson, Blackburn & Co of Leeds. On the death of the latter's sole partner, Mr Close, Whinney, Smith & Whinney became sole auditors, but the bank, then a purely Yorkshire concern, insisted that their auditors be resident in Leeds – hence Bailey's move north. In addition, the firm audited a number of landed estates which could be more effectively handled from Leeds than from London:[85] Lord Scarbrough's Wormersley Estate, the Welbeck Estates, the Earl of Harewood's Estates and the Duke of Buccleuch's Furness Estate.[86]

Two years later, in 1928, Whinney, Smith & Whinney opened

an office in Manchester. Unlike the case in Leeds, the decision was made to unite with an established, local firm, Thomas Smethurst & Co. Sir Thomas Smethurst, its senior partner and a former Lord Mayor of Manchester, wanted to retire but had no obvious successor. Whinney, Smith & Whinney wished to open a Manchester office to serve Dunlop Rubber (then a large and growing client with substantial plants and mills in Lancashire) more effectively. A merger with Smethurst had the advantage of providing a nucleus of local clients, a respected name and an introduction to the city's commercial world. Bailey, by comparison, had started almost from scratch in Leeds, building up his practice from professional contacts and friends; he recalled that Mr B. Lomas-Walker, a solicitor with Booth & Co, and the Yorkshire Penny Bank were both valuable sources of new work. As has been seen, Whinney, Smith & Whinney first encountered Smethurst through the Belsize Motors receivership. Soon afterwards various draft schemes for the sale of Smethurst's practice changed hands and a new partnership arrangement was concluded in October 1928.[87] As a result, W. D. Montgomery, a partner, was sent from London to take charge of the Manchester office, now called Whinney, Smethurst & Co.

Smethurst's practice was characterized by the three areas with which he had been most closely associated. Being born and brought up in Middleton, he was secretary of the Middleton Agricultural Society and audited the Middleton Corporation, the Heywood and Middleton Water Board and a number of businesses there. As Lord Mayor of Manchester he acquired a spread of city clients including the London & Manchester Oyster Company, the Railway Ticket Bureau, the Manchester Ship Canal, Port of Manchester Warehouses and the Mineral Water Association, and was secretary to a number of trade associations. Later he moved to Lytham on the Fylde coast and secured the audit of the Blackpool Tower Company and the Blackpool Ice Company, acted for a number of music-hall artists (including George Formby and Charlie Cairoli) and audited many theatres – the Manchester Palace of Varieties, the Queen's Hydro at Blackpool, the Empire, Preston, the Salford Palace, the Queen's, Alderley, and the Grand Theatre, Hanley.[88] The cotton industry formed an important proportion of his audit clients and although some (McKerracher & Sons, Sea Island Mills, Rivington Mill & Co, Duxburys Ltd and William Smith & Co [Preston]) were mills, he was more concerned with the merchanting and brokerage of the trade. J. Hobson & Co, A. J. Smethurst & Co and J. B. Beardsell amongst these provided some of the largest fees. Other local business clients included W. T. Rothwell and J. W. Lees (both brewers), Openshaw Brewery, J. W. & R. Healing & Co (rope makers), Mark Fletcher & Sons and Chadwick & Smith (both dyers and finishers of cloth) and I. H. Morris & Co (yarn agents).

Another firm that had also captured an entertainment niche in accountancy was Baker, Sutton in London. In 1916 they had a considerable number of theatres as clients – the Coronation Electric, Variety Theatres, Fredericks Electric Theatre, New Tivoli, Loughborough Playhouse, Empress Theatre of Varieties and the Prince's Theatre together with Artistic Novelties, Syndicate Varieties, Fredericks Belton Park Cinema and Boro' Theatre Billposting Co[89] to which by 1937 had been added the Regal chain of cinemas, Universal Cinemas, the Rotherhithe Hippodrome, the Garrick and Aldwych Theatres, together with the Margate Hippodrome, the last being acquired in 1923. This particular speciality was largely the result of contacts provided by an earlier client, A. E. Abrahams, an advertising company with extensive theatre interests.

In 1937 Montgomery was able to report of Whinney, Smith & Whinney's Manchester office that 'things are going ahead smoothly ... we had a considerable amount of work on the Dunlop audit this year, having taken over the audit of the footwear division at Liverpool, as well as certain work on two subsidiary companies at Manchester. The work on the Brigg's Tyre Group [which has since grown to become National Tyre Services] is also increasing and we have recently been engaged on a share valuation in connection with the proposed purchases of an additional holding for Dunlop.'[91] Finally, he added, 'there can be no doubt that conditions are improving in Manchester and even the cotton trade [a particularly depressed industry] is beginning to feel the benefit'.[92] Today the specialist textile character (the merchants, mill owners and cotton brokers that typified the client lists) has disappeared as the industry declined and experienced amalgamations. Only two cotton mills remain on the office's books, while electronics and general manufacturing have taken their place, reflecting the metamorphosis in Lancashire's industrial structure.

In Manchester three other firms of Victorian ancestry have

merged by various paths to form the present Ernst & Whinney office, each by the 1920s exhibiting some specialism which characterized the city's industrial and commercial life.* Parkinson, Mather & Co (founded in the 1860s by John Mather, son of William Mather, owner of the Salford Iron Works) was strongly orientated towards engineering and included Chloride, Ferrodo and Reynolds Chains amongst its audit clients. Trotter, Davies & Yearsley (founded by J. Townley Trotter in 1870) had a number of Jewish clients and was particularly strong in merchant houses, while the third, Shuttleworth & Haworth (founded c. 1870s), had a wide range of clients with concentrations in textiles and engineering.

Barton, Mayhew similarly expanded into the depressed north by merger with a local practice. In 1919 they amalgamated with H. W. & J. Blackburn, a Bradford practice with a branch in Leeds. Harold Barton and J. H. Blackburn, both of them Yorkshiremen involved with the English Institute, knew each other, and the latter, in old age, wishing to introduce some younger partners, proposed a merger; Barton, who had served under Leonard Coates in the Aircraft Costings Department, suggested that he too might join the practice. Blackburns had been established in 1844, having close associations with the English Institute – J. H. Blackburn had served on the Council for a record fifty-one years.[93] However, the merger proved in certain respects unsatisfactory and on expiry in 1929 was not renewed, Blackburns continuing through growth to become Blackburns, Robson, Coates & Co.

The opening of Buckley & Hall's Leeds office provides a further example of an accountancy firm following a client. W. B. Hall had married into a family closely connected with the West Yorkshire mining industry, which led to his being offered the audit of one of its smaller colliery companies, Robert Holliday & Sons. It was soon realized that such work could not be undertaken properly from Hull and accordingly an office was opened in Pearl Chambers, East Parade, Leeds, in 1924 under a manager, F. E. Holroyd, later to become a partner. The occasion was taken to change the firm's style to Buckley, Hall, Devin & Co, the

---

* Parkinson, Mather & Co merged with Barton, Mayhew in 1967, and Shuttleworth & Haworth in 1970, while Trotter, Davies & Yearsley joined Turquands Barton Mayhew in 1972 but left Ernst & Whinney in 1980.

Hull office later following suit. Because of its knowledge of the coal industry the Leeds office worked in collaboration with Thomson McLintock on the audit of the subvention given to the mining industry after the General Strike of 1926. When steps were taken in 1931 to amalgamate Holliday & Sons with a neighbouring colliery, Crawshaw & Warburton, to be undertaken according to a scheme prepared by W. B. Hall, this was opposed by a trustee in the bankruptcy of a former shareholder. The scheme, endorsed in the Railway and Canal Committee Court, was described by Mr Justice MacKinnon as being 'the most masterly document he had ever seen' conducted 'with the greatest possible ability, but with conspicuous fairness and industry'.[94] This public judgement did much to establish Buckley, Hall, Devin as auditors connected with the mining industry, further colliery clients being acquired including the Henry Briggs group. Nationalization of the coal industry (see p. 201) brought an end to this audit work, but in its place there was a considerable involvement in the allocation of compensation and subsequent liquidations. By the time this work was complete William Powell had become partner-in-charge of the Leeds office, which, largely at his instigation, merged with Whinney Murray in 1971, two years before the Hull office followed suit.

Ernst & Whinney's present Leeds office is the product of three additional mergers: in 1960 with Alfred Dobson & Co, in 1965 with A. E. Ellison & Co, and in 1971 with Smith & Garton, who also had a larger office in Huddersfield. The first was founded in 1922 and grew as a general practice based upon worsted mills, small engineering and textile businesses, farmers and personal tax clients in Leeds and its surrounding districts. Insolvencies were also a feature, the firm being responsible for liquidating Industrial Builders Ltd, who had been responsible for the erection of Quarry Hill Estate, a Le Corbusier-type experiment in the late 1930s to provide housing in 938 flats. Smith & Garton at Huddersfield, whose origins lie in the 1870s, like Wallace & Somerville in Edinburgh, was a firm with a strong local government connection. G. W. Smith acted as treasurer to the Kirkburton District Council, while Smith & Garton audited the Huddersfield and Brighouse County Borough Councils. Although a general practice, they enjoyed a strong link with road haulage in Huddersfield and Halifax, the office at the former dealing with as many as twenty hauliers – a few returning after de-nationalization in early

1950s – while their smaller-scale Leeds office had a number of East Riding gravel quarries as clients.

Not only did favourably situated City accountancy firms expand into the depressed areas of Britain, but young accountants left these regions of adversity for the South East in a general search for employment and brighter prospects. Glasgow, like Newcastle, was a city whose fortunes were based on trade, shipbuilding and mining. All were in decline and work was difficult to find, not simply for artisans but also for those professions which derived fees from their masters. Unemployment reached 27.7% of the insured population of Scotland in 1932 in sharp contrast to the 13.7% experienced in London and the South East.[95] While Glasgow itself had a total of 89,600 unemployed in 1936, Birmingham, a town of comparable size, suffered only 21,000.[96] Doubtless this prompted the clearly discernible drift of professionally qualified Scotsmen south not only to expatriate firms but to many English practices as well. In 1919 Brown, Fleming & Murray followed Thomson McLintock's lead and opened a London office.[97] Both Glasgow firms had important clients with City headquarters and they were concerned not to lose their business. In 1915 the Anglo-Persian Oil Company transferred their accounts department from 175 West George Street, Glasgow (where they had shared accommodation with Brown, Fleming & Murray), to London, causing their auditors to follow suit four years later.[98] With the resumption of peace, Thomson McLintock's London office (which until then had been largely engaged on war work for the government) also expanded rapidly and soon overtook its Glasgow parent.[99] In 1919 their respective fee incomes were £13,000 and £28,000; by 1927 McLintock's, London, had taken the lead and in 1933 extended the gap still further, to £159,000 as against £37,000.[100] The fact that Glasgow's fee income fell between 1927 and 1933, while London's continued to grow, is further evidence of the tragic regional disparities that existed in Britain. In part this explains why businessmen and politicians based in the capital did not always appreciate the gravity of the slump and hence did little to ameliorate its effects.

Once established in the City, these Scottish practices carefully preserved their national character, following a long tradition of Scots business and banking. As has been seen, the English and Scottish Institutes had different origins, which reflected their teaching and outlook. Brown, Fleming & Murray trained almost exclusively Scottish chartered accountants partly because they were limited by the English Institute's rule that no partner could have more than four articled clerks. There then being only three partners, Spens, Baguley and Habben, the last two both English members, the firm was encouraged to enter apprentices for the Scottish Institutes' examinations where no such limitation applied. Subsequently the number and proportion of Scottish-qualified partners increased. Even when Englishmen were taken on as apprentices, they were often entered for the Glasgow Institute's examinations and this prompted the three Scottish Societies to agree to allow them to attend prescribed legal classes in place of the compulsory university courses.[101] A Brown, Fleming & Murray partner, Mr T. W. Macdonald, was an official tutor in the Scottish law papers in the 1930s. It was common for apprentices and young accountants to join Territorial regiments in this period and Brown, Fleming & Murray's staff almost exclusively enlisted in the London Scottish. Golf, a most popular sport in Scotland, was not only their way of relaxing, but also provided an opportunity for meeting clients in an informal atmosphere. Matches were regularly arranged with Anglo-Persian Oil (Anglo-Iranian after 1935), a company with similar Scottish origins.

More important, Brown, Fleming & Murray behaved in business as if they were still in Glasgow. The strong connection between the mercantile community and Glasgow accountants, together with their close involvement in finance houses, has been outlined (see p. 81). In London, Ivan Spens (senior partner from 1919, and brother of Colonel Hugh Spens, senior partner in the Glasgow solicitors Maclay, Murray & Spens and later a director of Burmah Oil[102]) brought the Scottish practice of financial involvement south. Following the tradition in Glasgow, the firm advised a number of investment trusts, setting up a specialist department to assist the London & Provincial, London & Clydesdale, Capital & National, Railway & General, London & Montrose, London & Holyrood, British Steamship and United British Securities. Many City accountants then frowned on the holding of directorships, whereas in Scotland (and the English provinces) this commitment at board level, in companies where the partners concerned were not the auditors, was considered important and valuable. Scottish accountants felt that the help they could offer to companies far outweighed any putative loss of impartiality. Accordingly Brown, Fleming & Murray's London partners held directorships in the Scottish manner despite the disapproval of their closest English neighbours.

This was the period when Brown, Fleming & Murray were sharing 4b Frederick's Place with Whinney, Smith & Whinney – the connection arising from R. A. Murray's friendship with Sir Arthur Whinney. Initially Brown, Fleming & Murray occupied premises at 35 Walbrook, EC4,[103] moving to 1 Broad Street Place, Finsbury Circus, in May 1920 and finally transferring to 4b Frederick's Place in March 1922. They started with a few rooms but grew to occupy the fifth, third, most of the second and ground floors, while Whinney, Smith & Whinney had the basement, first and second floors.[104]

Although Brown, Fleming & Murray's Rule Book (1925) prohibited spare-time work, one of the two exceptions allowed was that: 'a member can be an agent for an insurance company'.[105] Milne's *The Accountant in Public Practice*, published in 1959, recorded with disapproval that insurance work was still a 'common occurrence'.[106] The other was that 'a qualified member ... can accept any tutorial position in connection with the various classes for articled clerks' – and this was encouraged. Again, this was a particularly Scottish tradition and persisted in expatriate firms far longer than in the older City accountancy practices.

Having looked at firms in the depressed areas and those which extended their operations to London, it is necessary, to complete the picture, to examine practices situated in areas of industrial growth, such as the Midlands. C. Herbert Smith & Russell in Birmingham and A. C. Palmer & Co in Leicester provide examples in this category. In 1927 the former took over the practice of Powell, Jerome & Co and in doing so acquired the audits of Joseph Lucas (electrical component manufacturers), Mitchells & Butlers (brewers), Ratcliffs (Great Bridge) Ltd and Laughton & Sons. With the upsurge of the motor industry in the 1930s, Lucas, already a public company, experienced rapid growth which was, to an extent, accelerated by the financial advice offered by their auditors. C. Herbert Smith & Russell were also secretaries to a number of trade bodies including the Paper Box Association.

In Leicester, A. C. Palmer & Co developed two major specialisms, in insolvency work which generated more than half their fee income in the 1930s (see p. 238), and in the accountancy of the shoe-making industry. They acted as secretaries to four related bodies: the Footwear Components Federation, the Boot and Shoe Manufacturers Association, the British Adhesive Manufacturers Association and a charitable body, the National Shoe Leather & Allied Leather Golf Fund. In addition A. C. Palmer audited the British United Shoe Machinery Co – a joint audit after 1944 when the company, desiring the services of a London auditor, suggested to A. C. Palmer's senior partner, T. F. Birch, that they select a practice with whom they could act jointly. Birch, a Council member of the English Institute, knew and respected Harold Barton, choosing Barton, Mayhew. This connection eventually led to a correspondent arrangement from 1961 and a full merger in 1972. The rise in C. Herbert Smith & Russell's fee income evident from 1932–33 (Fig. 3) reflects the nation's partial economic recovery and the boom of 1935 when firms like A. C. Palmer gained additional accountancy and audit work. The steady growth in fees after 1937 corresponds with progressive rearmament, which apparently saved business from another depression.

To conclude the first part of this chapter, we return to the depression itself. At home the slump was the major problem of the inter-war period, preoccupying politicians, economists, trade unions and business in general. Sir Arthur Whinney was President of the English Institute of Chartered Accountants in 1926–27 at the time of the General Strike and when regional unemployment and economic decline were beginning to bite. Because accountants had occupied strategic positions in the economy during the First World War, it was felt that they could again make a valuable contribution.[107] Their broad knowledge of business, experience in management and specialist financial and costing skills, it was argued, gave them a unique qualification to advise governments on policy and assist in its execution.

Sir Arthur Whinney delivered two presidential speeches in 1926. In his first, given at Bristol, he acknowledged the strides that accountants had made in the public's estimation, declaring that 'the profession has reached a stage at which its value and utility is recognised by those who but a short time since were ignorant of our existence', and added that this had resulted in leading accountants being 'called upon to act in an advisory capacity upon government committees and enquiries to render service to the industrial and financial interests of the country'.[108] However, his analysis of the problems besetting Britain in the 1920s (and speaking as President he was not presumably expressing his views alone) had a classical and highly conventional ring. He criticized the trade unions for, as he believed, an over-ready recourse to strikes, arguing that 'struggling as the country is, under the burden of crushing taxation [actually income tax was then only four shillings in the pound], it is in no condition to suffer a disaster of such appalling magnitude as the coal stoppage.' In a second speech prepared for the English Institute's London A.G.M. in June 1927 (though due to his sudden death it was never delivered, being published posthumously in *The Accountant*), Sir Arthur Whinney set out a policy designed to cure the country's economic malaise. Again criticizing the high level of direct taxation, he suggested that the only way out of the deepening recession was for people to work harder, while public expenditure was cut still further to pay for reductions in income tax. In addition, Sir Arthur Whinney proposed the formation of a 'Retrenchment Committee' to bring down government spending and trim bureaucracy through the amalgamation of various ministries. This, in turn, he argued, would allow the government to balance the budget, stimulate confidence in British business and boost exports.

To be fair, this view was at the time shared by the great majority of politicians, economists and Treasury advisers, though hindsight it may be seen to have been misguided and often cruel in its application. Even moderate expenditure by government was regarded as a wasteful use of resources and the concept of heavy borrowing and deficit financing appeared wildly unorthodox. The policy of retrenchment and balanced budgets largely ruled out any major initiatives to cure mass unemployment.[109] Hence, administrations, Labour, National and Conservative, stuck to a course of deflation and reduced expenditure. Fatalism and making the best of things were attitudes which affected the government as much as the individual unemployed, forcing Neville Chamberlain to announce in his 1933 budget speech that Britain was likely to suffer from heavy unemployment for another decade.[110]

At the time a number of public figures openly criticized government, economists and accountants for their common failure to act more positively. Sir Josiah Stamp argued in 1921 that the accountancy profession had failed 'to make a single substantial contribution to economic science over its own field of the analysis of the results of industry, although it has practically a monopoly grip of the required data'.[111] He continued to chide accountancy bodies for their lack of imagination and initiative throughout the

inter-war years. Stacey concluded that their outstanding characteristic was conservatism: they remained content 'to recommend
what they thought the general body of business would bear,
rather than recommending what was best for economic improvement'.[112] *The Economist* similarly attacked their 'too professional
attitude'. Later Stamp suggested that a 'want of proper facilities
for theoretical training is in part responsible for the scanty interest
displayed by accountants in the study of their craft' and its
application to practical policies. He drew the comparison with
America where 150 companies had been selected to provide
figures which when used collectively did not breach professional
confidence. These were processed by 'a neutral source, accountants and economists ... in order that an aggregate statement of
accounts may be obtained, giving fluctuations of turnover ...
price level and other details'.[113] Further, Stamp maintained that
accountants and academics should form a research committee to
assist the government. The failure to act in this way was partly
conditioned by business, which exhibited a reluctance to disclose
information even to a neutral source. In a period when a substantial proportion of the population endured great hardships not of
their own making, it is difficult to escape the conclusion that,
amongst many other causes, efficient policy making was hindered
by this failure to act with imagination and sympathy.

As the situation continued to worsen, in June 1930 Ramsay
MacDonald announced the creation of the Economic Advisory
Council comprising ministers, businessmen, union leaders, econo-
mists and one accountant, Sir William McLintock.[114] Other ac-
countants served on its various advisory committees, that on the
Iron and Steel industry involved Sir William Plender, while Sir
Gilbert Garnsey sat on the Marketing and Distribution, and the
Cotton Industry Committees, chairing that on Unemployment
Statistics.[115] Although Mowat concluded that the Economic
Advisory Council 'accomplished little',[116] it has recently been
argued that it was never in a position to influence events.[117] In
abeyance throughout the summer of 1931, over-large, divorced
from government and in fact very short-lived, the members of
the Economic Advisory Council never got a chance to show their
worth, though a number (mostly economists) joined the Committee on Economic Information, its more successful successor.
The Council was in fact the first attempt in Britain to recruit
economists into full-time government service and to create a

mechanism whereby outside experts could be consulted on a regular or informal basis.

In view of the depths reached by the slump, in February 1931 Philip Snowden, as Chancellor of the Exchequer, accepted a Liberal proposal for a retrenchment committee on the Geddes lines – during the 1921–22 recession Sir Eric Geddes chaired a committee which had reduced government spending by £86 million through cuts in teachers' salaries, education, public health and the abolition of the Ministries of Labour and Transport.[118] On this occasion Sir George May, until then Secretary of the Prudential Insurance Company, was appointed chairman, two of its six other members being accountants, Sir William Plender and Sir Mark Webster-Jenkinson.[119] Their Report, similar but more stringent than Geddes', published in July 1931, was described by Keynes as 'compounded of prejudice, ignorance and panic', being 'the most foolish document I have ever had the misfortune to read'.[120] They suggested that only £24 million of the £120 million required to balance the budget should be met by increased taxation and that £96 million should result from economies, two-thirds of this at the expense of the unemployed whose relief, already small, was to be cut by 20%. Again teachers' salaries were reduced, secondary school fees increased and the Road Fund abolished.[121] It is surprising to consider that following this economic philosophy the government wound-up its grants for public works and that most authorities were forced to economize on relief expenditure during the worst years of the slump when these schemes would have provided most assistance.[122] Cuts in unemployment benefit, salaries and the rest were not restored until 1934 when matters had eased appreciably through a recovery in world trade.[123]

Part II: Overseas

The geographical expansion of the leading accountancy practices, evident within Britain, was paralleled by a growth of overseas operations. Whinney, Smith & Whinney's earliest links were correspondent arrangements with other accountancy firms in the Dominions, concluded before the First World War as follows: David Fell & Co (Australia), George Ross & Co (New Zealand), Douglas Low & Co (South Africa) and Edwards, Morgan & Co (Canada). These associations, designed for mutual help in administrative matters concerning insolvencies, were accelerated by exchanging powers of attorney so that each could act on the other's behalf. At this stage, therefore, it was not solely a question of following clients as they expanded throughout the world by developing a network of Imperial branches, but a matter of improving their basic organization within the Dominions through agency arrangements.

However, two factors encouraged City practices to set up offices on the Continent during the inter-war years: the expansion of British and American financed businesses and the general disruption caused by the war to a slowly evolving Continental accountancy profession. Because of similar client interests and to cut costs, it made sense for Whinney, Smith & Whinney and Brown, Fleming & Murray to act in concert overseas, forming new partnerships, both named Whinney Murray, to run their Continental and Middle Eastern operations. Sir Arthur Whinney opened the first office at 7 Rue Richepanse, Paris, in 1920 (largely concerned with an Anglo-Persian subsidiary, Société Générale des Huiles de Pétrôle), while a second followed at Antwerp, consequent upon a merger with Marshall Rutherford, later that year. The latter's clients were mainly British or American companies domiciled in Belgium, though a considerable amount of work was conducted in Holland, where as yet no base had been established. A merger with Rees, Baguley & Habben, an English practice based in Germany* with a London office, resulted in the acquisition of the Berlin and Hamburg offices in 1924 and 1925 respectively, under the style Whinney Murray, Baguley & Co. The latter was particularly valued as Anglo-Persian Oil operated from Hamburg, which provided their first refinery in Germany, while a few local clients were also acquired, such as the U.F.A. Group, a Berlin and Munich based film maker and distributor. In 1934 William Harris-Burland set up a Warsaw office, being replaced in 1937 by Reginald Wilson, who had been much involved with the investigation of the Swedish Match Company's affairs at Stockholm. In 1935 an office opened in Oslo. Once in Warsaw, Wilson became particularly concerned with the funding arrangements for the Polish electrification, including their railways, which was largely undertaken by British and American businesses.

Not only for Whinney Murray, but also for other leading City accountants, the major force behind this territorial expansion was

* The firm, originally called Rees, Baguley & Co, was first founded at Berlin in March 1922, expanding later to Hamburg.

the pull of growing clients. Already in 1919 twenty-one of the 200 largest U.K. companies had overseas subsidiaries; by 1930 the number had grown to sixty-two and seventy-three in 1948.[124] Since these figures only record separately incorporated businesses, rather than branch offices, the degree of British involvement overseas is understated. In the wake of this phenomenon British accountancy firms opened their overseas offices. For example, Anglo-Persian Oil and its subsidiaries had an important network of distribution centres throughout Europe. Dunlop Rubber possessed a number of Continental plants and outlets, establishing a French company at Montluçon, Allier, in 1923 and a German factory at Hanau, near Frankfurt, which reopened after the armistice.[125] The majority of these subsidiaries in the 1920s were new and represented an attempt to capitalize on newly acquired technology and skills. It was also in part a search for raw materials - British Steel, for instance, integrating backwards into Spanish ore mines and railways.[126] Although much of the Continental firm's work was for British or American subsidiaries, often on behalf of their national accountancy practices, it had by the 1930s attracted a considerable number of local clients. On the outbreak of war in 1939, there was sufficient local work for the national staffs of Whinney Murray and Price Waterhouse in Germany to merge forming a new firm, Continental Treuhand, a practice which has since grown to major dimensions.

Ivar Kreuger's expansion into Estonia, Latvia, Yugoslavia and Rumania as sources for his rapidly growing match empire, and more importantly the complex frauds leading to his suicide in 1931, were instrumental in developing Whinney Murray's European operations.[127] Ernst & Ernst, as the New York auditors of the International Match Corporation (an American-based Kreuger subsidiary), had become increasingly worried about his European operations and tried to persuade the company to allow them to take matters further. A. D. Berning, of Ernst & Ernst, recalled that 'Kreuger & Toll had no American accountants or English auditors' and, as a Swedish company with a dubious financial history, did not relish their appointment.[128] In the event Kreuger's empire collapsed when his credit ran dry and his forgery of Italian government bonds and a dummy Danzig Bank were discovered.[129] The commission of inquiry appointed Price Waterhouse to conduct the lengthy investigation into Kreuger & Toll, while Ivan Spens, who spent much time working on the Continent, secured the reconstruction of their subsidiary, the Swedish Match Company, for Whinney Murray.[130] Having completed this work, Whinney Murray secured the audit of its East European branches.

Once Whinney Murray had established these European offices, they were approached by U.K. companies who were not their clients, but who had set up Continental outlets and wished to have British accountants prepare their accounts before they were sent home for incorporation or review. Thus a lot of the European firm's work was not in fact auditing but the drawing up of balance sheets and profit and loss accounts for parent companies based in Britain. Other work included the checking and revision of accounts prepared by local accountants before they were sent to the U.K. This required a knowledge of each country's business laws and tax regulations and meant that completed accounts had on occasion to be re-presented to meet British requirements. Where audits were performed reports often included a detailed analysis of internal controls and subsidiaries' accounts in the fashion of today's management letters. Continental offices, therefore, were often a source of additional business contacts within Britain.

As noted, Whinney, Smith & Whinney did not reopen their New York office in 1918 but concluded a correspondent arrangement with Ernst & Ernst (see p. 107). Similarly, as Ernst & Ernst's clients spread throughout Europe, they considered it prudent not to open British and Continental branches but in 1924 entered into a five-year working agreement with Whinney, Smith & Whinney, which continued to be renewed unchanged until 1958.

Barton, Mayhew and Turquand, Youngs also pursued an expansionist policy on the Continent, but both, because of client interest, moved into the Iberian peninsula. Barton, Mayhew were closely involved with the business interests of the Blandy family in the Canary Islands and Madeira, which induced them to open an office in Las Palmas in 1920. In 1921 they sent an English Institute prize-winner, L. I. Grant, to put up a brass plate in Madrid and before long he secured work from several sherry shippers in the south of Spain. Other offices in Lisbon and Paris opened in 1927, Oporto and Barcelona following in 1931 and 1932 respectively. Turquand, Youngs were similarly concerned with the wine and spirit trade. Their Malta office, set up in

1931–32 by D. W. Robertson, was designed to assist the audit of Saccone & Speed, the wine and spirit merchants, who supplied the British forces on the island; the Gibraltar office was founded shortly afterwards for the same reasons. Once established, local work followed, the Malta office auditing the Anglo-Maltese Bank, National Bank of Malta and Simonds Farsons, the island's only brewery. The firm had also opened offices in Paris (1922), Berlin (1932) and, as a result of the McAuliffe merger, acquired others in Madrid and Barcelona.

Whinney, Smith & Whinney and Brown, Fleming & Murray also co-operated in the Middle East where they had mutual interests. In 1921 Sir Arthur Whinney had sent one of his staff, E. J. Brown, to Iraq to supervise the realization of the surplus government stores (the property of Richard Thynne & Co, of whom Charles Cape was liquidator) associated with the running down of the British presence after the campaigns against the Turks and Germans in Mesopotamia. After a polo match at Basrah, he met a senior manager of Anglo-Persian Oil and discussed the practical problems of auditing operations in the oil fields. The situation had become acute with Anglo-Persian's decision to take over their own administration from the managing agents, Messrs Strick, Scott – a Middle East equivalent of Finlay Fleming in Rangoon. Accordingly, Brown, who knew the region well from the war, became the first Middle East partner in Whinney Murray, being resident at Basrah near the centre of Anglo-Persian's operations.

Offices at Basrah and Mohammerah (now Khorramshahr), Iraq's ports for Bombay and London, were followed by others in Baghdad, and at Haifa in 1927 when the Iraq Petroleum Company constructed a pipeline to the Mediterranean there. Although primarily concerned with oil, once established, the Haifa office attracted local Palestinian commerce, particularly the diamond trade. In 1928 the audit of the Bahrain government encouraged the establishment of an office there as well, though the audit itself was suspended at the height of the depression when a shortage of funds prevented payment of the fee. The audit has been held ever since.

The connection between client and the local accountant was strengthened by the remote nature of the oil fields. Different laws and customs meant that his acquaintance with national and regional conditions was highly valued. In 1920 the Armitage-Smith agreement clarified the terms which gave the Persian government

16% of the Anglo-Persian Oil Company's profits. The arrangement was in fact the product of a decade's dispute for which Sir William McLintock had been engaged to represent the Persian government, while R. A. Murray argued the oil company's case.[131] It was a complicated matter – definitions of profit were mixed up with local law and the particular circumstances of the industry – which doubtless served to bring client and auditor closer together. Indeed, Whinney Murray's work for the company went far beyond the minimum required for a satisfactory audit, offering detailed advice on accounting procedures and, in the case of damage to the pipeline in 1915, both technical and diplomatic expertise.

From 1927 Imperial Airways, a Whinney, Smith & Whinney client, started flights to Basrah, via Cairo and Baghdad. Because aircraft could not then fly safely in darkness, airports were designed with substantial overnight accommodation, which added to the scope of the accounting. With the completion of routes to Australia and India, Basrah became a refuelling point, strategically placed *en route* from London. As the airline's routes multiplied throughout the Middle East, Whinney Murray were repeatedly called to act as an intermediary in their discussions with local authorities. For example, in July 1933 the Baghdad office wrote, as was standard practice, to inform Imperial Airways that 'there is a new income tax law about to be passed, two of the clauses of which will directly affect the above company's assessment for 1933/34'.[132] Similarly the Haifa office handled their 'Indian, Iraq and Sudanese income tax payments'.[133] In 1935 Sidney Mearns, a London partner, wrote a prophetic letter to Mr Goord, partner-in-charge of the Baghdad office, noting that 'big schemes are afoot and I should think that work with Imperial Airways will greatly increase in the future'.[134] Whinney Murray's Middle East offices were sited not only along oil pipelines, but at the major airports on routes to India and Australia.

Turquand, Youngs exhibited a similarly far-flung expansion in the inter-war period. In 1938 they amalgamated with McAuliffe, Davis & Hope, a firm with a strong Far East practice (see p. 102), a connection which, in turn, introduced Turquand, Youngs to Arthur Andersen, the Chicago-based accountants, who had concluded a correspondent arrangement with McAuliffes in 1930 to represent them in Europe, South America and the Far East.[135] It was hoped that these loose ties might form the basis for a world-wide partnership, but the outbreak of war in 1939 ended such speculation.

Hence, by 1939 it was clear not only that trade followed the flag, but that accountants followed trade. British accountancy firms had spread around the globe to ensure that their growing international clients received an efficient and comprehensive service. In doing so they became important business organizations in their own right. However, their territorial expansion was temporarily curtailed in 1939 when war broke out in Europe, while its gradual extension to Africa, and in 1941 to the Far East, resulted in the closure of most of these offices – some of which never reopened after 1945. It is to the Second World War period that we must now turn our attention.

References

1 C. L. Mowat, *Britain between the Wars 1918–1940*, London (1955), p. 257.

2 Mathias, *First Industrial Nation, op. cit.*, p. 432.

3 George Orwell, *The Road to Wigan Pier*, London (1937), p. 75.

4 See Table II, p. 99.

5 Whinney, Smith & Whinney Audit Books, 1910 and 1933.

6 Barton, Mayhew Fee Journal 1921–1930.

7 Winsbury, *op. cit.*, p. 37.

8 Reader, *House in the City, op. cit.*, pp. 138–9.

9 T. C. Barker, *The Glassmakers, Pilkington: the rise of an international company 1826–1976*, London (1977), p. 322.

10 Alfred D. Chandler and Herman Daems (Editors), *Managerial Hierarchies: Comparative Perspectives on the Rise of Modern Industrial Enterprise*, Harvard (1980), Leslie Hannah, 'Visible and Invisible Hands in Great Britain', p. 42.

11 Roy Church, *Herbert Austin: The British Motor Car Industry to 1941*, London (1979), pp. 57–8.

12 *Ibid*, pp. 60, 63.

13 *Ibid*, p. 64.

14 Dunlop Rubber Co, Directors' Minute Book, No. 5 (1921–1923), 24 February 1922, p. 128.

15 Dunlop Rubber Co, Directors' Report, 1 May 1924, p. 2.

16 *Souvenir of the Pneumatic Tyre Majority Celebration 1888–1909*, London (1909), p. ii.

17 Dunlop Rubber Co, Directors' Report, 1925, p. 2.

18 Kathleen E. Dunlop, 'A History of the Dunlop Rubber Company

Ltd in England 1888-1939' (Unpublished Ph.D. Thesis, University of Illinois, 1948), p. 83.

19 Stacey, *op. cit.*, p. 108.

20 *The Accountant*, No. 3132, 15 December 1934, F. R. M. de Paula, 'The Form and Presentation of the Accounts of Holding Companies', p. 854.

21 19 & 20 Geo V, c. 23, 1929 Companies Act; *History of the Institute*, *op. cit.*, p. 75.

22 J. R. Edwards, 'Company Legislation and Changing Patterns of Disclosure in British Company Accounts 1900-1940' (Paper presented at the Third International Congress of Accounting Historians, London, 1980), p. 34.

23 *Ibid*, pp. 7, 35.

24 *Abacus*, Vol. 12, No. 1 (1976), P. S. Manley, 'Clarence Hatry', pp. 54-6.

25 *Abacus*, Vol. 13, No. 1 (1977), R. G. Walker, 'The Hatry Affair', p. 81.

26 P. N. Davies, *The Trade Makers, Elder Dempster in West Africa 1852-1972*, London (1973), p. 254.

27 *Ibid*, p. 258.

28 Noel Simpson, *The Belfast Bank 1827-1970, 150 Years of Banking in Ireland*, Belfast (1975), pp. 281-2.

29 Stacey, *op. cit.*, p. 150.

30 *Ibid*, p. 155.

31 Kitchen and Parker, *Accounting Thought and Education*, *op. cit.*, p. 96.

32 Edwards, *op. cit.*, pp. 24-6.

33 *Ibid*, p. 29.

34 *Ibid*, p. 38.

35 F. R. M. de Paula, *Developments in Accounting*, London (1948), p. 37.

36 Stacey, *op. cit.*, p. 155.

37 Information provided by Dr R. Ferrier, the BP Group Historian.

38 Sheila Marriner (Editor), *Business and Businessmen*, Liverpool (1978), T. A. Lee, 'Company Financial Statements: An Essay in Business History 1830-1950', p. 255.

39 Edwards, *op. cit.*, p. 38.

40 *Ibid*, pp. 15, 17.

41 *Ibid*, p. 13.

42 Leslie Hannah, *The Rise of the Corporate Economy*, London (1976), p. 92.

43 *Ibid*, p. 93; and W. J. Reader, *Imperial Chemical Industries, A History*, Vol. II 1926-1952, London (1975), p. 237.

44 Kitchen and Parker, *op. cit.*, p. 93.

45 *Ibid*, p. 85; and *Who was Who 1951-1960*, Vol. V, London (1961), p. 85.

46 Hannah, *The Corporate Economy, op. cit.*, p. 90.

47 Dunlop Rubber Co, Ref. 2468, Memorandum to the Board, 23 March 1934, p. 3.

48 *History of the English Institute, op. cit.*, p. 78.

49 *The Accountant* (1934), de Paula, *op. cit.*, p. 856.

50 Dunlop Rubber Co, Directors' Report and Accounts, No. 35 (1933), pp. 8-11.

51 De Paula, *Developments in Accounting, op. cit.*, pp. 91, 94.

52 Sir Gilbert Garnsey, *Holding Companies and their Published Accounts*, London (1936), p. 119.

53 R. G. Walker, *Consolidated Statements*, New York (1978), p. 210.

54 Mary Murphy (Editor), *Selected Readings in Accounting and Auditing Principles and Problems*, New York (1952), p. 169.

55 W. J. Reader, *Imperial Chemical Industries, A History*, Vol. I 1870-1926, London (1970), p. 374.

56 John Galsworthy, *To Let*, London (1921), Penguin edition, p. 136.

57 Hannah, *The Corporate Economy, op. cit.*, p. 90.

58 Stacey, *op. cit.*, p. 215.

59 De Paula, *Developments in Accounting, op. cit.*, p. 138.

60 C. H. Wilson, *A History of Unilever*, Vol. 1, London (1954), p. 273; D. K. Fieldhouse, *Unilever Overseas*, London (1978), pp. 32-3.

61 Wilson, *Unilever, op. cit.*, pp. 298-9, 303.

62 J. D. Scott, *Vickers, A History*, London (1962), p. 156.

63 *Ibid*, p. 157.

64 *Ibid*, pp. 162, 164-5.

65 John K. Winkler, *Five and Ten, The Fabulous Life of F. W. Woolworth*, London (1941), pp. 155, 158.

66 Barker, *Pilkingtons, op. cit.*, pp. 328-9, 335.

67 *Ibid*, p. 335.

68 W. J. Reader, *I.C.I.*, Vol. II, *op. cit.*, p. 158.

69 D. C. Coleman, *Courtaulds, An Economic and Social History 1940-1965*, Oxford (1980), pp. 30, 327.

70 *Ibid*, p. 31.

71 W. J. Reader, *Bowater, A History*, Cambridge (1981), p. 25.

72 *Ibid*, p. 48.

73 W. V. Bowaters (1926) Ltd, Board Minutes, 1926-1934, 20 January 1926, p. 3.

74 Reader, *Bowater, op. cit.*, pp. 48, 53.

75 Committee of Management (W. V. Bowaters) Minutes, 1926-1928, 2 July 1926, p. 1.

76 Bowater Paper Mills Ltd, Directors' Minute Book 1923-1928, 20 December 1927, p. 86.

77 Letter from the Belsize Motor Co to the Midland Bank, 14 September 1922.

78 Letter, dated 19 August 1924.

79 M.B.A. Acc 30/31, A Scheme for the Amalgamation of Companies engaged in the Cotton Industry, 8 February 1933.

80 E. Rosenbaum and A. J. Sherman, *M. M. Warburg & Co, 1798-1938, Merchant Bankers of Hamburg*, London (1979), p. 162.

81 *Ibid*, pp. 167-8.

82 Hannah, 'Visible and Invisible Hands', *op. cit.*, pp. 62-6.

83 Mitchell and Deane, *op. cit.*, p. 427.

84 Table II, p. 99.

85 Letter, 29 April 1926, from Sir Arthur Whinney to R. L. Latimer.

86 Memorandum from the Leeds Office, 21 August 1928.

87 Letter, 21 September 1927, from C. J. G. Palmour to T. Smethurst.

88 Typewritten list of Sir Thomas Smethurst's clients, *c.* 1920.

89 Baker, Sutton & Co Fee Book No. 1 (1903-1926), pp. 88, 90, 93, 95.

90 Baker, Sutton & Co Fee Book No. 3 (1936-1947), pp. 1, 57, 59.

91 Letter, 4 May 1937, W. Montgomery to C. J. G. Palmour.

92 *Ibid*.

93 *History of the British Institute*, *op. cit.*, p. 228.

94 *Yorkshire Evening Post*, 22 December 1931, and *Hull Daily Mail*, 23 December 1931.

95 M. P. Fogarty, *Prospects of the Industrial Areas of Great Britain*, London (1945), p. 5.

96 John Stevenson and Chris Cook, *The Slump, Society and Politics during the Depression*, London (1977), p. 57.

97 Winsbury, *op. cit.*, pp. 21-2, 29.

98 Information supplied by BP Group Historian.

99 Winsbury, *op. cit.*, p. 21.

100 *Ibid*, p. 22.

101 *History of the Chartered Accountants of Scotland*, *op. cit.*, p. 64.

102 *Who was Who 1951-1960*, Vol. V, London (1961), p. 1030.

103 Letters, 7 March and 11 March 1919, to Anglo-Persian Oil Company explaining the whereabouts of Brown, Fleming & Murray's new London office.

104 Letter, 21 May 1920, announcing change of premises to the Anglo-Persian Oil Company.

105 Brown, Fleming & Murray Rule Book (1925), p. ii (4).

106 K. L. Milne, *The Accountant in Public Practice*, London (1959), p. 39.

107 S. Pollard, *The Development of the British Economy*, London (1962), p. 55.

108 Sir Arthur Whinney's Presidential Speech, October 1926.

109 Stevenson and Cook, *op. cit.*, p. 61.

110 *Ibid*, p. 62.

111 Quoted from the *History of the English Institute*, *op. cit.*, p. 83 (from *The Incorporated Accountants Journal*, September 1921, p. 44).

112 Stacey, *op. cit.*, p. 118; and R. Lewis and A. Maude, *Professional People*, London (1952), p. 44.

113 *The Accountant*, No. 2656, 31 October 1925, p. 686.

114 Susan Howson and Donald Winch, *The Economic Advisory Council 1930-1939*, Cambridge (1977), p. 354.

115 *Ibid*, pp. 355, 356, 358.

116 Mowat, *op. cit.*, p. 359.

117 Howson and Winch, *op. cit.*, p. 2.

118 A. J. P. Taylor, *English History 1914-1945*, Oxford (1965), pp. 183-4.

119 *History of the English Institute*, *op. cit.*, p. 88; *ibid*, p. 287.

120 Taylor, *op. cit.*, p. 288.

121 Phillips and Maddock, *op. cit.*, p. 157.

122 Stevenson and Cook, *op. cit.*, p. 63.

123 Phillips and Maddock, *op. cit.*, p. 157.

124 Hannah, 'Visible and Invisible Hands', *op. cit.*, p. 57.

125 Dunlop, 'History of Dunlop Rubber', *op. cit.*, pp. 129, 130.

126 Hannah, 'Visible and Invisible Hands', *op. cit.*, p. 58.

127 Robert Shaplen, *Kreuger, Genius and Swindler*, London (1961), p. 123.

128 *Ibid*, p. 156.

129 *Ibid*, p. 142.

130 *Ibid*, p. 232.

131 Information supplied by BP Group Historian.

132 Letter, 29 July 1933, to Imperial Airways from Whinney Murray, Baghdad.

133 Letter, 17 September 1934, to Imperial Airways from Whinney Murray, Haifa.

134 Letter, 3 January 1935, to Mr Goord in Baghdad from S. Mearns in London.

135 *The First Fifty Years, 1913-1963, Arthur Andersen*, Chicago (1963), pp. 100-1.

CHAPTER 7

The Second World War

As in the First World War, accountants were recruited in 1939–45 either into the armed forces or as public administrators. However, the Second World War was both longer and more embracing in character. The genuinely world-wide nature of the conflict meant that the three services, campaigning from the frozen wastes of Norway to the monsoon jungles of Burmah, had to be supplied with equipment essential for their varied tasks in these highly varied conditions. In addition, the weapons of war assumed a technical complexity far beyond those of the First World War: the development and application of radar, atomic bombs, rocketry, larger and more effective tanks, aircraft, submarines, ships and munitions required an increasingly sophisticated logistics structure. Accountants, as a result, were in greater demand than they had been in 1914, being called to serve in ministries and departments and branches of the armed forces, which formed the essential back-up to men in action. For the first time civilians could not be shielded from the conflict. Blanket bombing, economic blockades and constant propaganda, now directly from Germany over the radio, meant that women, children and the aged were involved in a way that had never before been possible. The total nature of the war broadened and deepened the government's intervention. Accountants with costing, financial and management skills were often the state's professional instruments of action.

To a greater extent than before the First World War, there had been a considerable period of planning and preparation preceding the outbreak of hostilities. As early as 1935 the decision was taken by Baldwin's Conservative government to initiate a policy of rearmament.[1] From the outset the programme involved accountants, and when new plant and 'shadow factories', laid down for future use, were constructed, they costed and prepared the financial arrangements.[2] By 1938, 37.6% of all public expenditure was directed to the armed forces and rearmament, drawing an increasing number of accountants into industry.[3] Because of the urgency with which aircraft were needed, it was important for the government to ensure that contracts were accurately costed to prevent overcharging. Accordingly in 1936, with Sir William McLintock acting as mediator, the Air Ministry concluded an agreement with the Society of British Aircraft Manufacturers.[4] The failure to specify what was a suitable rate of profit and the view that companies with contracts to supply aircraft were making over-large profits at the taxpayers' expense led the Air Ministry to ask Lord Plender of Deloitte, Plender, Griffiths & Co to examine these businesses' accounts. He confirmed this impression and the Second McLintock Agreement, signed in July 1939, provided fixed prices for particular types of aircraft.[5] However, the resulting economies of scale which followed as production expanded still further meant that these rates too became over-generous and the government suspended the agreement in 1941. The Ministry of Aircraft Production then called in Barton, Mayhew to examine the accounts of various aircraft companies to obtain information which might form the basis for a fresh contract for costs and profits.[6] In the event the Second Agreement's two-year timescale proved too short for any meaningful results to be obtained. For the remainder of the war the government continued to negotiate individual contracts with the aircraft companies as the occasion demanded.

It was common during the 1930s for young accountants and their clerks to enlist in the Territorial Army. Consequently, when war broke out, many were trained, equipped and prepared for the conflict ahead. Indeed some form of military service (in the T.A. or Militia) became compulsory in July 1939, so that many conscripts had already received basic training by 3 September on the declaration of war. For example, twenty members of Whinney, Smith & Whinney left the firm on its outbreak to undertake full-time military service, while almost a hundred Price Waterhouse staff in T.A. or Volunteer Reserve units also went in September 1939. Whilst not introduced in the First World War until 1916, a Military Training Act in August 1939 instituted conscription in time of peace, a National Register being compiled in September; though objections followed from the trade unions, the controversy of 1915 was spared.[7] Inevitably the first to be called up were regular reservists, Territorials and the Militia, who amounted to over a million men between September and December 1939.[8]

Although the designation 'reserved occupation' included accountants, this only applied to qualified men of 25 years and over or those with ten years' experience.[9] Later, the demand for accountants in industry and government was such that this age limit was often waived and men under 25 were excused military service.[10] Despite this many exempted accountants volunteered for active duties – mostly as active soldiers rather than paymasters. In 1950 when Sir Harold Howitt addressed a meeting of 275 students, he conducted a straw poll to discover how many had served during the war; the answer was seventy-five, while a further twenty-five had completed post-war National Service.[11] After the war, as Whinney, Smith & Whinney's Rule Book shows, the firm continued to grant additional leave to members of their staff involved on training exercises in volunteer units.[12] Eighty-eight Turquand, Youngs' partners and staff joined the armed forces in the Second World War, Cooper Brothers provided 122 members of whom seven were killed and five wounded, and a total of fifty-eight enlisted from Whinney, Smith & Whinney, eight of whom were killed. Nevertheless, the proportion who served in the forces was lower than in the First World War, partly as a result of the broader scope and more rigorous enforcement of the reserved occupations and partly because the war had not generated the same enthusiasm, prompting men to volunteer despite their exemption.

In an attempt to avoid the hardship caused generally in 1914–15 to dependants of men killed in action both government and employers took steps to pay pensions and compensation. Whinney, Smith & Whinney, for instance, made provisions for their staff from October 1939. In the case of married men varying allowances were paid, ranging from 5/- a week to the member of staff and from 5/- to 15/- to the family so long as men were away in the forces.[13] In the case of 'single men with no responsibility to their homes, we are making an allowance of 10/- per week in augmentation of army pay'. Not only was Britain better prepared for war in 1939, there also existed a greater appreciation of the coming hardships. War was not greeted with wild patriotism (the memories of the trenches remained too close), rather the mood was one of 'release from unbearable tension, of slightly fearful determination and of grim resignation'.[14]

A number of accountants joined the forces as paymasters – C. J. M. Bennett, a partner in Barton, Mayhew, for example, became a paymaster in the Indian Army based at Meerut. However, the job had much altered from the First World War as the army kept pace with developments in civilian accounting. Until 1920 the forces' pay and finances had been administered by two bodies: the Army Pay Department, founded in 1878 and consisting of commissioned officers, and the Army Pay Corps, formed in 1893 and comprising military clerks. The instructions and records of the former reveal a complex and wide-ranging organization ordered to prevent fraud and encourage uniformity. The size of the Victorian armed forces and their deployment throughout the Empire necessitated rigorous accounting controls based around a monthly, rather than an annual, return.[15] Although not concerned with profits, it appeared, therefore, that army accounting produced advances in techniques relating to consolidation, integration and the coherent presentation of balance sheets. Yet the division of function between these two sections resulted in an inefficient organization, resolved in 1920 by the creation of a single united body, the Royal Army Pay Corps, while the Corps of Military Accountants, a unit established in 1919 following the demands of the First World War, finally merged with the R.A.P.C. in 1927.[16] Hence, by 1939 the armed forces were not only better equipped to fight the enemy, they also possessed an internal organization better able to regulate their complex financial dealings.

As in the First World War, accountants made an equally impressive contribution in their professional capacity as administrators. With the need to reorganize the nation on a war footing, it became apparent that there were critical shortages of skilled labour and professional expertise; this, at any rate, was the constant cry of the supply departments.[17] Laudable and selfless though the accountants' motives were in volunteering for active service, it can be plausibly argued that they might have been more profitably employed professionally in industry or public administration where their talents were at a premium. Early in 1939 over 6,000 members of the English Institute (from a total membership of 13,000) responded to an invitation from the President, C. J. G. Palmour, then senior partner of Whinney, Smith & Whinney, to enrol their names as being ready in time of war to undertake work for the government, while a further 3,000 had declared their intention to volunteer for military service.[18] At the request of the Minister of Supply, the Accountants' Advisory Panel, composed of civil servants and leading members of the profession, was formed in 1939 to select suitable accountants to perform government work.[19]

In fact, the Second World War, demanding more comprehensive public control and administration than the First, drew a greater number of accountants into government service in both senior and junior positions. Although the Ministry of Supply (a mammoth body handling all army equipment and that common to all three services) had not been set up until August 1939, the degree of state involvement even at this stage was far greater than it had been in 1914–15.[20] In addition the National government created four new ministries of a particularly interventionist character: Economic Warfare, designed to conduct the blockade against Germany; Food, which introduced a system of rationing and allocation; Shipping, to direct merchant ships and build more as they were sunk by U-boats; and Information, to inform the press, conduct propaganda and boost morale. The first three required accountants in large numbers to cost manufacturing processes, discover frauds or profiteering, and to cope with the vast bureaucracies that these ministries created and use their managerial skills to smooth their operation.

In June 1940 Churchill appointed Beaverbrook Minister of Supply and the half-hearted and desultory approach of the first two years was swept away. Port directors became dictators of docks, distributing imports in a co-ordinated fashion, while the railways were reorganized on a centralized basis. John Pears, for example, a partner in Cooper Brothers, became the Principal Controller of Costs at the Ministry of Supply, being responsible for costing contracts with private manufacturers, overseeing the accounts of the Raw Materials Division and auditing the many agency and Royal Ordnance factories. In 1943 and 1946 Whinney, Smith & Whinney were appointed by the Ministry of Supply to assist in the drawing up of capital assistance contracts. By the summer of 1941 the Board of Trade was undertaking the gigantic task of regulating the retail trade (a feat never attempted in the First War) and doing so with a staff expanded from 2,000 to 6,500.[21] Harold Barton, for example, served on the London Price of Goods Committee from 1939 to 1942.[22] The Board of Trade devised 'utility schemes' for furniture and many other domestic articles, which aimed to provide uniform goods of a reasonable standard.

The Goods and Services (Price Control) Act of 1941[23] provided for the appointment of inspectors who would assist the Local Price Regulation Committees in seeing that price orders were understood and observed. There were two grades of inspectors: the higher being qualified accountants capable of dealing with the more complicated cases and the second being unqualified but who could investigate the simpler infringements.[24] Experience had taught that enforcement relied on the proper keeping of records and the Act made provision for the furnishing of invoices and drawing up of books of accounts, often in a prescribed form. This wartime legislation may be seen, therefore, as having the unintentional effect of improving the level of accounting standards maintained by many businesses.[25] As well as controlling the prices of goods and services to the customer, the government also regulated manufacturers' prices.[26] This was usually determined by calculating their costs and adding a percentage profit margin. In the case of government contracts ministry accountants assessed the costs themselves on the work's completion or while in progress; for domestic goods manufacturers were left to do the costing themselves as Board of Trade accountants only had time to check a small proportion of the businesses involved.[27]

Clothes rationing, like food, operated on a points system to ensure that the reduced supplies were fairly distributed and did not go to the highest bidder, though inevitably a black market developed. Board of Trade accountants estimated in the early stages of rationing that goods worth millions of pounds had illegally reached the home market and that the bogus quota-holders who had supplied them earned many thousands in commissions.[28] Accordingly, in December 1940, a special investigation section was established in the Board of Trade's Accountants Division to track down black marketeers. Faked auditors' certificates were numerous and often attempts were made to bribe the investigating accountants, who had the task of checking traders' accounts, assisted in the fieldwork by ex-police officers.[29]

The success of a concerted U-boat campaign forced the government to tighten up food controls. By mid 1941 some weekly rations amounted to no more than what a respectable pre-war household would have thought sufficient for a single helping.[30] As in the First World War, the degree of government intervention and regulation deepened as the war progressed. Con-

trols initially imposed in a restrained and *ad hoc* fashion became
more intrusive and comprehensive as hostilities dragged on, the
employment of accountants increasing both in scale and significance.

H. O. H. Coulson, a partner in Barton, Mayhew, was seconded
to the Ministry of Food where he became its Director of Internal
Audit. Ware, Ward were appointed as South West Area Accountants to the Meat and Livestock Division. During their meetings at the headquarters in Colwyn Bay (decentralized to avoid
the bombing of London), they met accountants from Turquand,
Youngs who had been appointed South East Area Accountants
for the Meat and Livestock section of the Ministry of Food. This
early association aided a process of familiarization which was
much later to lead to thoughts of merger in 1960.

By coincidence, in the summer of 1939 Barton, Mayhew
bought a house at Weybridge against the contingency of war and
possible bombing of their London office. At the end of August all
their files had been taken there, while the tax department and a
skeleton audit staff had also moved to Weybridge. Two messengers, holding season tickets, travelled daily carrying suitcases containing the necessary documents required by the City office.
Neither J. F. T. Nangle, the partner-in-charge of the Weybridge
office, nor D. W. Robertson, who was barely 100 yards away at
Turquand, Youngs' newly opened emergency office, could guess
that thirty years later they would come together as joint senior
partners of Turquands Barton Mayhew.

In the 1930s C. J. G. Palmour had been invited by the Board of
Trade to serve on the newly formed Milk Marketing Board
(audited by Barton, Mayhew). In 1938 he had been elected President of the English Institute of Chartered Accountants, a post
which he continued to hold until 1944. As a result of his professional standing, Palmour was offered the chairmanship of Harland
& Wolff in Belfast, serving from 1942 to 1945. Having been
knighted in 1946 for sustained public service, Palmour then
advised the War Office on their system of accounting for stores.
In 1941 Harold Barton, then senior partner of Barton, Mayhew,
became Financial Director of the National Dock Labour
Corporation (serving until 1947) and in 1943, following his First
War experience in the Department of Aircraft Production, was
appointed Controller of General Aircraft Ltd.[31] In addition, Barton sat on the Higher Appointments Committee of the Ministry

of Labour and National Service from 1943 to 1944, when he succeeded Palmour as President of the English Institute.

Ivan Spens, senior partner of Brown, Fleming & Murray in London, had served in the First World War with distinction as an officer in the Cameronians, while his accountancy and general managerial skills were in demand during the Second.[32] He was Accountant General to the Ministry of Supply from 1939 to 1941, becoming Deputy Director-General of Finance and Accountant General from 1941 to 1942 and then Head of the Industrial Division of the Ministry of Production (1943-45). Reginald Wilson, a partner in Whinney Murray's Continental firm, on returning to Britain after the German occupation of Poland, joined the Ministry of Transport where in 1941 he became Director of Finance and in 1945 Under Secretary.[33]

Whinney, Smith & Whinney, along with most accountancy firms, had suffered at the outset from the loss of staff either to the services or government, and from the disruption caused to clients. In October 1940 Montgomery reported that conditions in the Manchester office were[34]

very difficult not only with constant interruptions caused by the second warning given by the 'look-out', but also travelling becomes more and more difficult and what with late arrivals in the morning and early leaving in order that the staff may be home before the black-out and night bombing starts, the hours of work are considerably curtailed.

In consequence of such hazards, as in the First World War, Whinney, Smith & Whinney's fee income initially fell from £71,657 in 1939 to £65,596 in 1941 (Fig. 4). The reduction is mirrored in audit receipts, which until then had reflected the firm's growth. Contributing the same percentage as in 1939 (73%) the revenue from audits had fallen from £42,765 to £35,922 (Table II). However, from 1941 until the end of the war, Whinney, Smith & Whinney's fees rose steadily in cash terms, reaching £112,532 in 1945. Brown, Fleming & Murray's fortunes exhibited a similar decline in the first three years of the war with a recovery in 1942; but in their case it was not sustained and their cash fees for 1945 were little more than those for 1939. Baker, Sutton also experienced hardships in 1941 and only regained their 1937 level of fee income in real terms in 1946.

The general rise in fees demonstrated by the graph of cash incomes (Fig. 4) may in part be explained by wartime inflation caused by shortages produced by the Battle of the Atlantic and by

Figure 4 The Second World War and Fee Income (1937–1948)

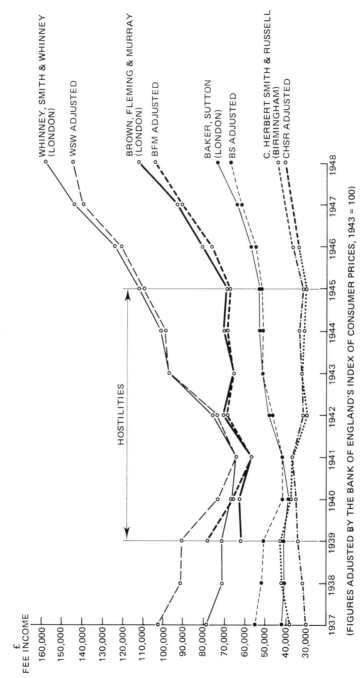

£
FEE INCOME

WHINNEY, SMITH & WHINNEY (LONDON)
WSW ADJUSTED
BROWN, FLEMING & MURRAY (LONDON)
BFM ADJUSTED
BAKER, SUTTON (LONDON)
BS ADJUSTED
C. HERBERT SMITH & RUSSELL (BIRMINGHAM)
CHSR ADJUSTED

HOSTILITIES

(FIGURES ADJUSTED BY THE BANK OF ENGLAND'S INDEX OF CONSUMER PRICES, 1943 = 100) deliberately heavy government spending designed to stimulate the economy in a war-winning effort to boost output.[35] Price rises intensified from 1939, reaching a peak in 1941, and were only then checked by severe rationing. They continued to climb from 1942 to 1945 but at a much slower rate as the U-boat menace was controlled, allowing supplies to arrive regularly in greater quantities, and as a series of Keynesian budgets regulated the economy more effectively.[36] Taking the Bank of England's index of consumer prices and recalculating the figures for 1937-48 with 1943 as the base year, the graph of fee income (Fig. 4) assumes a more pronounced aspect. The troubles of 1941 are depicted in much more serious light in view of the inflation of the late 1940s, suggesting not so much that practices took off in 1942, but that they, for the first three years or so, worked to regain the position they had held in the late 1930s.

Although we have spoken much about accountants involved in government work, this did not, in fact, benefit private practices to any great extent. Whinney, Smith & Whinney only derived 2.3% of their fees from such commissions in 1941 and 10.5% in 1945 – a mere £9,437. This was partly because staff seconded to the government became state employees, while work performed for the various ministries was not well paid, being undertaken from patriotic motives rather than financial gain.

Some additional work did result from the firm's appointment as trustees by the Custodian of Enemy Property when certain European companies with British subsidiaries were overrun by the German armies. It was common practice, however, to ask the English auditors of these subsidiaries to accept directorships in them as they were familiar with their operation. None was wound-up as they were protected on behalf of their owners, almost all being French nationals, to whom they were restored after the war. Ernest Whinney was appointed to the boards of six companies of which Whinney, Smith & Whinney were not the auditors, including Boucheron Ltd (jewellers), British & Saar Steel, Enfield Zinc Products Ltd, Enfield Rolling Mills (Aluminium) – which became an audit client in 1945 – and Kandem Electrical Ltd. R. L. Latimer, another partner, was appointed by the Custodian to the boards of some twenty-six companies including the textile business, Rodier Ltd, Fashion Silk & Rayon Weavers Ltd, La Soie Ltd, D. M. C. Thread Co (a subsidiary of Dollfus Miegel Cie) and Saint Frères Ltd, together with D. Pennellier & Co (bullion dealers) and St James's Restaurant Ltd (better known as Prunier's). He was later also appointed controller of two Japanese subsidiaries, Asano Bussan and Bessler Waechler. The time occupied by these directorships was not great and accordingly produced very little fee income. Cooper Brothers were given the more major task of running the financial affairs of the Belgian Shipping Fleet. Overseas, in Singapore on the outbreak of the Pacific War, both McAuliffe, Turquand, Youngs and Derrick & Co were appointed Custodians of Enemy Property, taking over Japanese assets, some of their staff already mobilized in the volunteer forces being released temporarily to deal with this extra work.

An area of increased but not substantial accountancy business was, as in the First World War, taxation. The imposition of an Excess Profits Tax (initially 60% but raised, almost by popular demand, to 100% in 1940)[37] meant work for accountants whose clients benefited from government contracts. In addition, the introduction of Purchase Tax and P.A.Y.E. (in the 1940 Finance Act) brought extra responsibilities for employers and their accountants.[38] Even in 1945 tax work only produced 7.5% of Whinney, Smith & Whinney's fees, a mere £6,733, a slight increase on the 1939 figures of 6.3% and £3,702, though the proviso has again to be made that the audit totals contain an element of undisclosed tax advice to audit clients. Because of taxation's growing complexity, the English Institute set up the Taxation and Financial Relations Committee in 1942 under the chairmanship of Harold Barton.[39] As the forerunner of the present Technical Advisory Committee, it drew up the first recommendations on accounting principles in an attempt to apprise members of new legislation and to a limited extent standardize procedures. William Carrington, a Whinney, Smith & Whinney partner, was chairman of its taxation sub-committee from 1942 to 1945.[40]

The Second World War had other important social consequences, which in turn were to exert a fundamental influence on the development of the accountancy profession. With so many men away in the forces, large numbers of women found work in industry, transport and as office staff. By 1939 they had already become prominent in clerical work. Naturally the civil service as a whole expanded greatly during the war, producing a disproportionate growth in the employment of women, such that the

95,000 women employed in the non-industrial civil service in 1939 had been swelled to 320,000 by October 1944 – 48% of the total.[41]

Accountancy firms of necessity had to employ women not simply as clerks, secretaries and telephonists, but also as audit staff and comptometer operators. Before the war it was common in many professions to sack females as soon as they married.[42] During the war scarcity of labour inevitably meant that married women were offered jobs and the old myths about their unreliability as employees were exposed. This pointed to an irreversible trend: a government survey conducted among private business at the end of the war showed a remarkable swing in public opinion with regard to the employment of women.[43] In 1931 a total of 1,152,000 women worked in public administration, commercial, financial and insurance occupations and as typists and clerks, almost doubling by 1951 to 2,286,000.[44] Accordingly qualified women, who had been discarded by accountancy practices in 1918, tended to retain their jobs in 1945.[45] Even if their numbers were not large, the principle at least had been established. In 1949 the Incorporated Society elected its first female Council member – then the only accountancy body with a woman on its governing committee.[46] Although women are still in a minority today, a change in present attitudes and the law, which may be seen to have its main origin in the exigencies of war, is now modifying the traditional male dominance of the accountancy profession.

By producing new methods of doing old jobs, introducing new management techniques and greater mechanization, the Second World War exercised a similar influence to the First, though to a much greater and longer lasting degree. It re-emphasized the importance of the accountants' skills and in doing so raised them further in public esteem, while a new generation received honours gained from public service. The state had never before been so completely involved in the economy and the general ordering of society. Post-war reconstruction, and the election of a Labour government dedicated to nationalization and social reform, meant that much of this involvement was of a protracted nature. For Britain there was to be no sudden withdrawal when peace came in August 1945.

References

1 A. J. P. Taylor, *English History 1914-1945*, Oxford (1965), p. 387.
2 M. M. Postan, *British War Production*, London H.M.S.O. (1952), p. 19.
3 Phillips and Maddock, *Growth of the British Economy, op. cit.*, p. 151.
4 William Ashworth, *Contracts and Finance*, London H.M.S.O. (1953), p. 117.
5 *Ibid*, p. 118.
6 *Ibid*, p. 119.
7 Arthur Marwick, *Britain in the Century of Total War*, London (1968), pp. 268, 269.
8 W. K. Hancock and M. M. Gowing, *British War Economy*, London H.M.S.O. (1949), p. 136.
9 Stacey, *op. cit.*, p. 212.
10 *History of the English Institute, op. cit.*, p. 93. C. J. G. Palmour was chairman of the Deferment Committee.
11 *The Accountant*, No. 3934, 13 May 1950, Sir Harold Howitt, 'The Profession of Accountancy', p. 538.
12 Whinney, Smith & Whinney Rule Book (1953), p. 9.
13 Memorandum from E. F. G. Whinney to W. D. Montgomery, 5 October 1939.
14 Arthur Marwick, *The Home Front, the British and the Second World War*, London (1976), p. 20.
15 *Financial Instructions in relation to Army Accounts, War Office*, H.M.S.O. (1886), pp. 7, 26-7, 30, 32.
16 *His Majesty's Regiments of the British Army*, London (1949), p. 103.
17 Hancock and Gowing, *op. cit.*, p. 144.
18 *History of the English Institute, op. cit.*, p. 92.
19 Stacey, *op. cit.*, p. 178.
20 Taylor, *English History, op. cit.*, p. 456.
21 *Ibid*, pp. 509-10.
22 *Who was Who 1961-1970*, Vol. VI, London (1972), p. 65.
23 4 & 5 Geo VI c. 31, 1941.
24 E. L. Hargreaves and M. M. Gowing, *Civil Industry and Trade*, London H.M.S.O. (1952), pp. 555, 559.
25 *Ibid*, p. 560.
26 *Ibid*, p. 578.
27 *Ibid*, p. 579.
28 *Ibid*, p. 111.
29 *Ibid*, p. 328.
30 Marwick, *Home Front, op. cit.*, p. 83.
31 *Who was Who, op. cit.*, p. 65; *The Accountant*, No. 4308, 13 July 1957, p. 40.
32 *Ibid*, p. 1063.
33 *Who's Who*, London (1969), p. 2723.

34 Letter, W. D. Montgomery to C. J. G. Palmour, 22 October 1940.
35 Henry Pelling, *Britain and the Second World War*, London (1970), pp. 115-16.
36 Hancock and Gowing, *op. cit.*, pp. 166, 201, 349.
37 *Ibid*, p. 163.
38 *History of the English Institute*, *op. cit.*, p. 95.
39 Kitchen and Parker, *op. cit.*, p. 110.
40 Magnus, *op. cit.*, p. 260.
41 Marwick, *Home Front*, *op. cit.*, p. 133.
42 *Ibid*, p. 140.
43 *Ibid*, p. 142.
44 Alan S. Milward, *The Economic Effects of the World Wars on Britain*, London (1970), pp. 31-2.
45 Coopers, *op. cit.*, p. 27.
46 Stacey, *op. cit.*, p. 217.

❀❀❀ CHAPTER 8 ❀❀❀

1945-1965

Producing possibly the greatest change in its history, the British accountancy profession experienced a startling transformation in the two decades after the Second World War. By 1945 Britain's economy had been distorted and exhausted by six years of total war. Many young accountants were overseas serving in the armed forces or seconded to the government, while the firms for which they had worked were understaffed, often being run by old men and relatively inexperienced women. Generally, accountancy firms, few having more than ten partners, remained small, analogous to solicitors', surveyors' or architects' offices. Within twenty years much of this had changed. Responding to the broadening needs of their expanding clients, by 1965 the largest accountancy firms had, by a process of growth and merger, formed international organizations with up to a hundred partners or more, who could call on a range of specialist departments to deal with taxation, special investigations, management problems and insolvency, while offering their articled clerks wider training facilities and opportunities. The character of the profession altered accordingly. New organizational structures had to be devised to cope with these greatly extended and expanded practices. Similarly, several professional bodies themselves amalgamated (in 1954 to form the Scottish Institute, and in 1957 when the English Institute of Chartered Accountants merged with the Society of Incorporated Accountants), pooling their resources to provide wider ranging advice and instruction. It is possible, therefore, that no profession has ever experienced such a fundamental metamorphosis in such a short period of time.

Initially the Labour government of July 1945 was presented with the daunting problem of re-routing an economy geared for war back to a peacetime path. Britain had taken a severe battering: overseas investments had been sold to the tune of £1,000 million; two-thirds of the small gold reserve of 1939 had been expended; domestic capital was run down; external debts were up by about £3,000 million and exports had dropped to a third of the pre-war level.[1] About $4\frac{1}{2}$ million men were waiting to be demobilized from the armed forces and a further $3\frac{1}{4}$ million civilians had to be redeployed from producing military equipment.[2] The government's first concern, therefore, was to minimize transitional unemployment and hasten economic recovery by ensuring that the demobilization of servicemen proceeded rationally. Accordingly, those whose skills were in greatest need were discharged first. Having set a list of priorities and staggered demobilization, the Labour government then turned its attention to implementing the programme of social reforms and selective nationalization.

Harold Barton, as chairman of the English Institute's Discharge Liaison Committee (it happened that Basil Mayhew had been secretary of the less successful Central Demobilization Board of 1918-20, of which Barton was also a member),[3] conducted negotiations with the Ministry of Labour to secure the speedy return of accountants required to assist the reconstruction of industry and commerce.[4] In addition, the various Institutes made concerted efforts to refresh and update the technical knowledge of returning servicemen.

The shift from private to public ownership not only meant that accountants' clients were affected by this reorganization, but that accountants themselves often became the instruments of its implementation. In 1946 the Bank of England, Cable and Wireless and Civil Aviation Acts, together with the Coal Industry Nationalization Act, were passed.[5] Thomson McLintock, a firm with experience in the coal industry, undertook colliery valuations, company liquidations and the calculation of compensation payments,[6] while William Carrington, a partner in Whinney, Smith & Whinney, served from 1948 to 1949 on the Central Valuation Board appointed to decide the apportionment of total compensation among the various coal districts. In 1955, when the Leicestershire Colliery & Pipe Co was taken over by the National Coal Board, the firm performed a separate valuation to assess the level of compensation to be paid. As a result of nationalization many local accountants lost the regular audit of private collieries as the work was transferred to the single firm of accountants (the audit of the nationalized industries usually fell to a large City practice) appointed by the Minister to deal with the coal industry in its entirety. For example, Buckley, Hall, Devin's Leeds office, which had been opened to serve certain colliery companies, lost a substantial part of its work following nationalization, though it did benefit in the short term from windings-up.

At first the form that the audit of the newly nationalized industries was to take created a source of some confusion. Such precedents as existed offered various possibilities: the accounts of the Coal Commission, for instance, were audited by the Comptroller and Auditor General before being examined by the Public Accounts Committee; those of B.O.A.C. were audited by public accountants – Whinney, Smith & Whinney – and then presented to Parliament. When the Coal Bill came to be drafted early thinking at the Ministry of Fuel and Power was to leave the whole of the district organization and branches to be audited by public accountants while the audit of the headquarters, which was in the nature of a huge holding company, was to be entrusted to the Accountant and Auditor General.[7] After some discussion it was felt that the audit ought to be entrusted entirely to public accountants rather than to civil servants and the Coal Bill, the first nationalization to pass through Parliament, set the pattern for subsequent legislation. The only major amendment to the Accounts Clause occurred in the Lords where the phrase 'to conform with ... the best commercial practice' was inserted to govern the presentation of the industry's accounts.[8] Only the Iron and Steel Bill, the last to be passed by the Labour Government, produced any changes, when a list of accountancy bodies, from which auditors could be chosen by the Minister, was included.[9]

Nationalization, by creating larger business units, also encouraged the growth of bigger accountancy practices. Those that gained the audit of the new nationalized industries (Whinney, Smith & Whinney, who had formerly audited Imperial Airways, were entrusted with the reconstructed B.O.A.C., see p. 206) often had to expand their operations in terms of staff, geographical location and the range of services offered following these appointments. Turquand, Youngs, who had been special auditors to the Electricity Commissioners (the body created in 1919 to oversee the industry and who from 1926 supervised the Central Electricity Board) in the inter-war period, were appointed South Western Electricity Area Board auditors in 1947 when electricity was nationalized and fourteen Area Electricity Boards created.[10]

Harold Barton, as a leading public accountant with administrative experience, was much involved in this reorganization. Knighted in 1947 following his wartime service as Financial Director of the National Dock Labour Corporation,[11] Barton also sat on the tribunal to determine compensation payable under the Cable and Wireless Act when they were incorporated within the overall structure of the G.P.O. In 1947, after the nationalization of public transport, he served on the two Railway Conciliation Boards appointed by the Ministry of Labour. In the following year Barton with Sir Alan Rae Smith of Deloittes became the first joint auditors of the British Transport Commission, which throughout its existence insisted on personal appointments rather than the nomination of accountancy firms.[12] Both Barton, Mayhew and Deloittes had a certain expertise in the field, the former in road haulage (being auditors of Southern Roadways and, after 1948, British Road Services), while the latter had long experience of railways as auditors of the Great Western and its successor, B.R. Western Region. As a statutory body designed to own all public transport, the B.T.C. supervised the railways, London Transport, provincial buses, canals, docks, steamer services and the travel agents, Thomas Cook.

Following his wartime work for the Ministry of Transport, [Sir] Reginald Wilson, a sometime partner in Whinney Murray, had been appointed as the British Transport Commission's Controller of Finance and Accounts. In contrast to most nationalized industries, he insisted that the original auditors of the various railway, canal and road companies be retained wherever possible to preserve a decentralized auditing system and to prevent practices from losing valued and established clients. Although British Railways' main regions mostly retained their pre-1948 auditing, the reorganizations affecting the other transport industries covered by the B.T.C. (which in 1952 was broken down into a number of separate bodies) streamlined the pattern of auditors. In the final shake-out Barton, Mayhew became auditors of Freight Services Ltd and National Carriers Ltd, Turquand, Youngs securing the audit of the National Bus Co.

Not only did post-war governments intervene more actively in the nation's economic life, they also sought to improve living conditions and a number of 'new towns' were planned to provide better housing and expanding industries with a conveniently sited workforce. The audits of the New Town Development Corporations were spread evenly among the leading City accountancy firms: in 1951 Whinney, Smith & Whinney were offered the audit of Bracknell, and Barton, Mayhew undertook Peterborough, while Brown, Fleming & Murray received that of Crawley. Sir Henry Benson of Cooper Brothers advised the Minister of Housing on the standard format of the town's accounts. However, once their construction was complete, the audit passed back to the New Towns Commission which was audited by Deloittes.

In general, the increased size and scope of business had for some time demanded changes in the statutes governing company accounts and their audit. Although pressure had been put on governments throughout the 1930s, nothing further had been done to regulate the financial conduct of business until the passing of the 1948 Companies Act.[13] Essentially this legislation provided for the fuller disclosure of company accounts; it prescribed the main contents and the manner of presentation of the balance sheet (specifying such items as investments, depreciation, debentures, premiums on share capital, aggregate capital and reserves), together with the form of the profit and loss account and the requirement to provide group accounts.[14] For the last, it required that 'the consolidated balance sheet and profit and loss account shall combine the information contained in the separate balance sheets and profit and loss accounts of the holding company and of the subsidiaries....'[15] In fact a few businesses had already produced fully consolidated accounts before the 1948 legal requirement, including Dunlops from 1934 and the Distillers Company in 1945.[16] For the first time all private companies were included within the regulations, which again meant much additional work for accountants. The Ninth Schedule contained important provisions governing the content of the auditor's report. Following the shortcomings evident from the Royal Mail case, the onus was on the auditor to declare 'whether in their opinion proper books of account have been kept by the company ... and proper returns adequate for the purposes of their audit', so that the accounts might present 'a true and fair view thereof'.[17]

Another novel feature was the Act's specification of who were qualified to perform these increasingly complex audits. Members of the English and Irish Institutes and the three Scottish Societies of Chartered Accountants, the Society of Incorporated Accountants and Auditors, together with the Association of Certified and Corporate Accountants, were alone deemed fit to undertake such tasks, though others might apply to the Board of Trade for approval.[18]

Writing in 1949 D. W. Robertson, a partner in Turquand, Youngs, recorded that the Companies Act had resulted in[19]

an increase in work, [but this] had to be undertaken with the handicap of the present extreme difficulty of finding satisfactory staff, which arises partly through the length and duration of the war and undoubtedly [because] nationalized industries and the Civil Service are continuously taking into their ranks accountants who are thus lost to the profession.

The immediate post-war years produced particular difficulties in the recruitment of qualified staff, as accountants, who had been seconded to industry or public administration, were tempted to remain, while nationalization created fresh opportunities for those attracted to the civil service and business. Seen against this background of state ownership and the continued growth of large companies, the prescriptions of the 1948 Companies Act caused certain accountancy practices to draw increasing numbers into their ranks in order to expand and develop their operations.

More precisely, the graph of fee income (Fig. 5) reveals that for some City practices, this was a period of steady and continuous growth. Whinney, Smith & Whinney's fees rose from £112,532 in 1945 (£167,958 calculated in real terms with 1955 as a base year) to £634,958 in 1964 (£490,315).[20] Similarly Brown, Fleming & Murray's fee income rose from £69,484 in 1945 (£103,553) to £196,905 in 1955 (£196,905).[21] Both firms' overall prosperity may be attributed to two factors: the acquisition of new clients, but more importantly the continued expansion of their largest listed clients. The main increase in their income was generated by rising audit fees, which in Whinney, Smith & Whinney's case rose from £56,632 in 1945 to £206,025 by 1960 (Table II), representing around 60% of total revenue throughout the period. The other area of expansion was in tax work, the firm's fees increasing from £6,733 in 1945 to £38,009 in 1960. Again the percentages did not vary much, ranging from 7.5 in 1945 to 14.2 in 1955. Although comparable records do not exist for Brown, Fleming & Murray, the continued growth of their leading audit clients (British Petroleum and Burmah Oil) suggests that similar forces lay beneath their expansion. The continuous rise in Turquand, Youngs' and Barton, Mayhew's real and cash fees may also be explained by the rapid growth of their leading audit clients; Arthur Guinness & Sons, J. Lyons, Courages, Consolidated

Figure 5 Predecessor Firms' Fee Incomes (1945-1965)

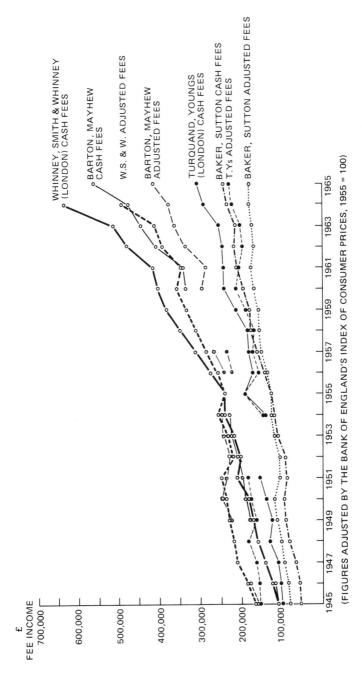

£
FEE INCOME

700,000

600,000

500,000

400,000

300,000

200,000

100,000

WHINNEY, SMITH & WHINNEY (LONDON) CASH FEES

BARTON, MAYHEW CASH FEES

W.S. & W. ADJUSTED FEES

BARTON, MAYHEW ADJUSTED FEES

TURQUAND, YOUNGS (LONDON) CASH FEES

BAKER, SUTTON CASH FEES

T.Ys ADJUSTED FEES

BAKER, SUTTON ADJUSTED FEES

1945 1947 1949 1951 1953 1955 1957 1959 1961 1963 1965

(FIGURES ADJUSTED BY THE BANK OF ENGLAND'S INDEX OF CONSUMER PRICES, 1955 = 100)

Goldfields, Norwich Union Group and I.D.V. for the former; Bowaters, Allied Suppliers, Ladbrokes, Westland Aircraft and Ronson Products for the latter. Turquand, Youngs also possessed three joint audits, Shell, Westminster Bank and Ind Coope – the last shared with Whinney, Smith & Whinney.

The graphs still reveal the influence of general fluctuations in the British economy, though they are less marked than in the nineteenth century, reflecting not only a much enlarged market but also more concerted and successful attempts to control cyclical variations. Whinney, Smith & Whinney's and Baker, Sutton's real fees both fell from 1950 to 1952 when business activity suffered as a result of costly wars in Korea, the Middle East and Malaysia together with the repayment of American loans.[22] A balance of payments crisis was finally checked in 1952 by import restrictions and 1953 saw a recovery in trade, the rise of accountancy fees in concert reinforcing the suggestion that the fortunes of these firms reflected economic trends. Two years later Britain's terms of trade worsened (also reflected in Whinney, Smith & Whinney's real fees for 1955 and probably in Turquand, Youngs' falling real fee income for 1956) and home production failed to satisfy rising demand drawing in an excessive volume of imports. Similarly, the balance of payments crisis of 1961 combined with general inflation appeared to have caused the reduction in the rate at which Whinney, Smith & Whinney, Barton, Mayhew and Turquand, Youngs grew.

Whinney, Smith & Whinney's audit of the British Overseas Airways Corporation proved of importance during this period as it grew to become an international client of major dimensions. With the nationalization of the airlines in 1946, the firm wound up Railway Air Services – an organization formed in 1934 by the four railway companies in association with Imperial Airways to fly certain U.K. routes – having previously performed some cost and audit work for them in Bristol. The amalgamation of British Airways and Imperial Airways in 1939 to create the British Overseas Airways Corporation gave Whinney, Smith & Whinney further work. However, when the war interfered with its operations, B.O.A.C. was closely controlled by the government, largely as a civilian adjunct to the R.A.F., and like so many similar bodies was headed by an accountant; during 1943 Sir Harold Howitt, senior partner in Peat, Marwick, Mitchell & Co and President of the English Institute in 1945-46, became its third chairman. In 1946 the European side of B.O.A.C., together with domestic services flown by the Associated Airways Joint Committee, was formed into a separate corporation, British European Airways, the audit of which fell to Price Waterhouse. Retaining B.O.A.C., in 1948 Whinney, Smith & Whinney also secured the audit of the International Air Travel Association's clearing house, which dealt with revenue from traffic exchanges between airlines, until the clearing house moved to Geneva in 1970. In due course the firm also acquired the audit of various B.O.A.C. subsidiaries and related organizations including the Airways Housing Trust, Airways (Corporation Joint) Pension Scheme and the British Airways (U.K. Staff) Friendly Society. When B.O.A.C. and B.E.A. merged in 1971 to form British Airways, Whinney Murray became its sole auditors.

Another factor encouraging further business within this field was the specialized nature of airline accounting. The main problems include revenue accounting (particularly complicated as most tickets are transferable on any nation's airline and therefore constitute in effect an international form of currency), the obsolescence of aircraft and their maintenance, together with the valuation of the stock of spares. Hence, as in brewing, oil, insurance or any area of specialist auditing, particular practices have tended to build up a list of similar clients. At present Ernst & Whinney audits British Airways, British Caledonian, Singapore Airlines, Middle East Airlines, Gulf Air and Saudia Airlines – the last three being attracted by Whinney Murray's Middle East coverage.

Baker, Sutton built up a considerable expertise in insurance broking accounts, having first gained the audit of Glanvill, Enthoven & Co at the turn of the century.[23] Willis Faber Ltd, Leslie & Godwin Ltd and a large number of individual brokers were also acquired as clients by D. C. Cann in the 1920s and H. E. Hann in the 1950s, while Baker, Sutton's merger with Gérard Van de Linde brought the audit of the Corporation of Lloyd's and two insurance companies. Other related audit clients included the Cornhill Insurance Co and Lloyd's Register of Shipping, such that at the time of their amalgamation with Ernst & Whinney in 1979, 35-40% of the firm's business lay in the field of insurance. More generally, this tendency for accountancy firms to specialize in particular areas of business (Turquands Barton Mayhew had, for instance, a virtual monopoly in sherry and port shippers from Spain and Portugal) heightened the emphasis on professional ethics. Clients operating within the same field were often rivals so that the auditor, whilst giving each the benefit of his total experience, had to take care that his advice remained unclouded by information derived from other companies' accounts. Growing specialization and polarization within accountancy both mean that such concentrations proliferated, making it all the more imperative that firms should behave with impeccable professional probity.

In a sense the character of the clientele is the essential governing factor for an accountancy practice. If all the clients are small (as they are for many provincial practices) then there is little incentive to expand geographically and limited demand for specialist services; indeed, the overheads are such that it is financially impossible to support such technical departments. However, the large City accountancy practice serving a number of multinational companies requires not only audit skills fitting their clients' particular forms of business, but also a range of specialist departments to provide the necessary back-up services, and an appropriate network of offices at home and overseas. As a result, the post-war period witnessed the creation of increasingly structured accountancy practices, performing a wider range of complex tasks. For example, at the end of the war Cooper Brothers' partners, who had been away in 1939-45, acknowledged that they were 'out of touch with current practice'.[24] In consequence, the firm's audit procedure was reviewed and new and more up-to-date methods adopted, specialist departments being set up to deal with executorship work, receiverships, investigations, registrar, share transfer, costing and secretarial work.

The continued growth in the size of client businesses and their demands for specialist services combined to provide a powerful impetus for larger accountancy practices. Such was the speed with which British Petroleum expanded in the early 1960s that Brown, Fleming & Murray were concerned that, without corresponding geographical growth, they might lose part or even all of the work. They did not gain the audit of BP's Canadian operations, for example, because the firm had no office there. When John Wilson, the senior partner in London, died unexpectedly in 1964, the dilemma over BP was a major factor in Brown, Fleming & Murray's earlier but as yet unanswered suggestion that they merge with Whinney, Smith & Whinney. Their shared office accommodation and combined Whinney Murray operations on the

Continent and in the Middle East provided a fitting prelude to full merger in 1965. Within the U.K. this gave them wider territorial coverage (though Brown, Fleming & Murray's Glasgow partnership did not formally join Whinney Murray until a year after the London firm) and the ability to extend their specialist departments. To this end Whinney Murray secured larger premises in 1967 at 57–67 Chiswell Street in an office block occupied jointly with a Brown, Fleming & Murray client, Burmah Oil.

In the nineteenth century Whinney, Smith & Whinney had experienced many changes of title as individual partners were admitted to or retired from the firm. With the adoption of the Whinney, Smith & Whinney style in 1894, the tradition of amendment of title to match the composition of the partnership ended. By contrast, Brown, Fleming & Murray had never altered their title – except to add Murray to Brown & Fleming in 1889. Yet it was appropriate in 1965 that certain leading elements from each name – 'Whinney' and 'Murray' – be selected for a new style to demonstrate the union of the two firms. The long-established name Whinney Murray had the added advantage of creating a coherent international presence. When Whinney Murray merged with Turquands Barton Mayhew and finally became Ernst & Whinney (see p. 223), the style became a matter of greater significance. As old staff loyalties to smaller units were stretched to embrace larger and potentially more remote organizations, a unified all-embracing title was designed to provide a cohesive force, consolidating the 'corporate identity'. In turn, the single style was recognizable to clients throughout the globe, offering an outward sign of increasingly unified accountancy practice and guaranteed professional standards.

There has been a general movement towards larger units through merger or association amongst the largest City accountants. For example, Brown, Fleming & Murray's amalgamation with Whinney, Smith & Whinney had been preceded by a more limited association with Thomson McLintock and Main Lafrentz to form McLintock, Murray, Main & Co to act for each other in America, Britain and Europe. Favouring a looser arrangement, Thomson McLintock operate a federalist system within Britain, where profits are not pooled but earned and retained by each autonomous regional office.[25] More commonly, however, merging practices adopted the single-firm concept where a unified partnership decided how the organization as a whole should act.

Certainly individual partners in small provincial practices had to sacrifice a measure of independence when they became part of a national firm. What they gained, by way of compensation, were the resources, back-up facilities and consolidated strength of that enlarged partnership. When firms remained linked only by federal ties, each office earning its own profits, there sometimes existed a disincentive to transfer work to where it would most effectively be performed.

It was often the case that less formal associations preceded full merger with a City practice. For example, before Ware, Ward (based in Bristol but diffused throughout the South West) amalgamated with Turquand, Youngs in 1963, a joint firm, Turquand, Youngs & Ware, Ward, had been formed three years earlier as a prelude to the final union.[26] The whole merger movement, if not actively initiated, was certainly facilitated by the repeal of the 'twenty-partner maximum' law in 1967, which allowed partnerships to have as many members as they desired. Firms had managed to get around the regulation by forming cross-partnerships on a geographical basis, though they naturally preferred that all their members should meet and reach decisions within a single integrated organization.

The background of expansion through merger and client growth provides the context within which the formation or development of specialist services should be viewed. In response to the rising levels and increasing complexity of taxation, Brown, Fleming & Murray had formed a separate tax department as early as the 1930s and they were in advance of general practice also taking the then uncommon step of referring the tax affairs of all clients to their specialist department as a matter of course. Whinney, Smith & Whinney had taken their first step towards the formation of a separate tax department in Edwardian times when Vernon Offord was diverted from general audit and accountancy work to concentrate on the provision of taxation advice to the firm's wealthier individual clients. In the early 1920s he was joined by William Carrington and W. D. Montgomery. William Carrington (having been President of the English Institute in 1955-56 and knighted in 1959) served on various official committees: from 1949 to 1951 as a member of the Royal Commission on Taxation under Lord Radcliffe and the two committees chaired by James Millard Tucker on Taxation of Trading Profits (1949-51) and Taxation Treatment of Provisions for Retirement (1950-53).

Later Sir William sat on an advisory panel to adjudicate on applications from companies wishing to leave Britain for tax reasons. The general importance of tax work is reflected in Brown, Fleming & Murray's deployment of staff in their London office, 20 (12%), out of a total 170, being in the tax department in 1962.[27]

The English Institute of Chartered Accountants similarly recognized the importance of taxation in the profession's work. Established in 1942, the Taxation and Financial Relations Committee,* under its first chairman, Harold Barton,[28] produced a number of research papers throughout the 1950s. By the early 1960s it was clear that taxation was simply one aspect of a growing range of specialist tasks performed by accountants. Accordingly the committee split into two: a Research Committee under Sir William Carrington for more general matters and a Technical Advisory Committee to deal primarily with tax, auditing and accountancy problems.[29] Although the Labour Government of 1945–51 did little, in fact, to change tax levels, this in itself did represent something of a break with the past in that it continued wartime levels of taxation in a period of peace.[30] As a result a fourfold increase in receipts from personal taxation occurred between 1938 and 1949 – a trend which was to be maintained despite changes of government almost unchecked throughout the 1950s and 1960s.

Another area of growing specialization for accountancy firms was in management services. In the 1950s practices increasingly developed costing and budgetary systems for their clients, while giving more general advice from their cumulative experience of business. Thomson McLintock began a management services department in 1959,[31] but because they were not yet large enough to support such a specialist (and then still slightly risky) enterprise, the matter was carried through in conjunction with Brown, Fleming & Murray and Mann Judd under the style McLintock, Mann & Murray.[32] The venture became a multi-discipline consultancy with a computer bureau and for many years the managing partner was not an accountant but an engineer (see p. 232).

The tendency for accountants to be recruited by industry, first evident in the inter-war period, intensified in the 1950s. In 1913 only 27.5% of the English Institute's membership were not in

* Renamed the Taxation and Research Committee in 1949 and the Technical and Advisory Committee in 1964.

private practice, but by 1939 this figure had risen to 51.5% and those in practice had fallen from 60.5% to 39.0%[33] – the remaining percentages being accountants employed overseas. In 1950 the total was divided 44.7% in practice and 55.3% in industry, commerce and public administration, while just over half of Scotland's chartered accountants fell into the last category.[34] When, in 1950, Sir Harold Howitt conducted his straw poll of about 275 students, he discovered that ninety had already decided to go directly into industry.[35] In response to this migration into management, in 1950 the English Institute decided that five of the forty-five Council seats should go to members who had moved from private practice into industry or commerce.[36]

The widespread recruitment of accountants into management posts not only reflected the increasingly complex financial structures produced by expanding companies but was also based on a much deeper appreciation of the accountant's potential contribution to business. For example in 1961 I.C.I. made a take-over bid for Courtaulds which the latter decided to oppose.[37] Calling upon Baring Bros, the merchant bankers, and Binder, Hamlyn & Co, the chartered accountants, to advise them, the latter under Anthony Burney were instrumental in preparing ammunition to demonstrate that resistance to the bid was well founded. Burney, amongst other tasks, drew up a document to show that Courtaulds' potential earnings were much greater than the I.C.I. terms implied and in a further memorandum set out a possible reorganization of the group with trade investments separated from manufacturing divisions.[38] These strong financial arguments enabled Courtaulds to ward off I.C.I.'s take-over bid.

In fact the take-over bid became a particular feature of the 1950s and 1960s.[39] It involved one company seeking to acquire the control of another usually by offering to buy out its shareholders at prices much above market quotations and to do so profitably because the balance sheet assets had been undervalued, or dividends had been kept unduly low in relation to earnings.[40] Accountants, therefore, occupied strategic positions on both sides of the bid, establishing the financial data and arguments with which the respective companies courted the shareholders.

At the same time as accountancy firms were refining and developing their services, important advances occurred in the techniques of auditing. In 1928, for example, the Midland Bank had been the first of the large banks to adopt a fully mechanized book-keeping system, consisting of electrically powered adding and ledger-posting machines.[41] The 1930s had witnessed the introduction of a whole range of office machinery – typewriters, duplicators and accounting machines (such as comptometers, pay roll listing and adding machines).[42] Montgomery reported from Whinney, Smith & Whinney's Manchester office in 1937 that their new comptometer 'is working well and will certainly enable us to get the work done with added speed and efficiency'.[43] For management the most important of these innovations were machines such as the Hollerith, which could process accounting data with great speed and which facilitated significant improvements in the collection and diffusion of information throughout large companies. Such technology, in turn, stimulated fresh thought about systems of management control. Machines continued to be used for certain aspects of auditing until the 1960s when the arrival of the computer heralded yet another major change.

Brown, Fleming & Murray were among the first to send staff on computer courses, and their training was facilitated by access to the McLintock, Mann & Murray computer.[44] However, it was not until the mid 1960s that accountancy firms had to take computers seriously. This was not so much to aid their own auditing procedures, as mechanical calculators had done, but because their major clients were now using computers as an integral part of their financial, costing and data storage procedures. Hence, it was necessary to develop new techniques to extract and analyse information from these companies' computers. In 1959, for example, British Tinken, a Whinney, Smith & Whinney client, installed a computer. After their merger with C. Herbert Smith & Russell in 1962, a Birmingham partner, John Masterton, was sent on an I.B.M. training course. Whinney, Smith & Whinney's larger scale allowed them to spare Masterton to teach other members of the firm computer techniques throughout 1965. Although this exercise was originally based in Birmingham, it soon made sense to establish a computer audit department in London where it later became part of the National Office concept (see p. 236).

Within Britain the continued growth of major accountancy firms posed great problems of internal organization. Unless partners opted for Thomson McLintock's decentralized solution, changes were needed. In the 'fifties and early 'sixties Whinney, Smith & Whinney's dozen or so partners still found it possible to meet around a table to discuss daily business and future policy as they had done for the previous hundred years. Only three provincial offices then existed – Leeds, Manchester and Birmingham – which could be easily contacted by letter or telephone. Having agreed to the single-firm concept, the merger with Brown, Fleming & Murray in 1965 virtually doubled the partnership and scale of the organization. Accordingly, in that year it became necessary to form an 'inner circle' of partners, the U.K. Policy Committee, who could act as delegates for the rest. Under this arrangement Britain was divided into regions, partners electing delegates from their ranks to express their views at policy meetings. Through this principle of regional representation, the essence of the accountancy firm's traditional partnership arrangement was successfully translated from its inception in the early nineteenth century to the present day. The adoption of a more structured partnership organization, in which some members devoted their time to client work and others to administration, in some senses marked a return to the small nineteenth-century firm where one member supervised the daily business while the other sought new assignments.

Although other professions (solicitors, doctors, surveyors and architects) have similarly moved towards larger units, none has formed practices on anything like the same scale as accountants. Apart from four or five specialized London firms, a large solicitors' practice might contain twenty to thirty partners, while a health centre might support ten doctors in general practice. This trend in accountancy has, of course, had repercusions for the profession as a whole. The polarization of accountancy practices into firms that are either very large or very small and the reduction in the number of medium-sized firms (where personal contacts were strong) and the consequent restructuring of the largest firms, has forced the English Institute to reconsider some of the rules governing the profession and the training offered to students (see p. 223).

In common with the largest practices the various professional institutes themselves have experienced growth and merger. The three Scottish Socisties (Edinburgh, Glasgow and Aberdeen) amalgamated in 1954, though in many respects thay had already been acting as one – for example, over examinations and disciplinary proceedings. In England the Society of Incorporated Accountants and the English Institute of Chartered Accountants united in 1957, when they took the latter's title and permitted all but a few members to call themselves chartered_accountants.

Greater emphasis was to be placed on formal education by the accountancy profession in the post-war era. More generally, there had been a move towards closer co-operation between the universities and industry in the Edwardian period.[45] In 1898 a Faculty of Commerce had been set up at Birmingham University following requests made by the city's business community, supported by Joseph Chamberlain, the major. Accountancy was an integral part of the course and Birmingham became the first English university to appoint a professor of accounting.[46] However the initiative was not widely accepted and when Cambridge University set up a course on Economics and Politics in 1903, no provision was made for accountancy despite an extensive debate. Alfred Marshall, the Professor of Economics responsible for the decision, argued that the subject was merely an extension of book-keeping, not a university subject but a practical skill.[47]

Following the criticisms voiced in the inter-war period, the English Institute, in conjunction with the newer universities, pursued a more positive policy towards education and research in the 1950s. The examination syllabus, which had been revised in 1944, reduced the emphasis on law in favour of accounting principles and introduced a separate paper on taxation, while costing and mechanized accounting were given greater prominence.[48] Degree courses, with accountancy, economics and law as the main elements, started at a number of provincial universities in October 1945. The Council established the P. D. Leake Professorship of Finance and Accounting at Cambridge (a chair oriented towards economics and national income accounting rather than the practical problems of company accounting) in June 1954 and P. D. Leake research fellowships followed at Balliol College, Oxford, together with others tenable at Oxford, London or Birmingham.[49] The closer association between academic study and accountancy practice partly resulted from the heightened complexity of company accounting and the growing volume of tax regulations, but also reflected a more inquiring attitude into these problems. The period also witnessed a general expansion in higher education with the result that the largest City and leading provincial accountants increasingly recruited graduates as articled clerks. By 1965 it was fairly common for teams to tour universities looking for suitable students with general qualifications in order to select them for training as chartered accountants (see p. 242). Although the numbers attending specific accountancy courses at university have grown greatly in the last twenty years, the majority of graduates recruited by the major City practices still come from other, often unrelated, disciplines.

Generally the two post-war decades were a time of continuous expansion in accountancy. The total fee income generated by accountancy firms grew by 43% between 1958 and 1969, which was 3% more than Britain's gross domestic product.[50] Accountancy practices which in 1959 employed 78,000 (excluding partners) expanded to the point where they had 89,000 staff by 1964 and 92,000 in 1969. The City of London alone had 370 accountancy practices in 1964-66 employing 11,407 staff, of whom 3,322 were women.[51] A similar picture may be painted of the other professional and service occupations. In 1959 a total of 85,000 staff worked for legal firms, which increased to 110,000 in 1968. Between 1959 and 1966 the numbers employed in accountancy and law grew by 19.2% and 22.4% respectively.[52] As the British service sector became increasingly important in terms of generating a greater proportion of national income and providing jobs, its growing productivity, and expansion in absolute terms, formed an essential component of the country's continued economic growth in the post-war period. More generally, in 1955 9.4 million (40.1% of the total working population) were employed in manufacturing and 10.7 million (45.7%) in services. By 1973 those engaged in manufacturing had experienced a real decline in their numbers, falling to 7.8 million (31.4%), while the service sector had continued to grow, reaching 12.5 million, or 50% of the workforce.[53]

This general expansion, witnessed at home, was mirrored in the overseas operations of major accountancy firms. Having established offices throughout the Iberian peninsula in the inter-war period, Barton, Mayhew now realized the potential of the vast Portuguese African colonies of Angola and Mozambique, opening offices at Luanda in 1954 and Lourenço Marques in 1961. They were not alone in this territorial adventurousness. With the end of hostilities in 1945, Whinney Murray set about re-establishing their Continental and Middle East practices. In Europe offices were reopened in Paris, Antwerp and Hamburg, while others were set up at The Hague (1958), Zurich (1959), Milan (1959) and Frankfurt (1962). Although much of the work followed from business connections established before the Second World War, further growth resulted from the flow of American investment into British and Continental manufacturing or commercial businesses, together with selective funding provided by the Marshall Aid Plan. For example, the Zurich office was principally opened to deal with the increase of American business in Switzerland. Growing United States influence in Europe encouraged Whinney Murray to strengthen their links with Ernst & Ernst – a direct source of work from American clients. Accordingly, when in 1958 Ernst & Ernst requested Whinney Murray to act for them on the Continent, North Africa and the Middle East, the initiative satisfied both sides, a partnership being concluded by which three Ernst & Ernst partners joined members of the Continental firm under the style Whinney Murray, Ernst & Ernst (see p. 245).[54]

The incentives for accountancy practices to expand overseas increased dramatically in the 1950s and 1960s. For although only 29% in a sample of 100 large U.K. companies had extensive overseas manufacturing interests in 1950, the proportion had risen to 58% in 1970.[55] By this date Whinney Murray's Continental firm had grown to employ 300 partners and staff based in sixteen offices spread throughout Europe and North West Africa, new offices having been opened in Stockholm, Copenhagen, Düsseldorf, Brussels, Madrid, Rome, Tripoli, Libya, Lagos and Monrovia, though the headquarters remained in Paris. Like the U.K. firm, these offices, under their senior partner, built up specialist departments for investigation and tax work, while management services had consultants based in Paris, Frankfurt and Milan. Accountancy in Europe is a particularly esoteric matter because each office (often serving a whole country) has to know the complexities of its national legal and tax requirements and this, allied to the language difficulties, can make it difficult to transfer staff from one office to another. Established to serve U.K. and transatlantic companies with European interests, the offices of the Continental firm preserved much of their original character and, though capturing some local work, they were at this time in essence the servants of British and American multi-nationals. This reality is reflected in their staffing, even as late as 1970 when nine of the twenty-nine partners and managers had come from Ernst & Ernst and five from Whinney Murray's U.K. firm.

A few members of Turquand, Youngs' Far East firm, many of

whom had suffered severely from imprisonment by the Japanese, helped to restart operations in 1946 when a substantial number of offices were re-established including Singapore, Penang and Kuala Lumpur, while new offices were set up at Kuching (1958), Kota Kinabalu (1959), Bangkok (1959), Malacca (1960), Sandakan (1961) and Sibu (1962). A portent for the future was created when in 1969 Whinney Murray asked Turquand, Youngs to act for them in Singapore, Malaysia and Thailand, a joint partnership being formed. Again there had been various alterations in the practice's style to reflect the changing emphasis of its composition. In 1946 the Derrick & Co element was removed from McAuliffe, Turquand, Youngs & Co's title as this merged firm had become fully integrated and then the name order was reversed when Turquand, Youngs purchased the McAuliffe practice (see p. 179). On the death of Sir Henry McAuliffe in 1951 the style reverted to Turquand, Youngs, providing the firm with a single recognizable name throughout the world.[56]

Generally, the two post-war decades witnessed the decline of Britain's interests in South America as the United States developed their influence there.[57] In common with this trend the McAuliffe offices in Brazil, Rio de Janiero, Para, Santos, and São Paulo, were sold to Arthur Andersen in the mid 1950s and those in Argentina (Buenos Aires) and Uruguay (Montevideo) allowed to merge with Price Waterhouse's South American firm.

To conclude the history of Ernst & Whinney, we must step into the 1970s to trace the evolution of the themes only introduced in this chapter – the merger movement within the profession, the drive towards greater specialization, the need to form international partnerships and greater government and institute regulations. The 1950s were in a sense watershed years between Britain as the oldest industrial nation geared temporarily for war and Britain fighting for survival in the tough competitive markets of a revived, reconstructed Europe and a wider world. It is against this economic battlefield that the firm's performance has to be judged in the latter part of the twentieth century.

References

1 Arthur Marwick, *Britain in the Century of Total War*, London (1968), p. 260.
2 Sidney Pollard, *The Development of the British Economy 1914-1967*, London (1969), p. 391.

3 *The Accountant*, No. 4795, 12 November 1966, p. 643.

4 Garratt, *op. cit.*, p. 247.

5 David Thomson, *England in the Twentieth Century*, Harmondsworth (1965), p. 220.

6 Winsbury, *op. cit.*, p. 84.

7 Sir Norman Chester, *The Nationalization of British Industry 1945-51*, London H.M.S.O. (1975), pp. 614-15.

8 *Ibid*, p. 619.

9 *Ibid*, p. 625; and Pollard, *op. cit.*, p. 381.

10 Channon, *Service Industries, op. cit.*, p. 233.

11 *Who was Who 1961-1970*, Vol. VI, London (1972), p. 65; *The Accountant*, No. 4584, 27 October 1962, p. 557.

12 Letter of appointment to Sir Harold Barton from the Ministry of Transport, 6 July 1948.

13 11 & 12 Geo 6, c. 38, 1948 Companies Act.

14 Stacey, *op. cit.*, p. 231.

15 1948 Companies Act, *op. cit.*, Eighth Schedule, section 17, p. 344.

16 Marriner, *op. cit.*, p. 254.

17 1948 Companies Act, *op. cit.*, Ninth Schedule, section 2, p. 348.

18 *The Accountant*, No. 3934, 13 May 1950, Howitt, *op. cit.*, p. 537.

19 *Arthur Andersen Chronicle* (1949), Robertson, *op. cit.*, p. 149.

20 Whinney, Smith & Whinney Day Books.

21 Brown, Fleming & Murray (London) Private Ledger 1939-1955.

22 Pauline Gregg, *A Social and Economic History of Britain 1760-1972*, London (1973), pp. 552-4; and A. J. Youngson, *Britain's Economic Growth*, London (1968), p. 174.

23 Baker, Sutton & Co Fee Ledger No. 1 (1903-1926), p. 1.

24 Cooper Brothers, *op. cit.*, pp. 16-17.

25 Winsbury, *op. cit.*, pp. 2, 74.

26 Ware, Ward, *op. cit.*, pp. 11-12.

27 Brown, Fleming & Murray (London) Minute Book 1961-1963, p. 76.

28 *History of the English Institute, op. cit.*, p. 101.

29 *Ibid*, p. 133.

30 Marwick, *Britain in the Century of Total War, op. cit.*, p. 359.

31 Winsbury, *op. cit.*, pp. 90-1.

32 In 1965 the style changed to McLintock, Mann & Whinney Murray.

33 Stacey, *op. cit.*, pp. 214-15.

34 *Scottish Chartered Accountants, op. cit.*, p. 93.

35 *The Accountant*, Howitt, *op. cit.*, p. 538.

36 *History of the English Institute, op. cit.*, p. 109.

37 D. C. Coleman, *Courtaulds, An Economic and Social History, 1940-1965*, Vol. III, Oxford (1980), p. 218.

38 *Ibid*, p. 224.

39 Pollard, *Development of the British Economy, op. cit.*, p. 431.

40 *Ibid.*

41 Edwin Green, *op. cit.*, p. 23.

42 Hannah, *Rise of the Corporate Economy, op. cit.*, pp. 86-7.

43 Letter, from W. D. Montgomery to C. J. G. Palmour, 4 May 1937.

44 Brown, Fleming & Murray Minute Book 1961-1963, 8 May 1962. Two members of staff 'booked to go on the I.C.T. introductory courses', p. 36.

45 Michael Sanderson, *The Universities and British Industry 1850-1970*, London (1972), p. 184.

46 *Ibid*, pp. 193, 195.

47 *Ibid*, p. 202.

48 *History of the English Institute, op. cit.*, p. 105.

49 *Ibid*, pp. 112-13.

50 John H. Dunning and E. Victor Morgan, *An Economic Study of the City of London*, London (1971), p. 240.

51 *Ibid*, p. 432.

52 *Ibid*, p. 241.

53 Leslie Hannah, *Management Strategy and Business Development*, London (1976): Derek F. Channon, 'Corporate Evolution in the Service Industries', pp. 214-15.

54 *Ernst & Ernst, op. cit.*, p. 77.

55 Derek F. Channon, *The Strategy and Structure of British Enterprise*, London (1973), p. 78.

56 Letter, 11 December 1950, which noted that 'the Eastern firm will be known from the same date as Turquand, Youngs & Co. . . . .'

57 Marwick, *Britain in the Century of Total War, op. cit.*, p. 260.

❀❀❀ CHAPTER 9 ❀❀❀

Today and Conclusions

The final chapter of this accountancy history sees the merger of Turquand, Youngs and Barton, Mayhew in 1972 and then their subsequent amalgamation with Whinney Murray in 1979 to culminate in the change of name to Ernst & Whinney in July of that year. However, these major alliances, which have been conducted without disturbing the style or outward form of the national firms concerned, conceal a significant number of provincial mergers. In the 1970s alone Whinney Murray amalgamated with the following practices: Smith & Garton based in Huddersfield and Leeds (1971), Fraser, Lawson & Laing, Glasgow (1973), Buckley, Hall, Devin, Hull and Leeds (1973–74), McWilliam, Smith & MacLean, Inverness (1976), Woolley & Waldron, Southampton (1977), and Mason & Sons in London (1977), while Turquands Barton Mayhew merged with Howell & Hanbidge, Sheffield (1974), Reid & Mair, Glasgow (1978) and Davidson Smith, Wighton & Crawford, Edinburgh (1978), having opened their own offices at Luton and Norwich in 1974 and 1976 respectively. Similarly, Whinney Murray had set up offices in Liverpool (1968) and Aberdeen (1975) without joining an established local practice. In September 1979 Ernst & Whinney amalgamated with Baker, Sutton a medium-sized City practice with a broad range of audit clients and a specialism in insurance accounting including Lloyd's underwriters and brokers. Most recently, in April 1980 Ernst & Whinney merged with Turquands Barton Mayhew's former correspondent firm in Belfast, FitzSimons & Cameron, to strengthen their U.K. coverage. It is as if the wheel of change suddenly began to accelerate in the late 1960s as the last fifteen years have witnessed a series of major amalgamations. Once started, the process appears to be almost self-generating, progressively gathering speed.★

★ Since the completion of the manuscript in December 1980 certain changes have occurred which affect Ernst & Whinney's U.K. firm but, because they lie beyond the study's timescale and their inclusion would delay publication, it was decided to leave the story as it stood.

In addition, almost as many internal administrative and organizational developments have taken place in the last decade as had been experienced in the previous century – such, however, is the pace of modern life. As before, changes in the structure and function of the accountancy profession reflect major changes in the business community which it serves. For example, the introduction of the English Institute's regulation, that firms should avoïd having a client which contributes more than 15% of its gross fees, was conditioned by the growth in scale of companies and a desire to prevent over-reliance upon a single source of income that might cloud professional independence.

Following the Whinney Murray merger of 1965, the second major amalgamation leading to the present Ernst & Whinney practice occurred in 1972 and was between Barton, Mayhew and Turquand, Youngs. Just as Whinney, Smith & Whinney and Brown, Fleming & Murray had co-operated overseas before their merger, so these other two firms had operated joint offices on the Continent (in France, Belgium, Italy and Switzerland) as a prelude, but with no presupposition, to formal amalgamation. When Turquand, Youngs severed their link with Arthur Andersen in 1957, they were left without a Paris office, so that Barton, Mayhew suggested they move into their premises and operate jointly under the style Barton, Mayhew, Horton & Turquand, Youngs, the practice being extended to Brussels and Madrid by 1961; the two firms subsequently opened a small office in Zurich together. The 1972 union was, as is customary, preceded by a gradual process of familiarization and discussion, being tested in an informal way in June 1969 when Barton, Mayhew arranged a cricket match to face for the first time in twenty-eight years a team from Turquand, Youngs.[1] Permitting a wider range of specialist services, the merger had advantages beyond those of absolute size. Turquand, Youngs had a strong West Country connection which complemented Barton, Mayhew's offices in Leicester and Manchester. Overseas both firms possessed offices in Spain which could unite with advantage, while Turquand, Youngs also operated an extensive practice in the Far East with additional branches in Ceylon, Malta and Gibraltar, Barton, Mayhew having already established themselves in Portugal's African colonies.

The merger between two leading international firms, Whinney Murray and Turquands Barton Mayhew, in January 1979 offered even greater operational and territorial advantages. The latter were represented in the following towns or districts not covered by Whinney Murray: Bristol, Exeter and Devon, Fifeshire, Leicester, Luton, Norwich and Sheffield; the former having offices in Birmingham, Aberdeen, Cardiff (following an amalgamation with Phillips & Trump in 1968), Huddersfield, Hull, Inverness, Leeds, Liverpool, Newcastle, Scunthorpe and Southampton, all towns in which Turquands Barton Mayhew were not represented. However, duplication did occur in the major commercial and industrial centres of Edinburgh, Glasgow and Manchester – and, of course, London. The union was further encouraged by a surprising degree of compatibility overseas: Whinney Murray's extensive Middle East practice matching Turquands Barton Mayhew's Far East firm, which was already acting for the former's U.K. and Continental firms. Although a measure of duplication existed on the Continent, Turquands Barton Mayhew's Iberian and Mediterranean strength complemented Whinney Murray's network throughout North West Europe and Scandinavia. However, the most important factor for the future proved to be the latter's close links with America through Ernst & Ernst, an area where Turquands Barton Mayhew were poorly represented. The exact nature of this overseas fit, like two halves of a jigsaw puzzle of the world, was remarkable when the size of the two firms is considered and it is unlikely that any other major accountancy merger could produce such complementarity. As most other leading accountancy firms have now concluded their own arrangements to cover the globe, it is unlikely that a merger on the Whinney Murray–Turquands Barton Mayhew scale could be arranged in the future.

A major feature of recent changes in British accountancy has been the decline in the number of medium-sized practices and the polarization of the profession between the largest national firms based in the City and the numerous small practices which flourish throughout the country. Although various criteria may be selected to define the size of accountancy firms (the number of partners or professional staff, annual fee income and geographical spread are all valid), there are today about twenty-five major practices employed at least 250 professional staff, excluding secretaries and ancillary workers, with over thirty partners and earning a U.K. fee income of over £3 million.[2] At the top of this list stand the so-called 'big eight', a group of practices which domi-

Map 2 The Location and Historical origin of Ernst & Whinney's principal U.K. Offices.

LEGEND:

WM(W) WHINNEY MURRAY (W.S. & W.)
WM(B) WHINNEY MURRAY (B.F. & M.)
TBM(T) TURQUANDS BARTON MAYHEW (T.Y.)
TBM(B) TURQUANDS BARTON MAYHEW (B.M.)
E&W ERNST & WHINNEY
(NOTE. THE DATE INDICATES EITHER WHEN THE
ABOVE FIRMS MERGED WITH AN ESTABLISHED
LOCAL PRACTICE OR SET UP THEIR OWN OFFICE)

nate the profession by virtue of their absolute size and range of operations. They each employ over 1,000 professional staff (some almost 3,000), have at least a hundred partners and earn U.K. fees in excess of £15 million per annum.[3] Some have suggested that they will 'continue to squeeze out the [remaining] medium-sized practices by taking over their larger clients',[4] while the small firms, operating in a different market, continue to prosper.

Although the number of accountancy firms recorded in the Stock Exchange yearbooks for the U.K. grew between 1948 and 1978 from 4,831 to 8,711, this expansion was accomplished through a disproportionate growth at the small end of the spectrum. The disappearance of many medium-sized practices has been clearly demonstrated by reference to the distribution of their listed client companies.[5] The number of medium-sized firms, that is those having more than three but less than twenty listed clients, fell from 206 in 1968 to 57 in 1978. The greatest percentage of public company audits was increasingly captured by the twenty largest firms. In 1948 they held 33.0% of listed audits; by 1979 no less than 68.9%. This trend becomes even more remarkable when the top ten accountancy firms are considered. In 1948 they audited 26.0% of listed companies, but had captured 56.1% by 1979.[6]

What, therefore, were the economic forces which compelled so many medium-sized accountancy firms to merge with the larger City-based practices over the last twenty years? Generally speaking it was not because their independent and growing clients deserted them for bigger auditors with wider coverage and services (though occasionally this has happened), but because these companies were themselves absorbed. Firms taking over other businesses normally wished their own auditors to perform the audit of their new subsidiaries. If, however, the former client were absorbed as a division, rather than a subsidiary, the audit automatically transferred to the accountants auditing the alligator group. The total number of public companies on the Stock Exchange has declined by 49% between 1948 and 1978 (from 5,978 to 2,955) as a result of bankruptcy, voluntary liquidation, but more importantly, through mergers.[7] The process of amalgamation and concentration being experienced by the business community at large had thus induced an equivalent momentum for amalgamation and concentration amongst accountancy firms. The fortunate auditors of the companies growing by merger themselves could reap the benefit – provided that they grew in scale and size equivalently and could offer the specialized services which larger more complex business structures demanded. Principally for this reason the number of accountancy firms with listed audit clients has fallen from 1,422 in 1948 to 511 in 1978, a reduction of 64%. Even in 1979 the top twenty accountancy firms gained a further forty-nine audit clients (from a directory of 2,107 quoted companies), representing 2.3% of the whole. In this redistribution the top ten gained on average 2.4 clients, the following ten achieved an average gain of 1.9, while those ranked 21 to 30 each lost an average of 0.3 listed clients.[8] These figures illustrate the increasing concentration of total audit clients among the largest accountancy firms as the total number of listed companies continues to decline. Moreover audit work is the biggest contributor to the overall fee income of these expanding accountancy firms, contributing in most cases at least 60% of their fees. Touche Ross quoted 60% for 1978, Arthur Youngs 70%, Peats 70% and Price Waterhouse 75–80%.[9]

The importance of this process of concentration which has had such profound effects upon the structure of the accountancy profession may be seen through an examination of the share of U.K. manufacturing output occupied by the hundred largest companies. In 1935 these hundred produced 24% of output, rising to 27% in 1958, 37% in 1963, and achieved 41% in 1968.[10] The figures show how industry has become progressively more concentrated as the expanding leaders have swallowed their lesser competitors and merged rivals. Accordingly, intermediate accountancy practices (usually serving a number of independent medium-sized businesses) suffered attrition as their biggest clients were taken over by large-scale operations and their audit transferred to the holding company's accountants. For example, Buckley, Hall, Devin (ranked second in Hull with nine partners) suffered from this process, which helped to persuade them, as both a defensive and progressive measure, to conclude a merger with Whinney Murray in 1973. As a result, they were in a position to gain work should Whinney Murray's larger clients take over businesses in their area. Equally important, they could offer existing clients a wider range of services and broader geographical coverage as a result of their link with a national and international practice. C. Herbert Smith & Russell, the largest independent Birmingham practice in the 1960s with four partners, were only intermediate in size in national terms. They believed that their largest or most rapidly growing clients, particularly Lucas, might be vulnerable to take-over or might demand services which they could not readily supply – hence their merger with Whinney, Smith & Whinney in 1962. In each case, the partners felt that some loss of autonomy would be more than outweighed by a gain in security and broadened horizons.

Another factor encouraging the growth of the leading accountancy practices is also closely connected with the character of their clients. Today's largest groups are not, as might be expected, highly concentrated in a geographical sense. In fact, they generally constitute a wide territorial spread of medium-sized plants united by organizational and financial links. Back in 1958 the hundred largest companies in Britain each only owned on average twenty-seven plants world-wide.[11] Hence the incentive for their accountants to open provincial and overseas offices was not great and most merely operated in the major manufacturing and commercial centres at home and on the Continent. However, by 1972 the hundred largest companies each possessed on average seventy-two plants (suggesting that their growth was largely by take over or merger), creating powerful pressures on the major accountancy firms to provide comprehensive coverage throughout Britain so that each plant could be efficiently audited by members of the same firm and the individual subsidiary accounts sent to the head office, often in the City, for consolidation and analysis. It was partly to facilitate the audit of Dunlop, for example, that Whinney, Smith & Whinney had opened their Manchester office in 1928. By the early 1970s Dunlop Holdings had grown to be the tenth largest manufacturing enterprise in Britain, with 130 factories operating in twenty-two countries, and employed 85,000 workers in the U.K. spread throughout the country in many plants.[12] Accordingly Whinney Murray's offices in Manchester, Leeds, Liverpool, Newcastle, Birmingham, Hull, Cardiff, Glasgow and London were all involved in the Dunlop audit. Similarly, Thorn Electric (ranked twelfth in 1972 with 82,000 U.K. employees and seventy factories throughout the world), which became a client of Whinney, Smith & Whinney when it became a public company in 1936, today provides work for Ernst & Whinney offices in Birmingham, Newcastle, Liverpool, Manchester, Leeds and London.

Meanwhile the smaller accountancy firms remained and multiplied. There are at least 12,000 practices with five or fewer partners in the U.K.[13] Within the City alone 370 practices flourished in 1964–66, of which only twenty each employed over a hundred partners and staff.[14] Most small accountancy firms primarily deal with the needs of the locality and their clients commonly include family businesses, private companies and individuals. As a result, their work mainly comprises the preparation of accounts, small audits, personal tax returns and general financial advice rather than the audit of listed public companies.

The process of polarization within the accountancy profession was clearly reflected at its upper end by the recent merger between Whinney Murray and Turquands Barton Mayhew. Although these two practices were large, individually neither was then among the accountancy giants at the upper end of the so-called 'Big Eight'. In October 1979 the united organization did, however, find itself among the top five firms in the U.K. with 200 partners and over 2,150 professional staff. Ernst & Whinney thus ensured that it was equipped to cope with the expansion requirements of existing and new clients. The former included Shell, National Westminster Bank,★ Norwich Union, Bowaters, Guinness, Ladbrokes, Westland Aircraft, Milk Marketing Board, National Freight Corporation and the Trustee Savings Bank inherited from Turquands Barton Mayhew, while British Petroleum, Midland Bank, British Airways, Dunlop Holdings, Lucas Industries, Burmah Oil, Thorn E.M.I., Bass, Smith & Nephew and Whitbread are all former Whinney Murray clients. Although Ernst & Whinney's primary concern for each of these clients is the annual audit, many companies require additional services such as tax advice, acquisition and other investigations, costing and internal accounting procedures together with information relating to overseas markets – all being provided by specialist departments.

A further feature of the growth in the scale of business had important repercussions for accountancy. Company expansion often proceeded through diversification of business commitments. For example, Dunlop Holdings at the time of their union with Pirelli had sixteen divisions devoted to the manufacture of wheels, vehicle suspensions, brakes, belting, aviation products, sports equipment and footwear.[15] Diversification followed

★ Both Shell and the National Westminster Bank are audited jointly, the former with Price Waterhouse (New York) and Klynveld Kraayenhof (The Hague) and the latter with Peat, Marwick, Mitchell & Co.

partly from the take-over of product-related companies and partly from a desire to extend the group's activities. Although only 25% in a sample of large U.K. companies could be considered as diversified in 1950, ten years later the proportion had risen to 45% and by 1970 was 60%.[16] As the earlier holding company structure had initiated consolidated accounting, so diversification was to have important implications for accountancy in the late 'sixties and 'seventies.

A recent study of 100 large U.K. companies found that by 1950 only 13 of them had adopted a multi-divisional structure, whereas by 1960 the proportion had risen to 30% and by 1970 to 72%.[17] The development was encouraged by the continued expansion in the size of businesses, and the need to obviate the tax problems related to a centralized group structure, while new markets, products and processes evolved on an international scale made it increasingly difficult to control and co-ordinate the multiplicity of operating decisions under a holding company-subsidiary company structure.[18] Such mounting complexity made the measurement of performance in different activities increasingly problematical with existing control systems. Accordingly, further decentralization and delegation of decision-making proved necessary if management were to supervise and plan efficiently.[19] The multi-divisional system called for enterprise to be divided into autonomous profit-centred units based on either product or geography. Because of more widely devolved responsibilities, the divisional head required more detailed accounts than the executive who had been in charge of a subsidiary. The central office, on the other hand, might require less, or at least more concentrated, information than before to enable it to monitor performance and make general policy decisions.

One of the early multi-divisional structures introduced to the U.K. arose from the recommendations by McKinsey & Co (the American management consultants) to the National Westminster Bank, following the merger of the National Provincial with the Westminster Bank in 1968.[20] Previously McKinsey had been called in 1959 to advise on the restructuring of Shell's administration in London and The Hague and had recommended the increased decentralization and devolution of power, the creation of Shell Chemicals as a separate company and the reorientation of senior directors from everyday management executive responsibilities to major policy questions.[21] Similarly the National Westminster Bank diversified by function as well as geographically in the course of the 1970s, acquiring its own finance house, and extending operations into leasing, factoring and insurance. Barclays and the Midland were forced by this success to follow suit. The former, however, had already taken a lead in overseas diversification, opening branches throughout the world, which in turn encouraged the National Westminster and the Midland (after 1973) to do the same.[22]

In the early 1960s Dunlop Holdings asked McKinsey & Co to design a decentralized product-division system. Like I.C.I., Dunlop, an early diversifier, had built up a large central office which had originally exercised tight control over its many subsidiaries. However, under the reorganization head office retained only the specialist departments, being restructured to co-ordinate and guide the activities of the newly created divisions.[23] The situation has since been further complicated by their union with Pirelli in 1971. Under this arrangement Dunlop acquired a 49% interest in Pirelli's Italian and European operations, together with a 40% share in their other overseas companies, while Pirelli in turn acquired a 49% interest in Dunlop's U.K. and European companies and a 40% interest in their other overseas companies.[24] The union necessarily involved close co-operation between Whinney Murray and Pirelli's Italian accountants. As always the accountancy firm needed to respond to the growth and changing organization of its client, wherever in the world business operations created the need for the accountant's presence.

Such changes in structure amongst the larger business organizations have induced equivalent developments in the administrative organization of the accountancy firms who serve them: there is a strong parallel with the way in which the largest accountancy practices have organized themselves. Like the multi-divisional company, they have a head office for policy making, co-ordination and the provision of specialist services, while each of their branches, overseas and at home, like the different divisions of a large business, is largely autonomous with a partner-in-charge responsible for its daily running. Although Ernst & Whinney's National Office in London acts as a profit centre, this is not normally the case with the head office of a multi-divisional company where the attribution of profits to its plants (especially when they are situated in different countries) is often a source of contention and brings much work for accountants as advisers on transfer pricing and the relative tax regulations. In addition, following the more general pattern throughout the service sector, there has been a certain amount of diversification within the profession. Accountancy practices, like the banks, now offer management consultancies; while accountants and solicitors both offer advice on taxation. Diversification, therefore, has led to each type of institution moving into areas traditionally held by others, so that established demarcation lines have become blurred.[25]

Here an important distinction ought to be underlined. As has been seen, in the Victorian period the professional accountant was often called upon not only to perform the statutory audit but also to draw up the company's balance sheet and later its profit and loss account. With the growth in the scale of business and the general diffusion of accounting knowledge in the early twentieth century, companies set up their own accounts departments not simply to keep a record of daily transactions but to draw up periodical balance sheets. Internal audit departments became increasingly frequent in the 1920s as the largest companies saw the need for costing and financial statements to aid management decisions. An important distinction developed, therefore, between the work performed by a company's own accountants and those appointed to undertake its statutory audit.

The transition by many groups from a centralized company to a multi-divisional structure had a great effect on their internal accounting departments. The devolution of responsibility multiplied the number of management positions within a given organization. Hence, the adoption of a multi-divisional structure generally necessitated improved and more sophisticated information systems.[26] This, in turn, has created an increasing demand in industry for qualified accountants not simply to assess the financial performance of divisions but to set up costing and management accounting systems suited to their particular operations. The migration of chartered accountants into business, already noted in the inter-war period, accelerated in the 1950s. In 1965 a survey revealed that 6.5% of directors of listed U.K. companies were chartered accountants.[27] A recent study of the English Institute's 68,000 members showed that 35% worked in industry and a further 6% in finance.[28] By 1980, 81% of chief financial officers in the 300 largest U.K. companies were chartered accountants. The reason for this trend is, as Anthony Sampson saw in the early 1960s:[29] '[Accountants] are the priesthood of industry; the more

fragmented and diversified a company becomes, the more important becomes the man who can disentangle the threads of profitability that hold it together.'

The growing complexity and scale of business operations led
companies to approach accountancy firms (usually their auditors
who had very detailed knowledge of their finances) to help them
reorganize their internal costings and accounting systems. To deal
effectively with these problems a number of management services
departments were set up by accountancy firms in the 1950s. A
common development in the 'sixties then became the creation of
a separate management consultancy firm (funded through the
partnership of the accountancy practice but often physically distinct and run by specialist and some non-accounting staff). In
other cases the management consultancy department was retained
within the practice, giving its operation a strong accountancy
base. However, the general recession in the early 1970s coupled
with the oil crisis of 1973–74 meant that fewer businesses could
afford such services. Whinney Murray at first operated a management service consultancy jointly with Thomson McLintock and
Mann Judd. Then in 1975 with the appointment of an engineer as
McLintock, Mann & Whinney Murray's managing partner, the
management advisory practice moved to City Gate House,
Chiswell Street, as a separate concern, leaving the share registration section and computer bureau, which had formed part of the
original facilities, in Granby House, Southwark. In the same year
Mann Judd withdrew and in January 1976 the enterprise came to
an end. As a result the accountancy-based management services
formerly organized through the joint venture reverted as part of
the original individual accountancy practices, Whinney Murray
setting up a separate department within the National Office
framework to deal with this work. In essence it provided businesses with cost and general information systems, advising on the
use of accounting machines and computers, while also offering a
financially orientated recruitment service. Initially the department
worked entirely for companies who were already audit clients,
but by 1979 this figure had fallen to 75–80% as it established a
reputation beyond the practice's immediate clientele.

Turquands Barton Mayhew operated their management consultancy service through a different system, being part of a consortium called Turquand, Youngs & Layton-Bennett. This, too,
was a separate operation, which by coincidence also had an en-

gineer as its managing partner and operated overseas. However, the 1979 merger brought an end to this consortium, when it was in part absorbed by a new Ernst & Whinney partnership comprising all management consultancy sections of the merged firm. The new partnership, now a member of the Management Consultancy Association, broadened its activities, widening the emphasis from accountancy-based advice, to embrace marketing, production and distribution policies and their practical implementation. Although formally part of the National Office structure, it operated as a separate partnership, which gave greater flexibility and enabled the operation to offer a broader range of services. Barton, Mayhew, like Whinney, Smith & Whinney before joining the McLintock, Mann & Murray consultancy in 1965, had its own management services department within the firm. This was incorporated within the Turquand, Youngs & Layton-Bennett consultancy after the 1972 merger.[30] Baker, Sutton, being of intermediate size and therefore restricted in the range of specialisms they were able to offer, provided coverage in this field by concluding a close correspondent arrangement in 1965 with Annan, Impey, Morrish & Co., a practice which specialized in management accounting.

In a sense, the progress towards Ernst & Whinney's present diversified practice in the U.K. may best be understood by an examination of its evolving organizational structure. The 1950s and 1960s witnessed the creation of various specialist departments, while territorial expansion, principally by merger and amalgamation with existing local practices, continued within Britain. An important step was taken in 1973 when a National Office was set up within Whinney Murray's London office at Chiswell Street, whose staff were divided between those working for clients in a specialist capacity and those concerned with the administration of the U.K. firm. The National Office umbrella, divided into two halves, now comprises on the Client Services side, Insolvency, Investigations, Computer Audit and Management Services, while the Support Services side consists of the Internal Finance and Accounting, Taxation, Technical and Training Departments. It was based in London as a matter of convenience – in a building which could accommodate the necessary numbers and suitably located in the City with good communications. National Office's role has been to advise regional offices when clients there demanded specialist services or created unusual problems. It remained the servant of Manchester or Inverness offices no less than of London, where it happened to be situated. Following the merger with Turquands Barton Mayhew in 1979, National Office extended its operations not simply as the firm's numbers increased but as economies of scale offered greater scope for spreading the overhead costs of these specialist departments.

The oldest and largest of Whinney Murray's specialist departments is taxation. All regional offices have partners or staff who are taxation experts, but with the rising volume of increasingly complex legislation and the resort to more frequent budgets to try to regulate the economy, it has proved necessary, in addition, to have a specialist organization within the National Office structure to study new tax legislation, to assist with training, compile booklets and periodicals and undertake research. Hence, in 1977 a National Tax partner, able to call on a technical group selected from London office to study specific tax problems, was appointed as a liaison officer between the senior partner, the provincial tax departments and the international partnership.

The recent increase in tax legislation has brought clients and accountants more closely together because of its very complexity, but the new laws have also embodied more deep-seated change. Until 1965 there had been very little alteration in the British tax system established by degrees from Peel's 1842 budget – major changes affected rates rather than its essential structure, kinds of taxes or the philosophy. As a result a considerable body of legal experience had been assembled through countless cases fought between individuals and the Inland Revenue. However, the mass of recent legislation with new forms of taxation, introduced from 1965, overtook many of these precedents and created a situation where great 'uncertainty regarding the interpretation and application of fiscal statutes'[31] meant that professional advisers often could no longer safely predict the outcome of the dispute with the Revenue. Tax accountants and solicitors were not always able to give definitive opinions. Consequently negotiations and compromise with the authorities has often displaced 'the settlement of disputed points by reference to the law'.[32] This, in turn, has drawn clients more closely to their professional advisers who, acting as intermediaries, are well placed to negotiate with the Inland Revenue. The influence of both civil servants administering the tax law and the accountants advising clients has been enhanced by this new complexity and uncertainty in tax legisla-

Figure 6 Ernst & Whinney's U.K. Firm Organization Chart, 1979

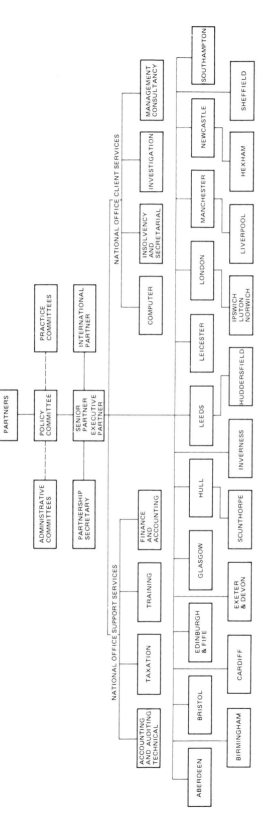

tion. The premium on expert, up-to-date information has sharply increased. Whereas in the past a local accountant might advise his clients efficiently from basic handbooks, now a telephone call to the specialist on a particular problem in the taxation department at London's National Office and regular supplements to the tax publications privately produced within the partnership and distributed to all regional offices are critical advantages for the large firm. And such special expertise normally can only be financed within the large national and international practices.

The growth in the size and complexity of the largest U.K. groups has encouraged the evolution of computer auditing, another important recent development. In 1970 Andrew Oakley, a manager, moved from Whinney Murray's Birmingham office to join the small London computer staff (originally set up by Brown, Fleming & Murray to cope with BP's use of computers). The department, growing in response to the widespread use of computers, became part of National Office in 1973 and, when Whinney Murray merged with Turquands Barton Mayhew, amalgamated with the latter's computer audit section. As well as having their own computer terminals, the department has developed a number of packages or programmes to suit the various computers used by British clients, which could be run as part of the audit procedure. The large accountancy firms have inevitably become important centres for the diffusion of these new computing skills through the business community. Whinney Murray's computer department has also taught staff from regional offices so that they too could run programmes without assistance from National Office. Within the City, where many of Ernst & Whinney's major clients also have their head offices and computer sections, the firm established direct links through the G.P.O. with company data banks. The use of the computer both reflects and encourages the development of sophisticated accounting techniques not only to monitor a company's financial performance more exactly but also in an attempt to measure its productivity and aid management decisions. Here, too, the ability to offer a specialist service has depended upon the large scale of operations.

Another specialist department is insolvency. Whinney Murray's Insolvency Department was formally established in 1973, also as part of the National Office concept. Like Computer Audit, which followed developments in the Birmingham office, the Insolvency Department arose from expertise gained in the provinces. W. G. Mackey, a partner in the Newcastle practice of Thomas Bowden & Glenton (which merged with Whinney Murray in 1968), had gradually built up a specialism in insolvency work during the 1960s, partially assisted by the region's overall decline, though the firm itself remained a general practice largely concerned with auditing, accounting and tax work. Having joined Whinney Murray, the experience which Mackey had gained meant that he was increasingly being appointed as receiver or liquidator not just in the North East but throughout Britain and occasionally to assignments with overseas connections. It made sense, therefore, to bring him and his small insolvency staff to London as part of National Office. The move in 1973 could not have been better timed as the Middle East oil crisis in that year combined with the recession to produce a host of bankruptcies in the crash of 1974.

Insolvency work can be divided into two distinct categories: receiverships, where an accountant is appointed by a bank or other lender to manage the business in the hope of disposing of those parts which are viable or to wind it up when reconstruction proves impossible; and liquidations, where the creditors of a bankrupt business appoint an accountant to realize the assets and distribute the proceeds. In both cases the appointments are made in the name of an individual and not the firm of which he is a member. In a sense, a receiver or liquidator is like a barrister in not being able to advertise (this in common with all other account-ants) and in having to build up a reputation and contacts on the basis of work successfully accomplished. However, a leading re-ceiver has needed the back-up facilities which only a major firm can provide as banks have been reluctant to appoint receivers from small firms when cases have proved complicated or protracted. Major insolvencies demand an insolvency administration with the experience and services commensurate with their size. In reality there are only a small number of receivers entrusted with major insolv-encies and all are members of the largest accountancy practices.

As in the nineteenth century, when the Overend & Gurney insolvency brought Whinney, Smith & Whinney fees for twenty-eight years (1866-93), receiverships can last a number of years. Although manpower demands are initially great when the stricken company has to be administered, the actual winding-up often tends to be a much less intensive but more protracted affair. Hence, the receiver may be called at short notice to deal with a rapid succession of insolvencies while his staff subsequently spend much longer in administering specific cases. Indeed, in 1974 Whinney Murray dealt concurrently with over fifty receiverships or liquidations.

Most receivers are, and have been, appointed by clearing or merchant banks as principal creditors, but a small proportion of appointments have been made by private individuals, corporations or government bodies who have put up risk and loan capital secured by debenture. In 1978 Mackey acted as receiver of British Tanners (being appointed by the Department of Industry amongst other lenders) and of a major oil refinery in Grand Bahama on behalf of an American oil company. For Whinney Murray, the Ernst & Ernst link helped both to provide contacts with American banks and businesses and to service insolvencies with international ramifications; while the firm's expertise in this field made overseas clients aware of the different range of facilities offered in the U.K.

Just as Whinney Murray's insolvency expertise was largely acquired through merger with a Newcastle practice, so too Turquands Barton Mayhew secured insolvency work through amalgamation with a provincial firm, in this case with A. C. Palmer of Leicester. Beginning in 1961, A. C. Palmer had been Barton, Mayhew's correspondents, but in 1971 the two merged, changing their style to Turquands Barton Mayhew in 1972, following the main amalgamation. Dating back to the inter-war period, this Midlands firm had built up an insolvency practice (for the year to 31 December 1933 their insolvency fees of £4,856 surpassed audit fees, then £4,118), which was subsequently developed in the post-war era by R. A. Haigh. The department's reputation had developed to the extent that when the financial crash of 1973–74 brought about the downfall of the 'secondary banks', Haigh's successor, Bill Sowman, was appointed in five of the ten foremost insolvencies. He was appointed receiver of Cannon Street Acceptances, First Maryland, David Samuel Trust and Burston Finance whilst also taking the liquidation of Jacobs Kroll. In each case, the attendant failures of the banks' borrowers drew a considerable amount of work to the Leicester practice, further enhancing its reputation and giving Bill Sowman a place in the national league of insolvency specialists. Indeed, true to the Overend & Gurney tradition, this exercise is still far from complete. The totally unexpected nature of the secondary banking crisis raised questions about the quality of information supplied in published accounts, which, in turn, was to have more general implications for the profession and lead to increasing demands for tighter accounting standards (see p. 248).

Ernst & Whinney's Investigation Department, though entirely separate, was most closely related to Insolvency. Whinney Murray's department was initially set up in 1974, a year after National Office, to be managed by another experienced provincial partner brought to London – Stephen Hall, originally a partner in Buckley, Hall, Devin, who had gained this expertise from commissions given by their client Hanson Trust. The department's work can be divided into six main categories: the preparation of specialist reports for the Stock Exchange (such as prospectuses or circulars for shareholders), examination of the financial position of companies being considered for purchase, assistance in the search for new businesses, the evaluation of investment projects, examination of the viability of businesses in debt and the valuation of shares in private companies and other assets liable to capital gains or capital transfer tax. From 1977 the department has advised the government on compensation payments to former shareholders following the nationalization of the aircraft and shipbuilding industries. Even though the specialist services are now organized through National Office, and seem to be a principal attraction of scale – reinforcing the influence of a powerful centre over the periphery – it is important to record that many had their origins in the provinces rather than London: partners from many provincial firms did not simply serve as a source of new audit clients, but also contributed expertise in highly specialized areas.

Whinney Murray's Accounting and Auditing Technical Department, responsible for keeping abreast of changes in accounting procedures resulting from government, Institute and European regulations, has advised the various regional offices on their implications and co-ordinated particular areas of expertise within a geographically extended firm. The Technical Department also worked in close contact with the Training Department to ensure that both students and qualified accountants on more advanced courses were apprised of latest developments both in the U.K. and overseas. Turquands Barton Mayhew's Technical Deparment, which had started in the late 1960s as a committee and developed when a partner was given part-time responsibility, expanded after the 1972 merger, finally amalgamating with Whinney Murray's section in 1979. Such departments had been encouraged by the growing complexity of audit work and by the English Institute's creation of the Accounting Standards Steering Committee in January 1970 (see p. 248), designed to regulate practice beyond the requirements of government legislation. Specialists were needed, therefore, not only to interpret and apply these regulations but also to make representation to the Institute's committees which ultimately influence legislation.

In the nineteenth century tuition was very much an *ad hoc* affair by which articled clerks under the guidance of a principal were left to study for themselves. Several retired chartered accountants have recalled how, when clerks, they were left to fend for themselves and could only proceed with a job having examined the previous year's audit – doubtless such an unsupervised approach claimed to build individual strength of character. Leading chartered accountants held student lectures (Frederick Whinney was much involved in such activity and delivered papers on railway accounts and the development of the profession) to help articled clerks through the examinations, although such tuition remained the individual member's responsibility, and the English Institute, in contrast to the Scottish bodies, has never formally assumed an educational role. Such a situation encouraged private enterprise. In 1884 H. Foulks Lynch founded his well-known correspondence college. He was, ironically, as his advertisement stated, 'a solicitor of twenty years experience in the preparation of pupils for law examinations'.[33] Indeed, until 1894 his staff was composed entirely of lawyers, when W. F. Wiseman, then a partner with Gérard Van de Linde & Sons (a firm which merged with Baker, Sutton in 1973), became the first qualified chartered accountant tutor.[34] As far as England was concerned these private establishments remained the only bodies offering tuition for the Institute's examinations in the nineteenth and early twentieth centuries.

During the inter-war period the expansion of the accountancy profession encouraged a number of practices to start correspondence courses and evening classes. Articled clerks paid for these facilities in addition to their premium, so that only the better-off could afford this extra tuition. However, in the 1960s a number of private residential or day colleges were set up to train accountants. These have since proliferated, doubtless encouraged by the largest accountancy practices paying for attendance on these college courses, having dropped the premium and begun paying their articles clerks a small salary (which has since risen to a modest living wage). Until the late 1950s each partner was allowed to supervise no more than two articled clerks, but following the merger of the English Institute and the Society of Incorporated Accountants together with the growth in the size of practices and the general increase in the proportion of qualified staff, this figure was first relaxed to four and then raised further on a formula basis. The expansion in the number of articled clerks (renamed students in 1973) allowed to accountancy firms has occurred in conjunction with the growth in the size of businesses. This, in turn, necessitated training procedures becoming more formalized and standardized. Day-to-day supervision of students' studies, work experience and welfare tends to be delegated to younger principals, so releasing their colleagues for specialist tasks and other roles.

With the standardization of training and the demise of Scottish tuition in London has come a search for improved teaching methods and the development of internal courses of instruction. Although Whinney Murray had always offered courses for articled clerks (Whinney, Smith & Whinney having begun them in 1960), the firm had neither achieved the size nor had it established the need to employ anyone full-time until 1967 when the first training manager was recruited. The department became part of National Office from the outset. While private colleges instructed students in accounting theory and were essentially concerned with the English Institute's examinations, the internal training departments of the major firms had a more pragmatic philosophy, their aim being to teach the practical application of accounting knowledge, introducing both qualified staff and trainees to their particular conventions and procedures. In addition, Ernst & Whinney's Training Department offered courses not solely for students but also for qualified staff, the majority being residential. Thus, there are now more specialized courses covering the latest technical developments in accounting and the peculiarities of particular branches of industry and commerce. Instructors' workshops, designed for members of regional offices selected to teach within the firm, help to ensure a similar standard of training.

Being smaller, Turquands Barton Mayhew's Training Department had developed similar teaching arrangements but on a reduced scale, and these, along with the other specialist sections, were integrated within the National Office structure in 1979. The main difficulties arising from a merger have tended to fall within these specialist areas where firms often had similar departments operating with slightly different philosophies, which offered scope for rationalization and compromise. Members of the audit and tax departments have not been affected by amalgamation in the same way because their operations were essentially governed by their clients and by geographical location (complementarity in these areas being a common cause of merger), though audit manuals and systems of quality control and review normally had to be revised in order to establish uniform procedures.

The provision of improved training courses, and the change of title from articled clerk to student, were partly a reflection of the increasingly complex and specialized nature of an accountant's duties, but they were also a recognition of the changed status of trainees entering the profession. In 1969 only 19% of articled clerks were graduates.[35] By 1979 72% of students had attended a university (the majority having studied subjects other than accountancy) and most of the large firms recruited only graduates. In addition, the numbers of women entering the profession rose dramatically. In 1969 only 2% of articled clerks were female; ten years later the proportion was 22%.[36] Also the transition from qualification to practising accountant has become less abrupt, softened by a two-year requirement to serve under a supervising principal on passing the final examination and to study for a minimum of forty hours in the year before a newly qualified member can practice on his own or be admitted to a partnership. Problems created by inflation accounting, new legislation and rules imposed by the E.E.C. have caused the Institutes to require new members to participate in compulsory classes (many of the major firms pre-empting or exceeding these regulations) after the fashion that doctors in general practice are compelled to attend periodic courses at hospitals to keep them abreast of developments in medical science.

With the creation of a National Office structure, Whinney Murray took the opportunity to revise the internal organization of the firm. As has been seen, the partnership had grown too large and cumbersome to allow all its members to discuss policy in a direct democracy, though there does remain the annual general meeting, an assembly of the partnership as a whole. Accordingly, the elected inner circle chaired by the senior partner – now called the U.K. Policy Committee – was administered by a newly created Executive Partner (with a four-year term of office), whose task it was to arrange meetings, agenda and implement decisions. However, as the firm expanded it became necessary to subdivide his responsibilities and in 1976 to appoint a Partnership Secretary to perform many of these administrative tasks, allowing the partners to continue to execute the jobs in which they were professionally most expert. The Partnership Secretary thus undertook *inter alia* the work normally done in a business by its company secretary.

Although Turquands Barton Mayhew had not been sufficiently large to establish a National Office framework, the 1972 merger had resulted in the creation of a sizeable practice which led to the reorganization of the firm in 1975. As in Whinney Murray an inner cabinet or Executive was formed comprising three partners (one responsible for finance, another for overseas offices and the third for the U.K.) and chaired by the senior partner. The Executive was, in turn, responsible to a Partnership Council consisting of the senior partner as *ex-officio* chairman and four elected members from London together with one partner from each of the principal provincial offices – Bristol, Exeter, Leicester and Manchester. Specialist departments were not grouped together but operated in a less structured fashion: technical and training had a partner responsible to the Executive, management services formed part of a separate consortium and the computer audit

Figure 7 Turquands Barton Mayhew & Co's U.K. Management Structure, 1972

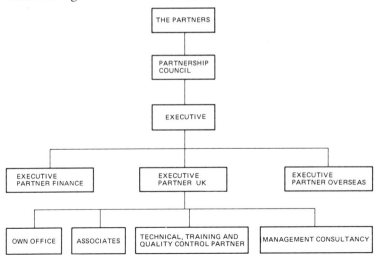

section was with the audit department. When Turquands Barton Mayhew amalgamated with Whinney Murray the latter's administrative framework in essence formed the basis for Ernst & Whinney's practice, with the former's partnership arrangement and specialist departments being integrated after some modification.

One of the most profoundly important developments in the recent history of the accountancy profession, exemplified by Whinney Murray and Turquands Barton Mayhew, and now Ernst & Whinney, has been the spread of business upon worldwide horizons. The largest accountancy firms have become as multi-national as their larger clients. Three major forces in the 1970s may be seen to have affected the growth and character of Ernst & Whinney's two principal constituent firms in the U.K.: Britain's membership of the European Economic Community, the strengthening of ties with the United States, and the increasing resort to legislation combined with the introduction of Accounting Standards (see p. 248). All reflect the growing international commitments of Britain, politically no less than in the structure and operation of business. Britain's entry into the Common Market in January 1972 encouraged Turquands Barton Mayhew to consider forming a European accountancy consortium to compete with the main eight firms with their strong American links. In 1973 they created a separate partnership with the Dutch practice Klynveld Kraayenhof & Co and the German firm Deutsche Treuhand-Gesellschaft to form Klynveld Turquands DTG & Co. Dutch and German practices had been selected in particular because they were two of the Continental countries with the most advanced accountancy techniques. The intention was to create a firm sizeable enough to offer a creditable alternative to the major Anglo-American accountants, Klynveld being the largest and DTG the second largest practices in the Netherlands and Germany respectively. Since the dissolution of this consortium, in September 1979 McLintock Main Lafrentz linked with Klynvelds, DTG and some other European firms to form Klynveld Main Goerdeler in pursuance of this same strategy.

At the same time businesses were forming trans-national, European consortia. For example, in 1971 Dunlop Holdings merged certain of their interests with those of Pirelli to create one of the world's largest tyre groups, pooling research and marketing together with a substantial exchange of shares in each other's companies. This had important repercussions for accounting practice.

From 1972 to 1976 a full set of 'union accounts' were published – a consolidation on a European scale – following in the pioneering tradition of F. R. M. de Paula, though this was not a legal requirement.

In addition, the E.E.C. has influenced accounting practices in Britain in a more direct and obvious fashion. The attempt to harmonize and co-ordinate the European economy has produced several directives designed to standardize accountancy procedures among member states. The Fourth Directive passed in 1978 has been amongst the most influential of these initiatives, containing regulations which governed the preparation and presentation of the balance sheet and the profit and loss account, all of which were originally to be incorporated within national laws by June 1980. To explain and assist their implementation both Whinney Murray's and Turquands Barton Mayhew's Technical Departments independently produced guides for clients and staff, while the Continental firm of Whinney Murray, Ernst & Ernst published a comprehensive multi-lingual series demonstrating the implications of the directive for each of the member states. Along with most other international practices, Whinney Murray's Continental firm moved its headquarters from Paris to Brussels in 1975, not simply to escape restrictive French regulations, but to be at the heart of the European community and in a position to exercise some influence over accountancy legislation. Klynveld Turquands DTG had similarly established its headquarters in Brussels.

In the event, the Klynveld Turquands DTG experiment was not successful and the consortium was dissolved in 1978. In fact one of its problems resulted from its very *raison d'être*; it lacked a viable connection with the United States. Although the Klynveld Turquands DTG practice had formed a partnership with the New York based American firm Hurdman & Cranstoun, the latter had already concluded a correspondent arrangement with Thornton Baker which meant that they were never in a position to refer work to the U.K., only to the joint practice in Europe. The American presence in the Western European Economy became so strong after 1945 that no sizeable international accountancy practice (serving multi-national business) could develop without a strong transatlantic partnership. Multi-national corporations were truly international in their operations and management, which meant that the largest accountancy firms had of necessity to open offices throughout the world, not least in America. In 1959 (see p. 217) Ernst & Ernst and Whinney, Smith & Whinney established Whinney, Ernst & Ernst firms in both Britain and America, whereby the former would act for Whinney, Smith & Whinney in the United States and the latter for Ernst & Ernst in Britain, while Whinney Murray's Continental and Middle East firms acted in these areas for clients of both Whinney, Smith & Whinney and Ernst & Ernst. This form of alliance was by no means uncommon amongst the largest City practices. In 1955, for example, Cooper Brothers had been approached by the major American practice Lybrand, Ross Bros & Montgomery to represent them in Europe. Accordingly their respective overseas offices were merged, the whole from 1957 operating on the Continent under the international style of Coopers & Lybrand.[37] Similarly, in 1964 Thomson McLintock formed an international practice with the American firm Main Lafrentz.[38] Deloittes had first come into contact with Haskins & Sells in 1905 when they had collaborated on the Hughes Insurance Company investigation. The relationship continued on a loose basis until 1952 when cross-partnership arrangements were concluded, the common name Deloitte Haskins & Sells being adopted in 1978.[39]

In July 1979 Ernst & Ernst on the one hand and Whinney Murray and Turquands Barton Mayhew on the other both changed their name to Ernst & Whinney, agreeing that they should operate throughout the world under the single style symbolized by a specially designed logogram and adoption of common stationery. Although the U.K., American, Continental, Middle East and Far East practices together with the Australian, Canadian and South African firms remained autonomous bodies and separate profit centres, special committees and an exchange of staff preceded the change of name in a strategy to harmonize procedures and philosophies to ensure that clients with outlets in various parts of the globe received a similar standard of service. In common with most of the big seven accountancy firms, the single style does not embrace a completely merged organization, but covers a group of unified practices each operating to agreed standards with highly developed administrative links. The various firms each have representatives on Ernst & Whinney International, the partnership designed to harmonize the running of the worldwide organization. The first chairman of this international body was Hugh Patterson, senior partner of the U.K. firm, who had long been a protagonist of the adoption of a single name by the U.K., American and other closely associated practices throughout the globe. Hence, members of these international practices have been asked to aspire to wider horizons. Victorian accountancy staffs owed one allegiance to thcir firm based, as it was, in a single town with powerful local connections. The twentieth-century expansion of practices at first nationally and then internationally has demanded a threefold loyalty (to the regional office, the national practice and to the world-wide organization), the extension being made easier by the adoption of a unified all-embracing style.

What then have been the implications of these closer links with the United States? Of the greatest importance has been the mutually beneficial exchange of work through each other's international clients. In the past, Whinney Murray had gained the audit of Coca Cola, Eli Lilly and Gulf + Western under this arrangement. As a concomitant, has come an exchange of views between Britain and America on accounting procedures and principles resulting in a measure of standardization. The different character of historical development in the economies produced distinct approaches to accounting problems. There are, for example, differences over the relationship between auditor and client, the general role of the accountant, the extent to which he should be involved in business and the degree to which work should be governed by law and Institute regulations. A suggestion with potentially far-reaching implications is that the American 'peer review' system ought to be applied to British accountants involved in the audit of American multi-national companies. This idea, by which one accountancy firm examines the procedures and administration of another to report on their adequacy and efficiency, had first been put forward by the Securities and Exchange Commission.[40] The scheme has been voluntarily adopted by most American firms as a demonstration to government that the profession is capable of regulating itself. Many American accountants have argued that the peer review logically ought to be extended to the British and European auditors of American-owned subsidiaries. So far the idea has been resisted, in favour of regulation by the Institutes, although more generally American accounting standards have influenced major European groups operating in the States, including Shell, I.C.I. and Unilever. At present members of the various international accountancy firms are discussing means to standardize internal procedures and philosophies to reflect world-wide operations, while others negotiate through the Institutes' committees with the American profession to harmonize external rules. Hence, both multi-national corporations and the big eight accountancy firms, through their transatlantic dealings, have indirectly spread accounting techniques and standards around the globe.

The third influence shaping Ernst & Whinney's methods of operation has been the change in attitudes towards business in general, reflected and moulded by government legislation and English Institute guidance. The latter had been issuing Recommendations on Accounting Principles from the early 1940s, but these were generally limited to encouraging companies to state their accounting policies and choose them from a reduced range of options. Although carefully considered, such proposals were not rigorous or mandatory. However, events conspired in the 1960s to put pressure on the various accountancy bodies to tighten up their regulations. Public comment was particularly stirred by the G.E.C. take-over of Associated Electrical Industries in 1967–68. When the latter produced a forecast endorsed by their auditors, which indicated a £10 million profit for 1967, G.E.C. instructed its auditors to investigate these figures and, on the basis of a different interpretation of stock valuations, they then calculated a potential loss of £4.5 million. The bulk of the difference was said to be due to 'matters of judgement'.[41] This case was followed by the Board of Trade's investigation under Sir Henry Benson of Coopers & Lybrand into the crash of John Bloom's Rolls Razor washing machine company, which had collapsed in 1964.[42] Although accountants were not directly brought into the proceedings, the case served to illustrate the difficulties of pursuing fraud prosecutions against companies which sought to exploit the broad range of accounting possibilities left by loose legislation.

In response to public pressure, therefore, the English Institute issued a declaration in December 1969 that it would devise rules to narrow 'the areas of difference and variety in accounting practice'. In January 1970 the Accounting Standards Steering Committee under Sir Ronald Leach (the then President) was set up to implement this promise.[43] The secondary banking crisis of 1973–74 revealed a further lack of precision in audit practice encouraging still more stringent regulations. In all, the Accounting Standards Committee has produced sixteen mandatory standards (Statements of Standard Accounting Procedure) covering a wide range of circumstances designed to restrict companies' options and to compel adherence to sound and fair procedures.

Standards imposed by the E.E.C. have further added to the complexity of accounts and represent a switch in philosophy from the concept of minimum disclosure towards standardized statements with little room for manoeuvre. Thus, tighter controls produced by domestic legislation, coupled with the attempt to harmonize accountancy standards throughout Europe, have extended the accountant's duties but at the same time have reduced the degree of discretion open to him. In the nineteenth and early twentieth centuries the almost total lack of audit regulation meant that Victorian and Edwardian accountants had a broad range of professional autonomy. Since then the accountant's field of action has greatly widened to include tax work, the audit of large groups and management accounting, but his freedom to perform these varied tasks is more closely circumscribed.

A third factor has assisted this fundamental shift of emphasis in the accountancy profession over the last twenty years: the growth of the large-scale practice. Millerson summarized the nineteenth-century ideal and keystone of the professions as one of trust. Associations, he argued, relied on the personal integrity of members, which in turn was founded on a belief in the innate probity of conduct required of an English gentleman.[44] The greater complexity and specialization evident in modern accountancy, combined with the great growth in size of a few firms (which necessarily reduced the level of personal contact between senior partner and partners, partners and their staffs), have switched the emphasis from self-regulatory professional conduct in the nineteenth-century sense towards more rigorous and binding codes of conduct of a very specific nature. Today students are of necessity taught more about the technicalities of accounting and the rules that have to be followed than their predecessors in the inter-war and immediate post-war periods. Indeed, the heightened extent of regulation (by government and Institutes) has removed some of the necessity for such self-imposed standards of discipline. For example, the 1967 Companies Act required still further information from the audit files and a greater degree of uniformity in the presentation of accounts.[45] The creation of larger units with their internal organizational structures has also curtailed something of the individual partner's former traditional autonomy, although it has broadened his scope in other ways by offering a wider geographical network and a range of specialist departments. Nevertheless as with any profession, despite the growing thicket of

regulations, personal probity remains the elemental basis of the
accountant's role. For instance, the English Institute's regulations
which limit the size of clients in relation to the size of the accountancy practice (no firm should have a client that contributes more
than 15% of its total fee income) were designed to avoid the
possibility of such a company exercising undue pressure on an
auditor concerned not to lose a substantial part of his business. In
the nineteenth century unscrupulous accountants (particularly
those not members of the professional bodies) doubtless gave in to
such suggestions, while the majority, guided by a strong code of
ethics, resisted temptation. Hence, the recent changes resulted not
simply from government legislation and larger accountancy
firms, but reflected more general shifts in society's attitudes towards the conduct of business – and in that sense were also influenced indirectly by changing standards and levels of expectation
in Continental Europe and America.

One further feature of recent years has been the increase in the
volume of government work offered to accountancy firms – an
inevitable consequence of an increasingly interventionist economic policy pursued by all administrations. Accountants, with
their technical skills, have always been valued members of inquiries of a financial nature. Having been appointed to the 1962
Commission of Inquiry into the sugar industry, C. J. M. Bennett,
a partner in Barton, Mayhew, served on a number of other committees including that into the pricing of certain contracts for the
overhaul of aero-engines by Bristol Siddeley. More specifically,
the number of Department of Trade investigations has increased
sharply since 1969 and since the Rolls Razor case most Inspectors'
reports have been published. For example, in January 1974, following the collapse of the secondary banks, John Whinney was
appointed as an inspector into the affairs of the Cornhill Consolidated Group* by the Department of Industry, while Peter Godfrey, then partner in charge of Whinney Murray's London office,
became an inspector engaged on the Rolls-Royce investigation,
having previously looked into the dealings of the Pinnock Finance Company in 1971. An early example of this type of work
for Whinney, Smith & Whinney had been Sir William Carrington's appointment in 1957 to examine the affairs of Hide & Co.
Dennis Garrett, senior partner of Turquands Barton Mayhew,

* Not to be confused with Cornhill Insurance, originally audited by Baker,
Sutton, now Ernst & Whinney.

was similarly involved in two Board of Trade inquiries, the first in 1970 into E. J. Austin International Ltd and the second, Burnholme & Forder Ltd in 1978, being a particularly tangled accountancy problem.[46] One reason for the heightened frequency of government investigations has been the growing complexity of business organizations, necessitating the appointment of a team of experts to unravel their financial arrangements, occasionally (as the Pinnock Report concluded) 'deliberately engineered' to confuse.[47] Or as the report on the Cornhill Consolidated Group argued in 1977, 'the practice of balance sheet window-dressing would seem to have gained partial acceptance by many professional accountants ... unless [it is] carried out to such a material extent that the auditors are of the opinion that the accounts do not give a true and fair view ... this situation could be substantially improved if the accountants' professional bodies issue guidance on the subject for members'.[48]

These appointments were partly a reflection of the state's more general intervention in the running of the economy, but also resulted from a growth in the size of companies, which brought into prominence the question of monopolistic and restrictive practices. The ambivalence of policy was such, however, that in some instances governmental intervention sought to promote mergers in order to create large-scale viable groups, while in others the object was the reverse – to prevent mergers or takeovers where a particular market might be dominated by one group. Professional accountants could profit on both counts, but most employment has been occasioned by the Monopolies Commission (indeed, Whinney Murray and Turquands Barton Mayhew were referred to the Commission over their own proposed merger), the Prices and Incomes Board and the Restrictive Practices Court calling upon accountancy firms to act as independent investigators.

Similarly, governments' attempts to control inflation have brought accountants more fully into advisory posts. The misleading nature of conventional company accounts in inflationary periods has long been understood in general terms, but the need for adjustment became pressing in the early 1970s when inflation accelerated and accountants were recruited to advise on new legislation. An application of a draft proposal, *Accounting for Changes in the Purchasing Power of Money*, published by the Accounting Standards Steering Committee in 1973, indicated that the accounts of

137 large listed companies for 1971 overstated their recorded earnings by on average 20%.[49] This paper put forward the current purchasing power school of inflation accounting. Monetary values subject to attrition from a depreciating currency, it was argued, should be adjusted by the retail price index so that all transactions were converted to the year-end constant values. The issue was particularly important in relation to whether depreciation should be charged according to historic cost or the replacement value of assets. Two objections were raised, principally by the Treasury: first, that general indices of price movements were not sufficiently precise to reflect accurately fluctuations in values affecting individual companies – for example, the huge rise in oil prices in 1973–74 demonstrated that specific prices could move wildly out of line with general inflation, which affected businesses differently according to their relative dependence upon the commodities in question; secondly, the government considered that this new accounting convention might encourage further inflation as companies could put up prices in advance of expected rises.[50]

Because of the doubts in 1973 the government appointed a committee under [Sir] Francis Sandilands to report on inflation accounting, the results of which were published in September 1975.[51] The report favoured a system of current cost accounting by which assets were included in the published accounts at their 'value to business'. This meant that the plant, equipment and other assets had to be revalued each year according to calculations of the current value of equivalent goods. This placed heightened responsibility on the auditor for his opinion and the judgement of any technical adviser. The major objection to this system was that it makes no adjustments for the general monetary effect of inflation. A comparison of results from one year to the next is largely meaningless if pounds remain unadjusted by the rate of inflation.[52] Even with the issue of S.S.A.P. 16, no general agreement has yet followed and one of Ernst & Whinney's Accounting and Auditing Technical Department's roles has been to explain the merits and application of such systems for clients and staff.

This brief history has sought to explain the evolution of Ernst & Whinney, and accountancy more widely as a profession, in the context of a developing business community. It is impossible to evaluate the efficient operation of modern business without an awareness of the contribution of the professional skills of the accountant to that efficiency. The accountant's role has been steadily enhanced in recent decades and today the demand for accountancy skills (and probably for all kinds of specialist services throughout the economy) is still increasing. Within the accountancy profession there are now eight major firms (in addition to Ernst & Whinney there are Arthur Andersen, Coopers & Lybrand, Deloitte Haskins & Sells, Peat, Marwick, Mitchell & Co, Price Waterhouse & Co, Touche Ross & Co and Arthur Young McClelland Moores & Co) who stand out in terms of numbers of partners and staff, their world-wide coverage and extent of specialist services. Although they cater for a wide range of clients varying in size and character, their recent growth may be most closely associated with the audit of the biggest multi-nationals and corporations. For example, Ernst & Whinney at present audits nine of the top fifty U.K. industrial companies,[53] not including the Midland and National Westminster Banks and British Airways. Most of the eight major accountancy firms originated in London and still have their British headquarters in or very near the City. The advantages of this location include proximity to the head offices of major clients, ready contact with other U.K. centres together with closeness to one another and the English Institute building at Moorgate. All of these are important because financial negotiations often call for consultations between bankers, lawyers and accountants and also between the accountants and other professionals acting for different clients.[54] Although many of the features of the nineteenth-century profession survive in small practices, a fundamental transformation has thus taken place among the largest accountancy firms. Their structure, scale, the scope of services offered, their clientele and the character of that relationship have all experienced change – and that clearly is not the end of the story. As long as the business community continues to evolve so too will the accountancy firms which serve it.

References

1 *Barton, Mayhew Bulletin*, Summer 1969.
2 *Financial Times Survey: Accountancy*, 3 July 1979, p. VII. The figures refer to the financial year 1978–79.
3 *Ibid.*
4 *Ibid*, Michael Lafferty, 'Changes in the Profession', p. II.

5 R. J. Briston, *The Accountants Magazine*, November (1979), 'The U.K. Accountancy Profession – the move towards monopoly power', p. 458.
6 *Ibid*, p. 459.
7 *Ibid*, pp. 458-9.
8 *Accountants Weekly*, 20 June 1979, p. 25.
9 *Ibid*, p. 28.
10 S. J. Prais, *The Evolution of Giant Firms in Britain*, Cambridge (1976), pp. 4-5.
11 *Ibid*, pp. 85-6.
12 *Ibid*, p. 222, figures for 1972.
13 *Financial Times Survey*, *op. cit.*, p. VIII.
14 Dunning and Morgan, *op. cit.*, pp. 432-3.
15 *Proposals to effect the union of the operating activities of the Dunlop Rubber Company Ltd and Pirelli S.p.A. and Société Internationale Pirelli S.A.*, London (1970), p. 9.
16 Leslie Hannah, *The Rise of the Corporate Economy*, London (1976), p. 174.
17 Channon, *Strategy and Structure of British Enterprise*, *op. cit.*, p. 67.
18 *Ibid*, pp. 238-9.
19 F. Clive de Paula, *Management Accounting in Practice*, London (1972), pp. 3-5, and R. Ian Tricker, *The Accountant in Management*, London (1967), pp. 33-4.
20 Leslie Hannah, *Management Strategy and Business Development*, London (1976), D. F. Channon, 'Corporate Evolution in the Service Industries', p. 219.
21 Anthony Sampson, *The Anatomy of Britain*, London (1962), pp. 434-5.
22 Derek F. Channon, *The Service Industries, Strategy, Structure and Financial Performance*, London (1978), pp. 61, 78.
23 Channon, *Strategy and Structure of British Enterprise*, *op. cit.*, p. 145.
24 *Proposals to effect the union of the Dunlop Rubber Company*, *op. cit.*, p. 8.
25 Channon, *The Service Industries*, *op. cit.*, p. 26.
26 Richard P. Rumelt, *Strategy, Structure and Economic Performance*, Harvard (1974), p. 156.
27 Tricker, *The Accountant in Management*, *op. cit.*, pp. 20-1.
28 *Financial Times Survey: Accountancy*, 13 May 1980, p. II.
29 Sampson, *Anatomy of Britain*, *op. cit.*, p. 466.
30 Edward Bishop, *The Debt We Owe, the Royal Air Force Benevolent Fund*, London (1979), p. 131. Barton, Mayhew's Management Services Department undertook an administrative survey of the Fund in 1971, the firm having been their auditors from the inter-war period.
31 H. H. Monroe, *British Tax Review*, No. 5 (1979), 'Fiscal Statutes: A Drafting Disaster', p. 269.
32 *Ibid*.

33 *Seventy Years of Progress in Accountancy Education, H. Foulkes Lynch &
Co Ltd*, London (1955), pp. 9, 11.

34 *Ibid*, p. 14.

35 Leon Hopkins, *The Hundredth Year*, London (1980), p. 42.

36 *Financial Times Survey* (1980), *op. cit.*, p. IV.

37 *C & L Journal*, No. 31, June 1979, p. 34. It was not until April 1973
that this style was used in the U.K. and America.

38 Winsbury, *op. cit.*, p. 133.

39 Hopkins, *op. cit.*, p. 62.

40 *Ibid*, p. 33.

41 *Ibid*, p. 122.

42 *Ibid*, pp. 80-2.

43 Although originally created by the English Institute, the
Accounting Standards Steering Committee has since become a body
which represents the profession as a whole, drawing its members from
the various societies, the word 'Steering' being dropped in 1976 to
reflect this change.

44 Millerson, *op. cit.*, pp. 163-4.

45 *The Companies Act 1967 Chapter 81*, H.M.S.O. (1977). Sections 3 to
11 require more detailed disclosure of information relating to
subsidiaries, shareholdings, directors' emoluments, staff salaries and
historical figures, pp. 2-10.

46 John Lloyd Eley and Dennis Garrett, *E. J. Austin International Ltd*,
H.M.S.O. (1972), and Thomas Dillon and Dennis Garrett, *Burnholme &
Forder Ltd (In Liquidation)*, H.M.S.O. (1979).

47 Basil Wigoder and Peter Godfrey, *Pinnock Finance Company (Great
Britain) Limited and Associated Companies. Investigation*, H.M.S.O. (1971),
p. 255.

48 David Calcutt and John Whinney, *Cornhill Consolidated Group Ltd,
Report*, H.M.S.O. (1981), pp. 281-2.

49 Prais, *op. cit.*, p. 277.

50 Hopkins, *op. cit.*, p. 138.

51 *Inflation Accounting: Report of the Inflation Accounting Committee*,
H.M.S.O. (1975).

52 Hopkins, *op. cit.*, p. 139.

53 *The Times 1000*, London (1979), pp. 20-6. Figures are for 1979-80.

54 Dunning and Morgan, *op. cit.*, pp. 434-4.

J
(
WHINNEY, SMITH
WHINNEY (London,

Mason & Son
(London, c. 1850)

F Woolley & Co
(Southampton, 1905)

Thomas Smethurst
& Co (Manchester,
c. 1870)

Joe Sharp & Co
(Huddersfield, c. 1870)

Harold E. Clarke & Co
(Birmingham, 1854)

Buckley & Hall
(Hull, 1903)

Holmes Dudley
& Co (Newcastle,
1847)

Charl
Cape

Woolley &
Waldron
(1925)

Thomas Bowden
Sons & Nephew
(Newcastle c.1860)

Sharp, Lampton & Co
(1907)

Sharp, Lampton &
Smith (1914)

Smith & Garton
(1919)

Scarr
& Burton

Buckley, Hall,
Devin & Co (1931)

1920

Alfre
(Leeds

Hamble & Glenton
(Newcastle)

1928

1939

1956

1956

1960

1962

Phillips & Trump
(Cardiff, 1935)

Thomas Bowden &
Glenton (1960)

1965

WH

Whinney Murray & Co's Genealogical Tree

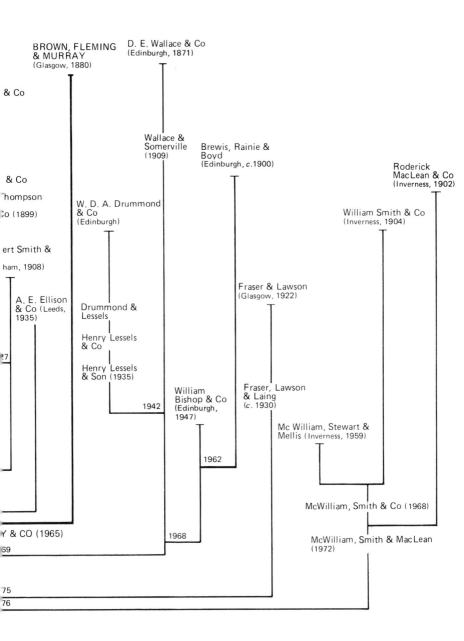

BROWN, FLEMING
& MURRAY
(Glasgow, 1880)

D. E. Wallace & Co
(Edinburgh, 1871)

& Co

Wallace &
Somerville
(1909)

Brewis, Rainie &
Boyd
(Edinburgh, c.1900)

Roderick
MacLean & Co
(Inverness, 1902)

& Co

hompson

Co (1899)

W. D. A. Drummond
& Co
(Edinburgh)

William Smith & Co
(Inverness, 1904)

ert Smith &

ham, 1908)

Fraser & Lawson
(Glasgow, 1922)

A. E. Ellison
& Co (Leeds,
1935)

Drummond &
Lessels

Henry Lessels
& Co

Henry Lessels
& Son (1935)

7

Fraser, Lawson
& Laing
(c. 1930)

William
Bishop & Co
(Edinburgh,
1947)

1942

Mc William, Stewart &
Mellis (Inverness, 1959)

1962

Y & CO (1965)

1968

McWilliam, Smith & Co (1968)

69

McWilliam, Smith & MacLean
(1972)

75

76

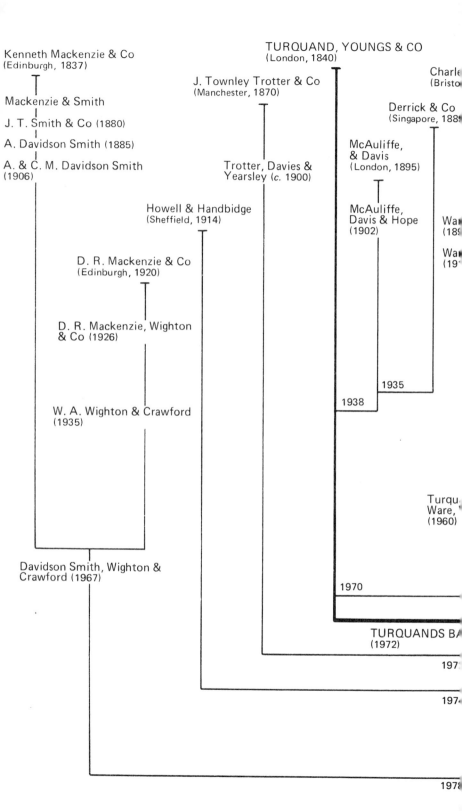

Kenneth Mackenzie & Co
(Edinburgh, 1837)

Mackenzie & Smith

J. T. Smith & Co (1880)

A. Davidson Smith (1885)

A. & C. M. Davidson Smith
(1906)

TURQUAND, YOUNGS & CO
(London, 1840)

J. Townley Trotter & Co
(Manchester, 1870)

Charle
(Bristo

Derrick & Co
(Singapore, 188?

McAuliffe,
& Davis
(London, 1895)

Trotter, Davies &
Yearsley (c. 1900)

Howell & Handbidge
(Sheffield, 1914)

McAuliffe,
Davis & Hope
(1902)

Wa
(189

Wa
(19

D. R. Mackenzie & Co
(Edinburgh, 1920)

D. R. Mackenzie, Wighton
& Co (1926)

W. A. Wighton & Crawford
(1935)

1935

1938

Turqu
Ware,
(1960)

Davidson Smith, Wighton &
Crawford (1967)

1970

TURQUANDS BA
(1972)

197

197

1978

Turquands Barton Mayhew & Co's Genealogical Tree

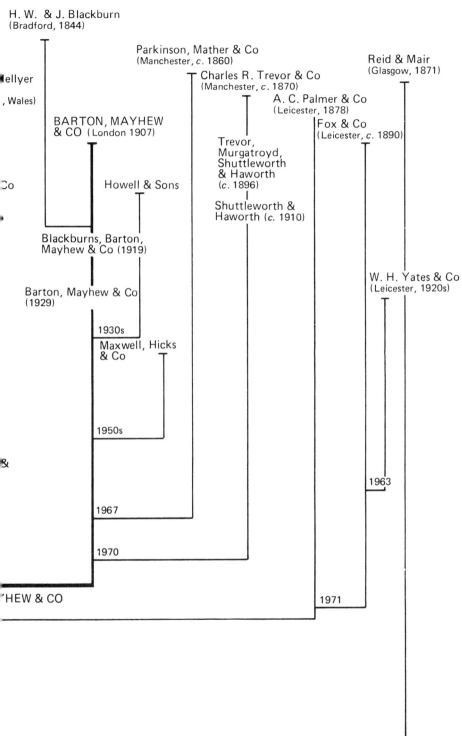

H. W. & J. Blackburn
(Bradford, 1844)

Parkinson, Mather & Co
(Manchester, c. 1860)

Reid & Mair
(Glasgow, 1871)

Charles R. Trevor & Co
(Manchester, c. 1870)

A. C. Palmer & Co
(Leicester, 1878)

ellyer

, Wales)

BARTON, MAYHEW
& CO (London 1907)

Fox & Co
(Leicester, c. 1890)

Trevor,
Murgatroyd,
Shuttleworth
& Haworth
(c. 1896)

Co

Howell & Sons

Shuttleworth &
Haworth (c. 1910)

Blackburns, Barton,
Mayhew & Co (1919)

W. H. Yates & Co
(Leicester, 1920s)

Barton, Mayhew & Co
(1929)

1930s

Maxwell, Hicks
& Co

&

1950s

1963

1967

&

1970

1971

'HEW & CO

❀ Appendices ❀

Fee Incomes of the Predecessor Firms (£s)

A

Year	Whinney, Smith & Whinney (London)	Turquand, Youngs & Co (London)	C. Herbert Smith & Russell (Birmingham)	Baker, Sutton & Co (London)	Barton, Mayhew & Co (London)
1848	221*				
1849	858				
1850	1,717				
1851	2,527				
1852	2,182				
1853	2,524				
1854	3,652				
1855	4,904				
1856	6,175				
1857	10,351				
1858	16,598				
1859	13,751	19,627			
1860	9,124	15,306			
1861	11,171	24,766			
1862	13,278	18,476			
1863	14,130	21,726			
1864	23,574	25,470			
1865	25,001	37,594			
1866	32,268	37,487			
1867	30,524	51,005			
1868	28,168	90,287			
1869	32,343	37,532			
1870	18,975	34,391			
1871	15,103	34,978			
1872		32,046			
1873		36,072			
1874	13,586				
1875	14,427				

* August–December only.

Year	WS&W	TYs	CHS&R	BS&Co	BM&Co
1876	11,609	47,270			
1877	10,315	36,041			
1878	11,310	34,181			
1879	25,203	39,196			
1880	14,054	36,378			
1881	12,133	37,838			
1882	10,232	28,701			
1883	12,470	27,697			
1884	14,810	27,949			
1885	12,399	27,296			
1886	12,825	28,774			
1887	13,255				
1888	15,167				
1889	15,208				
1890	14,318				
1891	16,302				
1892	17,280				
1893	13,308				
1894	11,511	31,826			
1895	10,603	41,532			
1896	13,031	35,678			
1897	13,178	38,889			
1898	11,775	40,526			
1899	13,090	40,385			
1900	15,015	45,003			
1901	15,997	41,184			
1902	20,929	43,760			
1903	15,560	38,697		5,785	
1904	16,864	42,072		4,123	
1905	12,884★	40,503		4,094	
1906	14,229			5,026	
1907	14,687			4,505	
1908	17,953			4,905	1,200
1909	25,379		1,437	6,068	4,900
1910	28,476	63,665	1,571	5,884	2,400
1911	24,247		1,992	6,254	3,500
1912	27,742		2,662	6,160	3,000
1913	30,458		3,637	6,806	4,500
1914	24,953		3,535	6,330	5,000
1915	28,756		3,817	6,696	7,500
1916	33,041		4,211	9,931	7,500
1917	28,325		5,009	14,932	11,000

★ 9 months only

Year	WS&W	TYs	CHS&R	BS&Co	BM&Co
1918	29,082		5,533	19,024	11,000
1919	38,051		7,590	26,206	11,500†
1920	67,983		9,320	28,904	
1921	83,564		9,667	25,551	16,732
1922	77,242		11,212	25,779	28,702
1923	83,464		12,161	27,680	19,482
1924	66,802		15,113		39,304
1925	77,360		16,751		32,671
1926	67,508		15,687	21,249	27,056
1927	74,237		14,303	24,631	32,147
1928	66,460		16,466	27,750	39,121
1929	65,754		15,336	31,268	30,122
1930	61,598		22,935	31,808	
1931	58,598		20,864	32,264	
1932	58,047		19,545	36,221	54,399
1933	60,536		22,999	35,605	64,977
1934	67,567		34,516	34,434	59,862
1935	61,744		35,742	36,674	66,891
1936	66,618		28,880	36,577	60,575
1937	79,482		30,534	42,398	61,831
1938	71,121		32,946	40,924	65,480
1939	71,657		34,546	40,806	
1940	67,705		34,839	38,163	68,434
1941	65,596		37,055	40,950	75,943
1942	76,266	95,874	31,561	47,507	86,897
1943	98,165	105,463	32,537	50,326	96,396
1944	105,799	107,063	33,318	52,572	105,740
1945	112,532	102,914	31,764	53,850	111,940
1946	124,637	103,606	36,389	56,810	124,504
1947	144,303	110,347		64,372	
1948	158,760	130,324	44,452	73,840	202,720 ×
1949	170,894	125,827	40,442	83,024	172,075
1950	181,264	137,520	54,975	91,921	180,835
1951	207,837	151,834	51,129	88,374	189,547
1952	201,495		61,489	96,418	203,616
1953	219,617		62,404	111,224	225,587
1954	242,623	138,744	66,001	117,468	236,566
1955	240,653	188,885	68,149	128,203	123,130‡
1956	276,839	170,103	72,462	144,696	247,014
1957	312,523	180,354	77,675	164,787	270,522

† Barton, Mayhew figures from 1908 to 1919 are estimates based on known profit figures.

Year	WS&W	TYs	CHS&R	BS&Co	BM&Co
1958	349,379	180,658	81,778	176,691	
1959	377,059	212,432	87,172	178,644	454,830 ˣ
1960	402,203	240,951	85,522	197,099	335,367
1961	413,677	241,599		207,706	345,443
1962	474,287	243,027		218,331	409,935
1963	514,289	251,686		214,283	448,789
1964	634,958	289,169		233,902	473,582
1965	546,103★	308,501		242,109	561,160

Note

Barton, Mayhew figures: ˣ = 18 months; ‡ = six months. ★ = 9 months.
The fees for both Whinney, Smith & Whinney and Turquand, Youngs & Co are for their London offices alone and do not include fees earned in their other regional or overseas offices.

B

Year	Brown, Fleming & Murray (London)		Year	Whinney, Smethurst & Co. (Manchester)
1939	62,822		1936	7,764
1940	62,926		1937	8,221
1941	57,390		1938	8,796
1942	70,577		1939	8,860
1943	65,540		1940	9,802
1944	70,454		1941	11,648
1945	69,484		1942	13,648
1946	80,195		1943	12,759
1947	94,245		1944	12,878
1948	112,525		1945	12,612
1949	116,151		1946	14,626
1950	124,891			
1951	139,161			
1952	143,044			
1953	159,820			
1954	168,754			
1955	196,905			

Numbers of Accountants in England and Wales

A From the census

1841	4,974
1851	6,138
1861	6,239
1871	9,838
1881	11,517
1891	7,930
1901	9,026
1911	9,499

Sources: The Census of England and Wales

1841	Occupation Abstract, Vol. xxvii (1844), p. 57.
1851	Population Tables, Vol. lxxxviii (1854), p. 65.
1861	Population Tables, Vol. liii (1863), p. xliv.
1871	Population Tables, Vol. lxxi (1873), p. 81.
1881	Occupation Abstract, Vol. lxxx (1883), p. xi.
1891	Occupation Abstract, Vol. cvi (1893–94), p. xii.
1901	Summary Tables (1903), p. 188.
1911	Summary Tables (1915), p. 134.

B Members of the Institute of Chartered Accountants in England and Wales

1880	not	*1887*	1,444	*1894*	1,991
1881	published	*1888*	1,576	*1895*	2,097
1882	1,193	*1889*	1,633	*1896*	2,189
1883	1,275	*1890*	1,678	*1897*	2,292
1884	1,316	*1891*	1,737	*1898*	2,399
1885	1,352	*1892*	1,796	*1899*	2,516
1886	1,371	*1893*	1,876	*1900*	2,623*

Note: * Figures for 1882–1900 are derived from the Institute's Annual Report.

	Total	In practice		Total	In practice
1900	2,702	2,013	1956	19,414	7,050
1905	3,399	2,329	1957	20,124	7,194
1910	4,192	2,701	1958	31,381†	9,827
1915	4,959	2,853	1959	32,579	9,991
1920	5,343	2,988	1960	33,867	10,183
1925	6,324	3,604	1961	35,228	10,476
1930	9,226	4,229	1962	36,581	10,821
1935	11,567	5,085	1963	37,880	11,020
1940	13,745	5,135	1964	39,293	11,223
			1965	40,759	11,397
1941	13,694	5,135	1966	42,457	11,504
1942	13,577	5,093	1967	43,742	11,764
1943	13,539	5,080	1968	45,500	11,986
1944	13,415	5,058	1969	47,652	12,169
1945	13,332	5,069	1970	49,725	12,354
1946	13,329	5,382	1971	51,660	12,593
1947	13,597	5,527	1972	53,908	12,953
1948	14,133	5,660	1973	56,425	13,432
1949	14,632	5,830	1974	58,954	14,148
1950	15,260	6,014	1975	61,718	14,635
1951	16,079	6,226	1976	63,370	15,027
1952	16,856	6,419	1977	65,362	15,635
1953	17,561	6,595	1978	66,891	16,225
1954	18,151	6,753	1979	69,168	17,076
1955	18,772	6,904	1980	70,095	—

† The jump in membership in 1958 is the result of the merger with the Society of Incorporated Accountants.

C Numbers employed in accountancy services (U.K.)

	Figures in 000s
1959	78
1960	79
1961	82
1962	86
1963	87
1964	90/89★
1965	93
1966	93
1967	92
1968	93
1969	94 (56 male; 38 female)
1970	95
1971	97/78★
1972	81
1973	82
1974	83
1975	86
1976	91
1977	90

★ Reclassification designated for this and subsequent years in series.

Source: Central Statistical Office, *Annual Abstract of Statistics 1963-1979*, H.M.S.O., 1959-60 = p. 110, 1961-62 = p. 113, 1963-64 = p. 115, 1965-69 = p. 127, 1970-72 = pp. 130-1, 1973 = pp. 134, 137, 1974-77 = p. 159.

Sources

1 Manuscript sources

(a) Whinney, Smith & Whinney: There are complete series of Day Books, Journals, Cash Books and Ledgers covering the period 1848-1964. The following records have proved the most useful: Day Books, Harding & Pullein (1848-1854), (1855-1858); Harding, Pullein, Whinney & Gibbons (1859-1864), (1865-1866); Harding, Whinney, Gibbons & Co (1867-1871); Harding, Whinney & Co (1874-1883), (1884-1888); Whinney, Hurlbatt & Smith (1888-1894); Whinney, Smith & Whinney (1894-1902), (1903-1905), (1905-1906), (1907-1911), (1912-1913), (1914-1920), (1920-1926), (1926-1932), (1932-1938), (1938-1944), (1944-1950), (1950-1955), (1955-1959) and (1959-1964).

In addition, there are: Harding, Whinney, Gibbons & Co Letter Books (1867-1902), (1892-1894) and (1892-1901), Frederick Whinney's Private Ledger (1886-1895), his Pocket Diaries (1854), (1860) and (1916), and Frederick Whinney's Personal Account Book (1851-1855). Other miscellaneous records include: Harding, Whinney & Co List of Companies in Liquidation (1877), Whinney, Smith & Whinney Audit Books (1910) and (1932), together with various Deeds of Partnership dated 1 November 1857, 29 December 1858, 20 January 1882 and 11 January 1903.

(b) Turquand, Youngs: Most of the firm's records were destroyed by fire but the following have survived: Private Ledgers (1858-1863), (1863-1868), (1868-1873), (1875-1883), (1880-1886), (1893-1898), (1899-1901), (1901-1905) and (1910), and the firm's Reports (1955-1965).

(c) Brown, Fleming & Murray: Both the Glasgow and London offices have very little historical material. It is as follows:
(i) Glasgow, Statement Books Nos. 2, 3, 4 and 6 (1890-1892), (1893), (1894-1895) and (1898).
(ii) London, Private Ledger (1939-1955) and Minute Book (1961-1963).

(d) Barton, Mayhew: Again the bulk of the firm's records were destroyed by fire and all that survives is a Fee Journal (1921-1930).

(e) Baker, Sutton: Fee Ledger No. 1 (1903-1926), No. 3 (1937-1947) and Private Ledgers (1903-1966) survive.

(f) Provincial Records:

(i) Manchester: Sir Thomas Smethurst's Private Letter Book (1885-1893); Shuttleworth & Haworth Letter Books (1874-1875) and (1894-1902); W. D. Montgomery's Correspondence File for Whinney, Smith & Whinney's Manchester Office (1933-1954).

(ii) Birmingham: C. Herbert Smith & Russell Ledgers (1908-1965).

(g) Miscellaneous Records:

(i) English Institute of Chartered Accountants, Minutes of the Council, Vol. B (1879-1880); Council Minute Book 'A' (1880-1885).

(ii) Imperial Airways, Audit File (1933-1940).

2 Personal recollections

The following is a list of retired members of Ernst & Whinney's predecessor firms who have provided valuable information.

Professor D. S. Anderson	R. L. Latimer
F. W. Bailey	T. W. Macdonald
C. J. M. Bennett	A. I. Mackenzie
H. O. H. Coulson	J. F. Moffat
F. H. Crop	J. F. T. Nangle
H. A. Cummings	J. S. Paine
R. B. Dixon	G. D. Paterson
P. H. Dobson	A. D. Paton
D. Garrett	H. P. Patterson
R. V. Garton	W. W. Powell
O. Guest	D. W. Robertson
Dr W. B. Hall	F. R. Williams
G. Hey	Sir Reginald Wilson
A. D. Knox	

Particular mention should be made of R. L. Latimer, who had been engaged on a history of Whinney, Smith & Whinney and who generously gave the author his detailed notes and workings, compiled after several years' painstaking research. H. O. H. Coulson, who is writing a personal history of Barton, Mayhew, lent material as well as correcting the text. F. R. Williams devoted much time to filling in the gaps for Brown, Fleming & Murray's London operations, particularly with reference to British Petroleum, while D. W. Robertson performed a similar role for Turquand, Youngs. However, it is difficult, and probably unfair, to single out individuals as all those in this list have devoted much time and energy to answer questions with great patience and forbearance; their help, interest and encouragement are much appreciated by the author.

3 Parliamentary Inquiries and Statutes

House of Lord's Sessional Papers, Vol. XXIX (1849), The Audit of Railway Accounts.

Reports of the House of Commons Committees, Vol. X (1867), Report from the Select Committee on the Limited Liability Acts.

Reports of the House of Commons Committees, Vol. VIII (1877), Report from the Select Committee on the Companies Acts of 1862 and 1867.

1719   6 Geo I c. 18, The Bubble Act.
1825   6 Geo IV c. 91, Bubble Repealing Act.
1831   1 & 2 William IV c. 56, Bankruptcy Court Act.
1834   4 & 5 William IV c. 94, Letters Patent Act.
1837   7 William & I Victoriae c. 73, Chartered Companies Act.
1844   7 & 8 Victoriae c. 110, Joint Stock Companies Act.
1844   7 & 8 Victoriae c. 111, Winding-up Act.
1844   7 & 8 Victoriae c. 113, Joint Stock Banks Act.
1845   8 & 9 Victoriae c. 16, Companies Consolidation Act.
1847   10 & 11 Victoriae c. 15, Gasworks Clauses Act.
1847   10 & 11 Victoriae c. 17, Water Works Clauses Act.
1848   11 & 12 Victoriae c. 45, Winding-up Act.
1849   12 & 13 Victoriae c. 45, Winding-up Act.
1856   19 & 20 Victoriae c. 47, Joint Stock Companies Act.
1856   19 & 20 Victoriae c. 79, Bankruptcy Act.
1862   25 & 26 Victoriae c. 89, Joint Stock Companies Act.
1867   30 & 31 Victoriae c. 127, Railway Companies Act.
1868   31 & 32 Victoriae c. 119, Regulation of Railways Act.
1869   32 & 33 Victoriae c. 71, Bankruptcy Act.
1869   32 & 33 Victoriae c. 83, Bankruptcy Repeal Act.

1870 33 & 34 Victoriae c. 61, Life Assurance Companies Act.
1871 34 & 35 Victoriae c. 41, Gasworks Clauses Act.
1874 37 & 38 Victoriae c. 42, Building Societies Act.
1875 38 & 39 Victoriae c. 60, Friendly Societies Act.
1883 46 & 47 Victoriae c. 52, Bankruptcy Act.
1900 63 & 64 Victoriae c. 48, Companies Act.
1907 7 Edward VII c. 50, Companies Act.
1908 8 Edward VII c. 69, Companies Consolidation Act.
1928 18 & 19 George V c. 45, Companies Act.
1929 19 & 20 George V c. 23, Companies Consolidation Act.
1948 11 & 12 George VI c. 38, Companies Act.
1967 15 Elizabeth II c. 81, Companies Act.

4 Trade directories

The Post Office London Directory (1842), (1844-47), (1850-57), (1859-60), (1870), (1875) and (1880).

Pigot's London and Provincial New Commercial Directory (1822-23), (1827-28), (1836) and (1840).

Slater's General and Classified Directory of Manchester and Salford (1863), (1865), (1871-72), (1884), (1886), (1893) and (1898).

The Post Office Directory for Manchester (1873).

The Business Directory of Manchester (1868-69).

5 Printed sources

Arthur Andersen, *The First Fifty Years 1913-1963*, Chicago (1963).
Ashworth, William, *Contracts and Finance*, London H.M.S.O. (1953).
Fifty Years, The Story of the Association of Certified and Corporate Accountants 1904-1954, London (1954).
Babbage, Charles, *On the Economy of Machinery and Manufactures*, London (1835).
Bailey, J. D., *A Hundred Years of Pastoral Banking, A History of the Australian Mercantile Land and Finance Company*, Oxford (1966).
Barker, Ernest, *The Development of Public Services in Western Europe*, Oxford (1944).
Barker, T. C., *Pilkington Brothers and the Glass Industry*, London (1960)
The Glassmakers; Pilkington: the Rise of an International Company 1826-1976, London (1977).

Baxter, W. T. and Sidney Davidson, *Studies in Accounting*, London (1977).

Booth, Benjamin, *A Complete System of Book-keeping*, London (1789).

Bradshaw's Railway Manual, Shareholders' Guide and Directory, London (1869), (1890) and (1900).

Brief, Richard P., *Business History Review*, Boston (1966), 'The Origin and Evolution of Nineteenth Century Asset Accounting'.

Briston, R. J., *The Accountants Magazine*, November (1979), 'The U.K. Accountancy Profession – The move towards monopoly power'.

Brown, Richard, *A History of Accounting and Accountants*, Edinburgh (1905).

Carr Saunders, A. M. and P. A. Wilson, *The Professions*, Oxford (1933).

Carus-Wilson, E. M. (Editor), *Essays in Economic History*, Vol. I, London (1954), H. A. Shannon, 'The Limited Companies of 1866–1883'.

Cave, Alan, 'Professionalism and Industrial Relations' (unpublished L.S.E. research paper, 1976).

Chandler, Alfred D., *The Visible Hand, The Managerial Revolution in American Business*, Harvard (1977) and Herman Daems (Editors), *Managerial Hierarchies: Comparative Perspectives on the Rise of the Modern Industrial Enterprise*, Harvard (1980), Leslie Hannah, 'Visible and Invisible Hands in Great Britain'.

Channon, Derek F., *The Strategy and Structure of British Enterprise*, London (1973).
The Service Industries, Strategy, Structure and Financial Performance, London (1978).

Chatfield, Michael (Editor), *The English View of Accountants' Duties and Responsibilities 1881–1902*, New York (1978).

Checkland, S. G., *Scottish Banking, A History 1695–1973*, Glasgow (1975).

Chester, Sir Norman, *The Nationalisation of British Industry 1945–1951*, London H.M.S.O. (1975).

Church, R. A., *Kendricks in Hardware, A Family Business 1791–1966*, Newton Abbot (1969).
Herbert Austin: The British Motor Car Industry to 1941, London (1979).

Cipolla, C. M., *The Fontana Economic History of Europe*, Vol. III, Brighton (1976), R. M. Hartwell, 'The Service Revolution: The Growth of Services in the Modern Economy 1700-1914'.

Coleman, D. C., *Courtaulds, An Economic and Social History*, Vol. III, *Crisis and Change 1940-1965*, Oxford (1980).

Cooke, C. A., *Corporation, Trust and Company*, Manchester (1950).

Cooke, John, *The Compting House Assistant or Book-keeping made easy*, London (1764).

A History of Cooper Brothers and Co, 1854-1954, London (1954).

Cooper, Ernest, *Proceedings of the Institute of Chartered Accountants in England and Wales*, London (1921), 'Fifty-seven Years in an Accountant's Office'.

Corley, T. A. B., 'Communications, Entrepreneurship and the Managing Agency System: The Burmah Oil Company 1886-1928' (unpublished Reading University research paper, 1979).

Cory, Isaac, *A Practical Treatise on Accounts, Mercantile, Partnership* ... London (1839).

Crick, W. F. and J. E. Wadsworth, *A Hundred Years of Joint Stock Banking*, London (1936).

Crouzet, Francis, *Capital Formation in the Industrial Revolution*, London (1972), Sidney Pollard, 'Capital Accounting in the Industrial Revolution'.

Davies, P. N., *The Trade Makers, Elder Dempster in West Africa 1852-1972*, London (1973).

Deloitte and Co, 1845-1956, Oxford (1958).

De Paula, F. Clive, *Management Accounting in Practice*, London (1972), and Frank A. Attwood, *Auditing Principles and Practice*, London (1976).

De Paula, F. R. M., *Developments in Accounting*, London (1948).

Dicksee, Lawrence R., *Auditing, A Practical Manual for Auditors*, London (1892).

The Student's Guide to Accountancy, London (1897).

Business Methods and the War, Cambridge (1915).

Dodson, James, *The Accountant, or, the method of book-keeping deduced from clear principles*, London (1750).

Duffy, I. P. H., 'Bankruptcy and Insolvency in London in the Late 18th and Early 19th Centuries', Oxford D.Phil. Thesis (1973).

Dunlop, Kathleen E., 'A History of the Dunlop Rubber Co in England 1888-1939', University of Illinois Ph.D. Thesis (1948).

Dunning, John H. and E. Victor Morgan, *An Economic Study of the City of London*, London (1971).

Edwards, J. R. and C. Baker, *Accounting and Business Research* (1978-79), 'Dowlais Iron Company: Accounting Policies and Procedures for Profit Measurement and Reporting Purposes'.

Ernst and Ernst 1903-1960, A History of the Firm, Cleveland (1960).

Fieldhouse, D. K., *Unilever Overseas, The Anatomy of a Multinational 1875-1965*, London (1978).

Seventy Years of Progress in Accountancy Education, H. Foulks Lynch & Co, London (1955).

Garcke, Emile and J. M. Fells, *Factory Accounts, Their Principles and Practice, A Handbook for Accountants and Manufacturers*, London (1887).

Garnsey, Sir Gilbert, *Holding Companies and their Published Accounts*, London (1923).

Garratt, A. A., *History of the Society of Incorporated Accountants 1885-1957*, Oxford (1961).

Green, Edwin, *The Making of a Modern Banking Group, A History of the Midland Bank since 1900*, London (1979).

Hall, P. G., *The Industries of London since 1861*, London (1962).

Hancock, W. K. and M. M. Gowing, *British War Economy*, London H.M.S.O. (1949).

Hannah, Leslie, *Business History*, Vol. XVI, London (1974), 'Takeover Bids in Britain before 1950: An Exercise in Business Pre-History'.

The Rise of the Corporate Economy, London (1976).

Management, Strategy and Business Development, An Historical and Comparative Study, London (1976).

Hargreaves, E. L. and M. M. Gowing, *Civil Industry and Trade*, London H.M.S.O. (1949).

Hartwell, R. M., *The Industrial Revolution and Economic Growth*, London (1971).

Hein, Leonard W., *The British Companies Act and the Practice of Accountancy, 1844-1962*, New York (1978).

Historical Accounting Literature, London (1975).

History of the Institute of Chartered Accountants in England and Wales 1870-1965, London (1966).

History of the Chartered Accountants of Scotland from the Earliest Times to 1954, Edinburgh (1954).

Hopkins, Leon, *The Hundreth Year*, London (1980).

Howson, Susan and Donald Winch, *The Economic Advisory Council 1930-1939*, Cambridge (1977).

The Institute of Municipal Treasurers and Accountants, A Short History, London (1960).

Irving, R. J., *The North Eastern Railway Company 1870-1914, An Economic History*, Leicester (1976).

Kaye, Barrington, *The Development of the Architectural Profession*, London (1960).

Kitchen, J. and R. H. Parker, *Accounting Thought and Education: Six English Pioneers*, London (1980).

Lisle, George, *Accounting in Theory and Practice, A Text-Book for the Use of Accountants*, Edinburgh (1899).

Encyclopaedia of Accounting, 6 vols, Edinburgh (1903-04).

Littleton, A. C., *Accounting Evolution to 1900*, New York (1933), and B. S. Yamey, *Studies in the History of Accounting*, London (1956).

Magnus, Philip, 'The History of the Institute of Chartered Accountants in England and Wales 1880-1959', unpublished typescript (1959).

Malcolm, Alexander, *A Treatise of Book-keeping, or Merchants Accounts*, London (1731).

Manley, P. S., *Abacus*, Sydney (1976), 'Clarence Hatry'.

Margerison, Tom, *The Making of a Profession*, London (1980).

Marriner, S., *Business and Businessmen: Studies in Business, Economic and Accounting History*, Liverpool (1978).

Marwick, Arthur, *The Deluge, British Society in the First World War*, London (1965).

Britain in the Century of Total War, London (1968).

The Home Front, the British and the Second World War, London (1976).

Women at War 1914-1918, London (1977).

Mathias, Peter, *The Retailing Revolution, A History of Multiple Retailing in the Food Trades based upon the Allied Suppliers Group of Companies*, London (1967).

The First Industrial Nation, London (1969).

Journal of European Economic History (1973), 'Capital Credit and Enterprise in the Industrial Revolution'.

McKendrick, Neil, *The Economic History Review*, Vol. XXIII (1970), 'Josiah Wedgwood and Cost Accounting in the Industrial Revolution'.

Millerson, Geoffrey, *The Qualifying Associations*, London (1964).

Milne, K. L., *The Accountant in Public Practice*, London (1959).

Milward, Alan S., *The Economic Effects of the World Wars on Britain*, London (1970).

Montgomery, Robert H., *Fifty Years of Accountancy*, New York (1939).

Mortimer, Thomas, *A General Dictionary of Commerce, Trade and Manufactures*, London (1810).

Mowat, C. L., *Britain between the Wars 1918-1940*, London (1955).

Murphy, Mary (Editor), *Selected Readings in Accounting and Auditing, Principles and Problems*, New York (1952).

Olsen, Donald J., *The Growth of Victorian London*, London (1976).

Oschinsky, Dorothea, *Walter of Henley and Other Treatises on Estate Management and Accounting*, Oxford (1971).

Parker, R. H., *Management Accounting: an Historical Perspective*, London (1969).

British Accountants: a Biographical Sourcebook, London (1981).

Parry, Gordon, *National Mortgage and Agency Co of New Zealand*, Dunedin (1964).

Perry, William, *The Man of Business and Gentleman's Assistant, Book-keeping by Single and Double Entry*, Edinburgh (1774).

Pike Russell & Co, An Account of a London Firm of Chartered Accountants 1903-1973, London (1973).

Pixley, Francis W., *The Profession of a Chartered Accountant*, London (1897).

Pollard, Sidney, *The Genesis of Modern Management*, London (1965).

The Development of the British Economy 1914-1967, London (1969).

Pollins, Harold, *Accounting Research*, Vol. VIII (1957), 'Railway Auditing - A Report of 1867'.

Postan, M. M., *British War Production*, London H.M.S.O. (1952).

Prais, S. J., *The Evolution of Giant Firms in Britain*, Cambridge (1976).

Pulling, Alexander, *A Practical Compendium of Law and Usage of Mercantile Accounts*, London (1846).

Reader, W. J., *Professional Men, The Rise of the Professional Classes in 19th Century England*, London (1966).

Imperial Chemical Industries, A History, Vol. I, London (1970), Vol. II, London (1975).

Metal Box, A History, London (1976).

A House in the City, A Study of the City and the Stock Exchange based on Foster & Braithwaite 1825-1975, London (1979).

Bowater, A History, Cambridge (1981).

Richards, G. E., 'History of the Firm [Price Waterhouse], The First Fifty Years, 1850-1900', typescript (1950).

Robertson, D. W., *The Arthur Andersen Chronicle* (1949), 'Turquand, Youngs, McAuliffe & Co'.

Robinson, Howard W., *A History of Accountants in Ireland*, Dublin (1964).

Rosenbaum, E. and A. J. Sherman, *M. M. Warburg & Co 1798-1938, Merchant Bankers of Hamburg*, London (1979).

Rumelt, Richard P., *Strategy, Structure and Economic Performance*, Harvard (1974).

Russell Limebeer, A London Firm of Chartered Accountants, London (1978).

Sampson, Anthony, *The Anatomy of Britain*, London (1962).

Sanderson, Michael, *The Universities and British Industry 1850-1970*, London (1972).

Scott, J. D., *Vickers, A History*, London (1962).

Shaplen, Robert, *Kreuger, Genius and Swindler*, London (1961).

Slater Lewis, J., *The Commercial Organization of Factories*, London (1896).

Snell, Charles, *The Tradesman's Director; or, a short and easy method of keeping books of accompts*, London (1697).
The Merchants Counting House: or, waste-book instances, London (1720).

Solomons, David, *Studies in Costing*, London (1952).

Stacey, Nicholas A. H., *English Accountancy, A Study in Social and Economic History 1800-1954*, London (1954).

Stevenson, John and Chris Cook, *The Slump, Society and Politics during the Depression*, London (1977).

Stewart, James C., *Pioneers of a Profession, Chartered Accountants to 1879*, Edinburgh (1977).

Tann, Jennifer, *The Development of the Factory*, London (1970).

Taylor, A. J. P., *The First World War*, London (1963).
English History 1914-1945, Oxford (1965).

Thompson, F. M. L., *Chartered Surveyors, The Growth of the Profession*, London (1968).

Thomson, H. Byerley, *The Choice of a Profession*, London (1857).

Tricker, R. Ian, *The Accountant in Management*, London (1967).

Viney Merretts, Chartered Accountants for 150 Years in the City of London, London (1978).

Walker, R. G., *Abacus*, Sydney (1977), 'The Hatry Affair'.
Consolidated Statements, New York (1978).

'Ware, Ward & Co, A History of the Firm 1867-1971', typescript, Bristol (1973).

Welch, Charles and W. T. Pike, *London at the Opening of the Twentieth Century*, London (1905).

Who was Who 1916-1970, Vols I-VI, London (1929-72).

Williamson, Harold F. (Editor), *Evolution of Internal Management Structures*, Delaware (1975), Peter Mathias, 'Conflicts of Function in the Rise of Big Business: The British Experience'.

Wilson, Charles, *A History of Unilever: a Study in Economic Growth and Social Change*, London (1954).

Unilever 1945-1965, Challenge and Response in the Post War Industrial Revolution, London (1968).

Winsbury, Rex, *Thomson McLintock & Co, The First Hundred Years*, London (1977).

Witty, Richard A., *How to become a Chartered Accountant*, London (1906).

Woolf, Arthur H., *A Short History of Accountants and Accountancy*, London (1912).

Worthington, Beresford, *Professional Accountants: An Historical Sketch*, London (1895).

Yamey, Basil S., H. C. Edey and H. W. Thomson, *Accounting in England and Scotland*, London (1963).

The Historical Development of Accounting, A Selection of Papers, New York (1978).

✸✸ INDEX ✸✸